W9-DIL-964

Assessing the Business Environment

Assessing the Business Environment

Guidelines for Strategists

C. W. RONEY

QUORUM BOOKS
Westport, Connecticut • London

HD
30.28
.R6615
1999

Library of Congress Cataloging-in-Publication Data

Roney, C. W. (Curtis W.), 1942–
    Assessing the business environment : guidelines for strategists /
C. W. Roney.
        p.   cm.
    Includes bibliographical references and index.
    ISBN 1–56720–235–7 (alk. paper)
    1. Strategic planning.   I. Title.
HD30.28.R6615   1999
658.4′012—dc21   99–13716

British Library Cataloguing in Publication Data is available.

Library of Congress Catalog Card Number: 99–13716
ISBN: 1–56720–235–7

First published in 1999

Quorum Books, 88 Post Road West, Westport, CT 06881
An imprint of Greenwood Publishing Group, Inc.
www.quorumbooks.com

Printed in the United States of America

The paper used in this book complies with the
Permanent Paper Standard issued by the National
Information Standards Organization (Z39.48–1984).

10 9 8 7 6 5 4 3 2 1

Contents

Illustrations

FIGURES

EXHIBITS

Preface

In 1999, Commercial Planning Consultants became a quarter century old. During the past 25 years, we've had the privilege of serving many companies' chief executives in preparing their strategic plans of business, enhancing their planning procedures and helping to implement them. During that time, we have learned a lot about strategic planning principles and their application in different industry settings. Now, we believe it is time to share some of what we have learned with other planning professionals. Accordingly, we have begun to assemble procedural guidelines for planning managers' use in organizing and conducting their firms' planning functions.

Our approach to compiling these guidelines has been evidentially oriented. Wherever possible, we are attempting to identify empirical evidence that confirms the appropriateness of methodological principles in specific environmental settings. We have found that firms in some industries most successfully follow planning procedures which are not suited to other industries. Similarly, some techniques are more applicable to firms in growing markets than those in mature or declining markets. Indeed, we are learning that many technical contingencies of this nature must be observed for planning procedures to succeed. However, most planning texts seem to suggest, mistakenly, that the same procedures may be used regardless of industry differences or environmental circumstances.

Our strategic planning methodology follows a fairly classic three-stage sequence: gathering evidence, making strategic decisions, and implementation. We began our mission of defining planning principles at the first stage, gathering evidence, by compiling guidelines for assessing the firm's internal capabilities. That work went quite satisfactorily. Next, we moved to procedures for gathering evidence about the external environment. But, there, we hit a snag. When we searched for empirical evidence regarding the efficacy of alternative environmental assessment methods, there didn't seem to be any! We found ourselves dealing with a multitude of theories and technical disciplines—for example, macroeconomics, microeconomics, market research, demographics, and forecasting. While there is abundant literature on each of those topics, very little of it is focused on applications to strategic planning.

As our research into environmental assessment methodology employed in strategic planning progressed, we became convinced that a concise collection of guidelines is seriously needed because current methodology is uncodified and scattered through hundreds, if not thousands, of documents in the professional literature. Indeed, there was no single, consolidated source of environmental assessment principles for planning managers to consult until this volume was compiled.

The dearth of codified environmental assessment principles is especially frustrating to graduates of business schools that teach modern principles of strategic management. According to current doctrine, all general managers should know strategic management principles and be capable of directing, if not conducting, the strategic management functions of their firms. According to those same precepts, the general manager should develop a firm's internal capabilities consistently with environmental opportunities or problems for maximum competitive advantage. Doing so requires the manager to conduct assessments of internal strengths and weaknesses as well as the external environment. While internal capabilities assessment should be a relatively straight forward matter, environmental assessment is more difficult, because external drivers of a firm's performance potential are much harder to discern than those within. Moreover, as explained earlier, there are no consolidated guidelines for conducting an environmental assessment. In our research, we looked extensively for texts on this subject and found only one (Stoffels, 1994) which, while helpful, is focused primarily on environmental scanning rather than strategic planning. So, we decided to compile this reference specifically for strategic planning purposes.

As we compiled the evidence and theory conveyed in this book, we gained greater appreciation of planning managers' frustrations as they attempt to perform environmental assessments in the course of strategic planning. For instance, consider the growth/share matrix which often is used in strategic analysis prior to setting objectives. How can a manager use the growth/share matrix without a reliable estimate of the firm's and competitors' market shares or a credible forecast of the industry's or market's growth? To which sources can the planning manager refer for guidance in attempting to diagnose relationships between a firm's performance potential and driving forces in the environment, let alone to forecast potential changes in those relationships? What diagnostic and prognostic techniques are available to identify core competences that will be needed in future markets? Fortunately, there is a rich, albeit uncodified literature where methodologies for performing such assessment tasks may be found. Those methods simply haven't been compiled in one volume before.

Thus, this book was prepared for those managers who must understand what can (and cannot) be known about their firms' external environments and how best to attain that knowledge. They include chief executives of small- and medium-size firms who must prepare their own business plans with limited staff assistance; chief operating officers of divisions in larger corporations who have similar planning responsibilities; planning executives of large companies; and technical specialists who are responsible for environmental assessment functions in larger corporations. Those are the "planning managers" to whom several passages of this book refer.

Comprehensive strategic planning is difficult enough even with a codification of relevant environmental assessment principles. Without such guidelines, application of techniques such as the growth/share matrix, the multi factor matrix, the directional policy matrix, the market evolution matrix and other strategic decision-making approaches is practically infeasible. Thus, it is not surprising that their use often is unsuccessful. Similarly, all of the currently popular "shareholder value" approaches to setting financial goals make fundamental assumptions about firms' potential growth, the duration of business cycles, and points in industry life cycles where the potential for adding value becomes negligible due to competitive convergence of returns toward capital costs. Shareholder value approaches also require planning managers to have considerable forecasting skills. Thus, planning managers who focus on maximizing shareholder value must have many of the environmental assessment skills that are discussed in this book.

As we compiled these guidelines, we tried to strike a balance between methodological comprehensiveness on one hand, and pragmatism on the other. This is not a procedure manual. Instead, it is a concise handbook which hopefully covers its subject matter comprehensively but compactly. Plenty of references are provided for those who wish to explore particular topics in greater detail and, thereby, obtain methodological sophistication. This book explains the scope of assessment methodologies available to planning managers but does not explain how to perform all of them, which would require a volume of encyclopedic proportions.

To assemble this collection of assessment principles, it has been necessary to delve deeply into the professional literature, consulting virtually hundreds of references. Some of the sources that we consulted are rather old. (For instance, Gompertz, 1820; Kondratiev, 1926; Schumpeter, 1939; Katona, 1951; Schoffler, 1955; and Simon, 1957.) Many of the classic methodologies are still valid today. While they often have been overlooked by modern methodologists, we have not hesitated to employ such authorities, regardless of their publication dates.

Environmental assessment principles really have not changed much in the past quarter-century. Many techniques that were used in the past still are used today—including structural economic analysis, demographic analysis, statistical analysis and most forecasting procedures. In this respect, the methodology of environmental assessment has not changed nearly as rapidly in recent years as other management science disciplines. But, even in the musty annals of environmental assessment (EA), changes are beginning to occur. Thus, in this book, readers will find discussions of some exciting, new approaches including the linkage of econometric modeling to input-output tables, multivariate statistical techniques and scenario forecasting. The new North American Industry Classification System (NAICS), which will replace the Standard Industrial Classification (SIC) code beginning in 2000, also represents a step foreword. NAICS will provide analysts with a much more refined framework for market segments' analysis.

In the Appendices, which we have called "An Informational Tool-Kit," planning managers will find several useful reference materials. Among these are illustrative tables which may be used to translate SIC codes into the new NAICS classification categories, and instructions for obtaining a complete collection of cross-reference tables from the government. Also in the appendix, readers will find several other planning aids including demographic trends and projections for the United States and other industrialized nations; economic and demographic data describing trends in composition of the world's markets; a directory of sources from which analysts may obtain a great deal of data describing trends in domestic and world economies, industries and markets; another directory, listing economic forecasting firms and their services; and a ten-year forecast of the U.S. economy recently released by the Bureau of Labor Statistics. These reference materials should provide valuable resources for planning managers and technical EA specialists. We use them frequently in our own practice.

Compilation of these assessment principles reflects the effort of our firm's entire staff. I am especially grateful to Christopher C Titer who manages the technical operations of our firm and conducted many of the projects from which the procedures contained in this manual were derived. I also am grateful to Felecia Gardner who typed this manuscript, late at night, too many times. While special credit is owed to those persons and all the members of our firm who have contributed to this volume, it is dedicated, most of all, to the community of planning professionals with whom we have practiced our trade during these past twenty-five years.

C. W. Roney

Part I

General Methodology

CHAPTER 1

The Vital Role of Environmental Assessment in Strategic Planning

This is a handbook of environmental assessment principles for managers who formulate their firms' strategy. Its purpose is to provide methodological guidelines for understanding forces in the relevant economy, industries and markets which can influence a firm's performance potential and, therefore, shape strategic decisions. The strategic planning process requires adaptation of a firm's internal capabilities to problems and opportunities in the business environment. Most approaches for accomplishing such a rationalization conform to a model approximately like the one depicted in Table 1.1.

As Table 1.1 suggests, planning managers' tasks are addressed to discovering opportunities for the most rewarding deployment of their firms' resources. Planning decisions depend both on demand for the firm's output and availability of inputs—physical resources including labor, materials and equipment as well as intellectual resources such as skill and technology. But, even superior resources may not provide a competitive advantage if they are not available when and where they are needed, or if competitive rivalry is prohibitive. Therefore, planning managers must be skilled at assessing present and potential environments within which their firms' resources can be acquired and deployed. This book provides planning managers with guidelines for performing such environmental assessments in order to diagnose and anticipate strategic targets of opportunity.

THE STRATEGIC PLANNING PROCESS

Procedurally, strategic planning is a rational, integrative discipline. Its approach is to gather evidence with which management can reconcile a firm's internal capabilities to the external environment and, then, make decisions to employ the firm's resources for maximum commercial advantage. As the procedural planning model in Figure 1.1 discloses, environmental assessment provides virtually half of the evidence required to make strategic planning decisions. (The other half is assessment of internal capabilities.) Thus, firms are competitively vulnerable to the extent that their plans are not well grounded in environmental assessment. Conversely, firms that have superior environmental assessment capabilities probably enjoy a significant strategic advantage over their less insightful competitors.

Table 1.1
The Strategic Fit Paradigm

Internal Capabilities

Environment:	Strong	Weak
Favorable	Targets of Greatest Opportunity Strategy: Exploit Competitive Advantage - Invest resources for maximum returns	Targets of Potential Opportunity Strategy: Improve Competitive Capabilities - Invest limited resources - Evaluate and reinvest as warranted by returns
Unfavorable	Areas of Low Return Strategy: Transfer skills to targets of greater opportunity - Harvest resources for redeployment	Danger Zone Strategy: Avoid; Escape; Mitigate - Don't invest resources here! - Divest/redeploy resources

Source: author

Management is usually able to assess the firm's internal capabilities definitively. But, assessing the external environment is much more difficult because the required evidence is not as readily available or as easy to interpret. Therefore, environmental assessment (EA) proficiency is quite rare, even in large corporations. In fact, surveys discussed in the next chapter have disclosed that most firms' chief executives do not appreciate the importance or understand the methodology of comprehensive environmental assessment, which is one reason why firms often do a poor job of it. Clearly, then, firms that are proficient in EA functions should have superior planning capabilities, as well.

Figure 1.1
The Strategic Planning Process

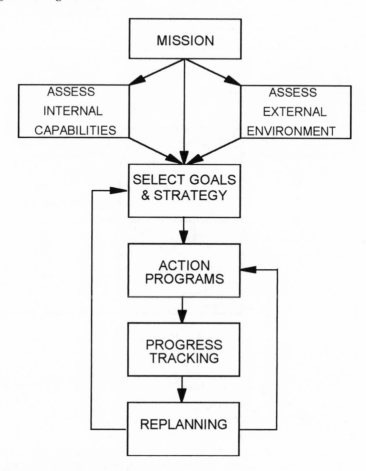

PORTFOLIO APPROACHES TO
STRATEGIC DECISION MAKING

Portfolio methods of assessing corporate and business level strategy have become common in strategic planning procedures. Four of the most frequently employed portfolio planning approaches, each of which relies on an accurate environmental assessment for its validity, are discussed in the following paragraphs.

The Growth-Share Matrix

The original portfolio approach took its genesis from research by the Boston Consulting Group (1968) that demonstrated how unit costs decline with experience in production. Industries where participants can benefit from learning effects provide firms with opportunities to gain a competitive advantage by seizing strategic initiative and capturing high market shares. (Henderson, 1984) This model also recognizes the advantages (and cash flow concomitants) of relative market or industry growth. Thus, the "growth share matrix" provides an opportunity to evaluate portfolios of products or businesses by considering their market shares and growth potentials, jointly (see Figure 1.2).

Figure 1.2
The Growth-Share Matrix

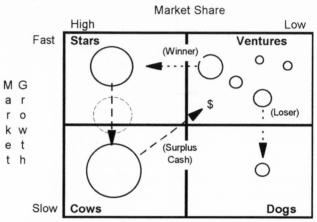

Circle size denotes product or business sales.

Original Concept: Boston Consulting Group

An ideal corporate portfolio of businesses (or a single business portfolio of products) would contain one or more *cash cows* (high shares of mature, slow growth markets) that generate surplus cash flows; several small *ventures* (low shares of embryonic and/or fast growth markets) into which surplus cash flows should be invested in search of future growth in earnings; and a smaller number of *stars* (high shares of fast growth markets), which presumably generate a lot of earnings but not much cash since they are growing and require sustained influxes of working capital and capacity additions. Only a small portion of *ventures* probably will become *stars*. Others will be unsuccessful and fall into the fourth quadrant (*dogs*) of low share businesses or products in slow growth markets. Dogs and other unproductive ventures must be eliminated from the portfolio, according to the doctrine of this approach.

Some empirical research has both confirmed and refuted validity of the growth-share matrix. While the basic concept seems sound, *cash cows* and *dogs* both may be capable of better earnings than the hypotheses underlying this model suggest (Hambrick, MacMillan, and Day, 1982; Woo and Cooper, 1982). Moreover, as explained later, the present rate of market growth is not as important, for planning purposes, as the forecasted rate. But, a common mistake is to classify businesses and products based on their past growth, versus their anticipated growth. In any event, quite a lot of environmental assessment work must be done well if portfolio methods like this one (or others) are to be used successfully.

We should acknowledge, here, that just about all generally accepted approaches to forming strategy (not just portfolio methods) require an assessment of the commercial environment for effective implementation. For instance, in their widely acclaimed work, *Competing for the Future: Breakthrough Strategies for Seizing Control of Your Industry and Creating Markets for Tomorrow,* Hamel and Prahalad (1994), challenge management to develop core competences today that will be required to compete in future markets and industries. But, the authors never explain how to forecast industries' and markets' future success requirements. The principles that appear later in this book provide guidelines for doing so and, thereby, for implementing both resource-based approaches to strategy formulation, like Hamel and Prahalad's (1994), and "positioning" approaches such as the portfolio methods discussed in this section.

Three Other Matrix Approaches

Three variations of portfolio methodology, none of which is used as often as the growth-share matrix, are described briefly in the following paragraphs. Consider, first, the GE/McKinsey multifactor matrix, developed jointly by the two firms for which it is named. This concept recognizes that market or industry attractiveness may result from characteristics other than growth alone. For instance, industry profitability, concentration, barriers to entry, and substitution potential, also are relevant considerations. Moreover, a larger, 3x3 matrix is used to provide analysts with an opportunity to distinguish market positions that are either significantly above or below the norm (Figure 1.3).

Figure 1.3
The Multi-Factor Matrix

		Industry Atttractiveness		
		High	Average	Low
	Strong	Invest	Invest	Manage Selectively for Earnings
B S u t s r i e n n e g s t s h	Average	Invest	Manage Selectively for Earnings	Harvest Or Divest
	Weak	Manage Selectively for Earnings	Harvest Or Divest	Harvest Or Divest

Original Concept: McKinsey & Co. & GE

Figure 1.4
The Directional Policy Matrix

Future Industry Attractiveness

	Attractive	Average	Unattractive
Strong	Leader	Growth	Cash Generation
Average	Try Harder	Custodial	Phased Withdrawal
Weak	Double or Quit	Phased Withdrawal	Disinvest

(left axis label: Functional Performace Potential)

The directional policy matrix (Robinson, S.J., Hitchens and Wade, 1978; Hussey, 1978) is similar to the multi-factor matrix except that assessment of industry attractiveness is based on its future prospects; not the present. Similarly, a firm's functional performance potential is more important than its present capability (see Figure 1.4).

Hofer's (1977) product/market evolution matrix (see Figure 1.5) employs the life cycle concept, in an interesting variation of the previous three approaches. In this technique, each industry is portrayed as a circle on the matrix. Its horizontal position reflects the industry's evolutionary status; the vertical position reflects a firm's strategic market position; and the wedge reflects its market share. While this technique isn't used frequently, it does provide a long-range planning perspective and compresses a lot of information into a single protocol. (Also see Hofer & Schendel, 1978; page 34.)

Figure 1.5
The Product/Market Evolution Matrix

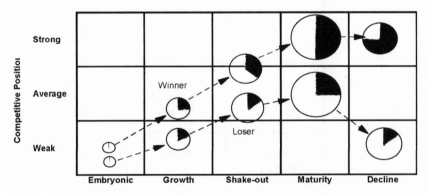

Stage of Growth/Market Evolution

Circle size denotes size of market or segment in which the firm competes.
Wedge size denotes products' share of those markets.

Original Concept: Hofer, 1977

The Vital Role of
Environmental Assessment

For strategic planners, the methodological challenge to using all of these portfolio approaches is the same. A sound environmental assessment must be performed before classifications of industry or market attractiveness can be re- lied upon—and before any of these models (or others) can be a valid description of the firm's strategic situation.

The importance of EA methodology for success in strategic planning is re- flected quite clearly in these portfolio models which often are used to select strategic objectives. For instance, the widely used growth-share protocol as- sumes that a strategist knows a great deal about both the growth potentials of relevant markets and competitors' shares of those markets. Similar matrix ap- proaches assume that the strategist understands various other environmental dimensions, including market attractiveness, the firm's industry position, life cycle stage, and so on. However, in most instances, practitioners really have very little information about their industries' and markets' growth potentials, market shares and other structural characteristics. Therefore, without evidence developed by environmental assessment, these widely used matrix protocols lack validity and cannot be used with confidence. For those reasons, sound en- vironmental assessment is a necessary prerequisite to effective strategy selec- tion.

THE PURPOSE OF THIS BOOK

Many firms fail to do an adequate job of environmental assessment in strategic planning. This often is because they have no practical guidelines for doing so. The purpose of this book, therefore, is to make the work of environ- mental assessment easier for planning managers to do, by providing a frame- work of generally accepted principles that explain what can be known about the external business environment and how to gain that knowledge through analy- sis, forecasting, and assessment of alternative futures.

The previous paragraphs demonstrate that before management can make strategic decisions, it must form an assessment of the external circumstances within which it intends to do business, both presently and in the future. But, because the external environment's scope—economy, industry, and markets— is so broad, complex, and dynamic, management needs concise guidelines for performing EA functions which are relevant to strategic planning. Thus, pro- fessional business planners and top-level executives who are responsible for their firms' plans and planning procedures[1] all need this collection of generally accepted environmental assessment principles.

Surprisingly few texts on the methodology of environmental assessment have been written. The most recent may be Stoffels' (1994) text on scanning. However, no prior work covers the entire scope of environmental assessment required for strategic planning. Equally important, no prior text on EA meth- odology has been based on the body of empirical evidence which demonstrates

alternative methods' relative effectiveness. This book was written in an attempt
to fill those two voids.

SCOPE AND APPROACH

The scope of an environmental assessment must include the broad economy and the specific industry (or segment) within which a firm competes, as
well as the communities of customers (markets) which are or may be served
(see Table 1.2). Each of these dimensions, of course, is multifaceted. For instance, an industry may be assessed in terms of its products, their substitutes,
competitors, regulation, technology, resource requirements, operating characteristics, and financial performance norms. Each of those dimensions, in turn,
must be assessed in terms of trend, present condition, apparent direction, and
potential for change. With such a broad scope, it is not surprising that so many
general managers—especially those in smaller firms—treat EA procedures su-
perficially in their planning methodology. Only large corporations are able to
afford specialized staffs with the technical skills to comprehend the full scope
of EA functions completely.

In fact, it is not necessary (or always possible) for most firms, large or
small, to employ specialists in all environmental disciplines. Certainly technical skills in each area are valuable assets. But practitioners of the planning art
have learned that they do not need to be theoretical experts in all of the EA
disciplines to apply the principles that are relevant to selecting goals and strategy. Rather, strategic environmental assessment integrates and applies technical elements of many specialized disciplines to a firm's planning procedures.
An analogy might be the difference between pure science practiced by a theoretical physicist and the applied science of a mechanical engineer. Planning
professionals are more like engineers than pure scientists.

Table 1.2
Scope of Environmental Assessment

	Economy	Industry	Markets
Past/Trend	1-1	1-2	1-3
Present	2-1	2-2	2-3
Future	3-1	3-2	3-3

The remaining contents of this book are presented in seven chapters.
Chapter 2 provides a broad overview of environmental assessment practices and
results of empirical research that demonstrate how widely and effectively those

practices are employed. After completing that chapter, planning managers should be generally well-informed with regard to both the scope of EA methods that are available to them and the extent to which businesses have incurred competitive advantages or disadvantages through the use and neglect of those methods. Chapters 3, 4, and 5 describe methods for assessing the firm's present situation in its relevant economy, industry, and served markets.

Chapter 6 is devoted to a survey of conventional forecasting methods. Chapter 7 addresses issues of uncertainty in environmental assessment. Methods for defining alternative futures through the use of scenario forecasting and contingency planning are described in that chapter. Finally, Chapter 8 concludes by summarizing the scope of environmental conditions that can be known with confidence and the range of techniques that may be used to acquire knowledge about them. From that final chapter, strategic managers may take some comfort in their knowledge that generally accepted methods to assess impacts of the commercial environment on their firms' performance potentials and strategic alternatives either exist, or do not exist.

Readers should be warned that this book has not been written for those who seek simple solutions to complex problems. Neither strategic planning nor environmental assessment lend themselves well to shortcut approaches; and no simplified, cookbook answers will be found here. Instead, you will find occasional admissions that technical voids exist where generally accepted principles remain to be discovered. In those places, this book challenges academicians to reinforce the environmental foundations of strategic planning methodology where procedural guidance is lacking in the empirical and/or theoretical literature.

It has been necessary to condense a large body of empirical evidence and theory regarding analysis and forecasting of the commercial environment in this book. In some cases, it was not possible to describe all available authorities. However, liberal citations of references throughout the text are intended to enable professionals who wish to learn more about the principles summarized here to do so readily and, thereby, to select EA methods for use in their businesses with greater confidence. Similarly, it is not the purpose of this book to explain every environmental assessment methodology in detail. That would require compiling a volume of encyclopedic proportions. We will leave such a daunting task to others! However, by referring to the EA principles in this handbook, and the citations of research or theory on which they are based, planning managers should be able to draw solid conclusions regarding the extent to which environmental circumstances of their firms can be understood through the application of formal assessment procedures.

NOTE

1. Throughout the remainder of this book, we will refer to those professionals and executives, collectively, as "planning managers."

CHAPTER 2

Scope and Approach of Environmental Assessment

A rational selection of strategy is based on a firm foundation of evidence regarding the commercial environment. In this book, the planning manager will find guidelines for diagnosing forces in the economy, industry, and markets that influence a firm's performance potential. This book also describes methods and procedures for forecasting environmental opportunities and problems that fundamentally may influence the scope of feasible strategy, and assessing environmental risks that necessarily pervade any business environment. This chapter provides a broad overview of those environmental assessment (EA) functions.

We begin by defining the scope of the commercial environment. Next, a more rigorous discussion summarizes research that has been done to discover the importance of several structural factors that must be addressed by environmental analyses. The discussion then turns to a few studies that have been performed to define the scope of formal EA practices in American Industry and their acceptance. The chapter concludes with a more precise definition of EA functions' scope and a discussion of challenges faced by planning managers in balancing pragmatism against comprehensiveness of EA procedures.

SCOPE OF THE BUSINESS ENVIRONMENT

The scope of any business environment most conveniently may be divided into three substantive dimensions:

- The general economy,
- The firm's industry, and
- Relevant markets.

Each of those dimensions will be described in the following chapters.

We define *the general economy* simply as a system wherein all goods and services of any relevance to the firm are produced and consumed. One may describe such a system generally in terms of expenditures by consumers, producers, and governments. The community of firms that choose to supply the same goods or services constitute an *industry*. Communities of individuals, firms, and other organizations (including government) that consume an industry's goods or services comprise its *markets*. Thus, an economy consists of inter-dependent supplier industries and consuming markets. Each of these three dimensions—economy, industry, and market—provides a different perspective on the same system. It is equally possible to describe an economy in terms of national income accounts, industrial output of goods and services, or the markets' consumption of goods and services (Exhibit 2.1).

Exhibit 2.1
Scope of the Business Environment

Markets	Domestic (U.S.)			Foreign (Non U.S.)		
	Consumers	Producers	Government	Consumers	Producers	Government
Industries						
Domestic	**A.**			**B.**		
Durables	**DOMESTIC CONSUMPTION OF DOMESTIC PRODUCTION**			**EXPORTS**		
Non-durables						
Services						
Total						
Foreign	**C.**					
Durables	**IMPORTS**			-	-	-
Non-durables				-	-	-
Services				-	-	-
Total				-	-	-

Gross Domestic Product = Quadrant A+B   Domestic Demand = Quadrant A+C
Domestic Consumption = Domestic Demand ± Inventory Fluctuation

It often is necessary to evaluate a firm's business environment in terms of all three dimensions (economy, industry, and markets). Moreover, because comprehensive business planning addresses methods and procedures for preparing the firm to conduct its mission in both present and foreseeable environments, the scope of this volume also must take into consideration the following three chronological dimensions of assessment:

- Analysis of current environmental trends;
- Forecasting future environmental conditions; and
- Assessment of contingencies or alternative futures.

Since the business environment must be described in terms of both its substantive (economy, industry, and market) and chronological (present, future, and contingent) dimensions, the scope of a business environment's assessment may be summarized as in Exhibit 2.2. The contents of this exhibit confirm that conducting an environmental assessment indeed can be a complex task.

Exhibit 2.2
Scope of a Commercial Environment Assessment:
Illustration of Contents

	Economies	Industries	Markets	Scope
Analysis of Present Conditions and Trends	National income accounts, monetary variables, price levels, saving, business cycles	Performance norms, industry structure, competitive rivalry, critical success factors, input/output tables, competitors' capabilities	Sources of demand: consumers, producers and government; purchase decision dynamics; demographics	Diagnosis of the present situation, trends, and critical success factors
Forecasting	Time series extension; trend-cycle models; econometric models; experts' opinions; long waves	Analogies, growth curves, input-output simulation, technological forecasting, life cycle forecasting	Demographic forecasts: socio-psychological models; industrial purchasing models; econometrics; hybrids	Prognosis of most likely future business conditions
Contingencies and Alternate Futures	Systemic shocks, impacts of structural shifts due to geo-demographics, regulation; resource shifts	Potential impacts of structural shifts; competitors' entry or exit; new technology; new materials; new regulations	Potential impacts of shifts in consumer needs, industrial requirements, life styles, work styles	Scenarios describing impacts of changes in fundamental forecasting assumptions
Scope	Economic conditions in nations where the firm does business	Products, substitutes, suppliers, competitors, entry barriers, performance norms	Buyers' willingness and ability to purchase the firm's products and/or services	**The Commercial Environment**

A planning manager must analyze the present nature of relevant economic, industry, and market conditions before attempting to forecast them. Until an accurate understanding of each substantive element is achieved through fundamental analysis, planning managers are like physicians who prescribe treatment without first conducting a diagnosis. Only after an accurate diagnosis of the firm's environmental elements has been accomplished, will it be possible to forecast business conditions validly and then to prescribe a correct strategy. Indeed, failure to diagnose the relationships of a firm's performance potential to elements in its external environment, before attempting to forecast impacts of changes in the environment, probably is one of the most lethal pitfalls to which planning managers succumb.

Because they are external to the enterprise and beyond management's control, environmental factors impose risk on all firms. Since we cannot control the firm's environment, it is necessary to prepare for a realistic range of potential eventualities in the economy, industries, and markets where a firm does business. Although we cannot control these factors, it is possible to minimize adverse consequences of changes in them, and to maximize potential benefits, by being adequately prepared. In such cases, forewarned is forearmed, and the competitor who reacts fastest often will be the most successful.

Thus, the planning manager is well advised to consider a reasonable range of alternative futures ("contingencies") for which strategic responses should be available. Such alternative futures—although not as likely as the plan's prevailing environmental assumptions—may be so consequential that it is prudent to monitor the environment in order to detect emergent increases in contingencies' likelihood. If necessary, management can develop contingent strategies more fully and make them ready for implementation if and when an alternative future becomes more likely than the prevailing plan's assumptions. On such occasions, a change in strategy may be required.

To summarize, the firm whose management is better prepared for potential shifts in external business conditions (contingencies) than its competitors often can react faster and more effectively than they can. Consequently, the firm with superior environmental assessment capabilities (and contingency plans) should enjoy a significant (if not decisive) competitive advantage.

COMPOSITION OF THE
RELEVANT ENVIRONMENT

The scope and composition of environmental influences on performance potential have been subjects of several multivariate statistical studies. Duncan (1972) conducted one of the earliest and most influential of those studies. His findings disclosed four clusters of variables revolving around customers, suppliers, sociopolitical dynamics, and technology. Bourgeois (1978, 1985) concluded that accuracy of managers' perceived uncertainty and their consensus regarding uncertainty could modify the effects of those factors on performance potential.

Daft, Sormunen, and Parks (1988) found that "strategic uncertainty" stems from six independent environmental sectors: economic, competitive. customer, technological, regulatory, and sociopolitical. From this perspective, impacts of each sector on strategic uncertainty can be measured by the interaction of their importance, complexity and dynamism. Thus,

$$SU = I(C+R), \quad \text{where:}$$

SU = strategic uncertainty
I = importance
C = complexity
R = rate of change

Various statistical studies have been done to test the validity of Duncan's factors. Such studies generally have found the same (or nearly the same) few factors. For instance, Boulton, Lindsay, Franklin, and Rue (1982) found Duncan's four factors to be prominent in their data. Those researchers also demonstrated significant interindustry differences in these factors' importance. Jain's (1984) research attempted to modify the structural model slightly. While keeping the technology factor separate, he combined the customer and supplier factors into a single "economy" factor. Narayanan and Fahey (1987) also used the same structure (economy, social, political, technological) to subdivide one of three broader categories that they called the macroenvironment. The other two broad dimensions were industry/competition and the firm's internal environment.

In contrast to the foregoing findings that 4 to 6 clusters of variables comprise the fundamental environmental factors that are capable of influencing a firm's performance potential, Kudla's (1978) extensive survey demonstrated that, in practice, firms' environmental assessment functions tend to focus primarily on competitive and technology issues much more than the others. Surprisingly, the firms in Kudla's study focused least often on demographic forces. Thus, when assembling evidence on which to base their strategic decisions, planning managers often overlook important, even very basic, factors in the environment.

Based on the combined results of these studies, it may be concluded that any comprehensive assessment of the firm's business environment should consider at least ten families of variables within three dimensions. They are listed in Table 2.1.

Table 2.1
Scope of the Business Environment

Economy	**Industry**	**Market**
Macro-economics	Competitors	Customers
Regulation	Suppliers	Demographics
Other political factors*	Product/Services	Other sociological factors **
	Technology	

* Monetary policy, governmental stability, military conflict. ** For instance, consumer tastes and styles.

At a given time in any particular industry or market, each of these dimensions may be more or less important, and they may act with unequal force. Significant interindustry and individual firm differences typically exist as well. Therefore, diagnosing the firm's sensitivity to such factors is one of the planning manager's most challenging responsibilities.

The environment is so broad in scope that it probably is impossible for most firms to perform a truly comprehensive assessment. Fortunately, that usually is not necessary. Instead, a few driving forces in the general economy, industry, or served markets will be more influential in determining a firm's performance potential than others. These forces often are called critical success factors, or, CSFs (Leideker and Bruno, 1984). It is vital to identify such factors and focus the firm's environmental assessment efforts on them.

Critical success factors—and, therefore, the EA functions that are addressed to them—differ between industries. J. E. Prescott (1986) has shown that differences in the influences of environmental forces on financial performance potential are more likely to be in degree than in direction. But, since interindustry, and intra-industry differences in the strength of CSFs can be significant, the EA function's effectiveness will depend on an accurate CSF diagnosis. Voluminous literature has been addressed to the methodology of critical success factor assessments (for instance, see Leideker and Bruno, 1984; J. E. Prescott, 1987; and King, 1987). Essentially, such assessments consist of sensitivity analyses, many (but not all) of which can be performed statistically.

Effective critical success factor analysis should benefit later stages of the planning process considerably. Thus, identification of CSFs with strong influences on the firm's competitive or financial success potential should disclose specific internal capabilities that must be strengthened to a point where they are sources of distinctive competitive competence. These particular competences may be designated as critical core competences (CCCs) to distinguish them from others which may not be mandatory. Exhibits 2.3 and 2.4 depict the diagnosis and development, respectively, of CSFs and CCCs.

For example, if fuel's availability, or costliness were discovered to be critical for a firm's success during the environmental assessment stage of planning, subsequent assessments of internal capabilities' strengths and weaknesses should focus on maximizing the firm's competitive advantages and minimizing its risks, insofar as the acquisition and use of fuel is concerned. The firm may have other unique strengths or weaknesses, but these are critical. Accordingly, planning deliberations might pay special attention to procurement methods, commodity market hedging, inventory planning, refining of crude materials, or developing technological approaches to using alternative fuels—all because fuel is diagnosed as a critical success factor.

In the strategic planning process, management devises approaches to achieving or sustaining competitive advantage by enhancing the firm's ability to exploit critical success factors. When it is not possible to exploit a CSF, management's strategy may seek ways to circumvent it—perhaps by outsourcing or developing substitute resources through technological innovation.

In any event, decision-making steps in the strategy selection process must reflect an assessment of critical success factors in the business environment.

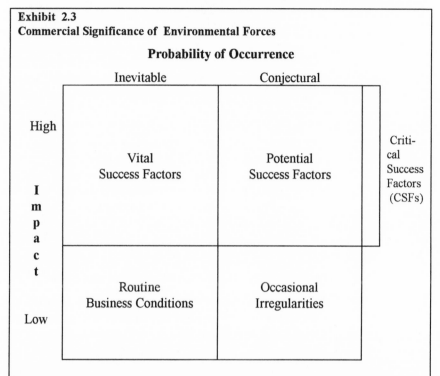

Exhibit 2.3
Commercial Significance of Environmental Forces

Probability of Occurrence

	Inevitable	Conjectural	
High	Vital Success Factors	Potential Success Factors	Critical Success Factors (CSFs)
I m p a c t			
Low	Routine Business Conditions	Occasional Irregularities	

Vital Success Factors (VSFs):   Inevitable environmental conditions with high impact. Distinctive core competence to deal with VSFs is required for long-term commercial success. Examples: increasing scarcity of important raw materials; imminent regulatory ban on use of chemical components, such as HCFCs.

Potential Success Factors (PSFs): Contingencies which, if realized, could change the way an industry's or market's participants do business, but whose emergence is uncertain. Examples: Perfection of low cost fuel cells for autos; entry/exit of important competitors; a potential product substitution; significant shift in distribution channels. Contingent strategies must be available for implementation if/when PSFs' likelihood becomes sufficiently high.

Routine Business Conditions and Occasional Irregularities: The firm's operating resources and managerial functions should be sufficient to deal with these forces without needless stress.

EXHIBIT 2.4
How Critical Success Factors Influence Strategic Planning

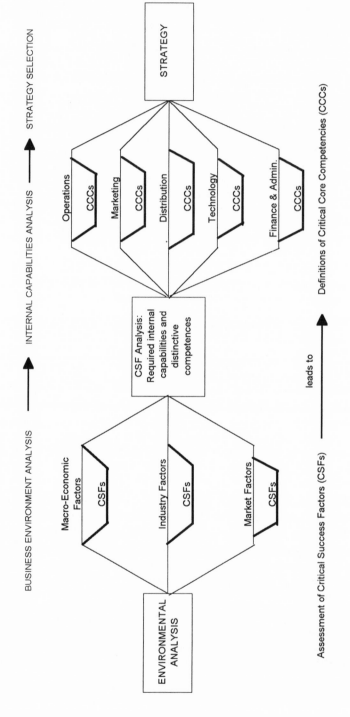

THE PRACTICE AND ACCEPTANCE
OF ENVIRONMENTAL ASSESSMENT

Klein (1973) conducted one of the earliest formal examinations of environmental assessment as an ingredient of comprehensive business planning. After studying several case histories, he developed the argument that strategic planning procedures typically do not incorporate adequate environmental assessment functions. Subsequently, researchers and theorists have drawn essentially the same conclusion: most firms' environmental assessment functions are underdeveloped and don't make reasonable use of EA tools that are available to them. Consequently, their planning methodologies are commensurately impaired. Virtually no studies have concluded that environmental assessment functions typically are developed to a state of general proficiency in any industry, but many have found to the contrary.

It is generally accepted that environmental assessment should make a fundamental contribution to goal setting and strategy formulation (Fahey, King, and Narayanan, 1981). However, Godiwalla et al. (1980) demonstrated that environmental uncertainty, caused by an interaction of environmental dynamism and complexity, can increase the difficulty of strategy selection. Of the two dimensions, dynamism (i.e., volatility) was more influential than complexity on the accomplishment of large industrial firms' goals and objectives during the severe recession of 1973–1974 (see Figure 2.1).

Figure 2.1
Impact of Two Environmental Uncertainty Dimensions
on Perceived Difficulty of Accomplishing Goals and Objectives
(Percent Increase in Difficulty between 1973 and 1976)

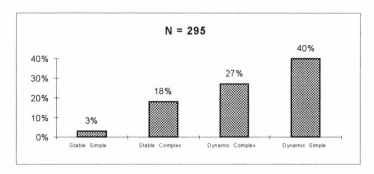

Source: Adapted from data reported by Godiwalla, et al. (1980)

Thomas (1980) conducted a survey which demonstrated that the very largest companies tend to conduct environmental scanning more often than others. Subsequently, in a more extensive survey, Diffenbach (1983) developed similar conclusions. However, even in large corporations, a majority of presidents did not confirm the usefulness of EA functions. Executives from smaller firms' actually acknowledged the importance of environmental assessment for strategic planning more often than large firms, even though the incidence of EA functions was lower. Jain's (1984) research similarly demonstrated that the largest corporations tend to have environmental assessment functions much more often than others. Larger firms also performed such functions more proficiently than smaller firms (Figure 2.2).

Figure 2.2
Impact of Firm Size on
Development of Scanning Practices (N= 186)

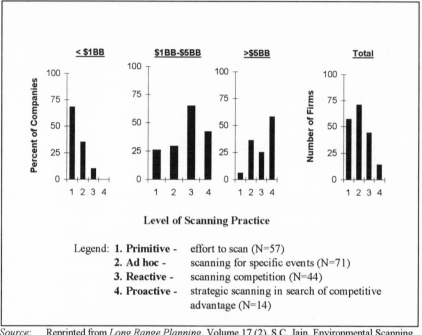

Source: Reprinted from *Long Range Planning*, Volume 17 (2), S.C. Jain, Environmental Scanning in U.S. Corporations, p.118, Copyright © 1984, with permission from Elsevier Science.

Of course, top management's acknowledgment of EA functions' importance can determine their effectiveness. Thus, Javidan (1984) showed that chief executives' awareness of environmental factors determined the extent to which corporate strategic planning employs environmental assessment functions. Daft, Sormunen, and Parks (1988), studied the effect of environmental uncertainly on "scanning" behaviors of 50 manufacturing companies' chief executives. As strategic uncertainty of environmental elements that were judged important to the firm increased, so did scanning behaviors. Correlations between environmental uncertainty and scanning were highest among firms with the highest rates of return, suggesting the potential for return on investments in EA functions.

To summarize the results of these surveys, it seems that formal environmental assessment tends to be a luxury in which only the largest companies indulge. However, even large firms' executives have not universally accepted the value of environmental assessment functions. Thus, EA functions' value in strategic planning remains to be practically accepted by a majority of corporate executives, notwithstanding their obvious potential to enhance competitive advantage.

THE ENVIRONMENTAL ASSESSMENT PROCESS: GENERAL METHOD

During the 1950s and 1960s, businesses conducted managerial planning in a fairly orderly environment that Drucker (1969) characterized as an age of continuity. However, commencing with the Arab oil embargo of 1973–1974 and the ensuing economic recessions of 1974 and 1981, management was forced to question the reliability—if not the validity—of basic environmental assumptions in its strategic plans. The result was a heightened interest in understanding the business environment better. This understanding was needed to strengthen strategic planning methods which, according to some, had taken the environment too much for granted (Kiechel, 1982).

State of the Art

Conjecturing on typical weaknesses of EA functions' effectiveness, Fahey, King, and Narayanan (1981) concluded that as the 1980s began, firms still were performing environmental assessments primarily for the wrong reason—in response to crises. They also found that forecasting horizons usually were not long enough to accomplish the anticipatory purposes of environmental analysis and that the methods employed were not very sophisticated. The most frequently employed methods of forecasting in their survey sample were trend extrapolation and scenarios. Similarly, Diffenbach (1983) concluded that expert opinion (86%), trend extrapolation (83%), and evaluations of alternative scenarios (68%) were the most frequently used forecasting methods.

Jain (1984) concluded that among most of the corporations included in his large survey, the level of environmental analysis functions typically was either primitive or only slightly more advanced than that. In this study, Jain found Delphi forecasting approaches to be the most popular. In another extensive study, Klein and Linneman (1984) concluded that environmental assessment was not yet an effective or widely accepted function; senior managers in only 48% of the 445 large firms surveyed concurred that EA functions had become important parts of their strategic planning procedures. Moreover, there was general dissatisfaction with forecasting methods, which most frequently included trend extrapolation and scenario building.

Firms with the most highly developed environmental analysis functions among those surveyed by Klein and Linneman (1984) tended to have made a significant commitment to strategic planning. They had more extensive experience in planning, longer planning horizons, more highly developed forecasting and analytic skills. They also were in more rapidly changing business environments. One other distinguishing characteristic was particularly interesting: EA functions of foreign firms tended to be more highly developed than those of U.S. firms.

There also is a strong suggestion in these studies' findings, that simple trend extrapolation and non-quantitative Delphi or scenario forecasting methods often are preferred over more rigorous, quantitative methods.

Balancing Pragmatism and Comprehensiveness

Exhibit 2.5 portrays the strategic information flow in a typical EA procedure. Some variations are much simpler; but many are more complex. Environmental assessment functions that can be conducted simply actually may be more effective than complex processes exemplified by Segev's (1977) elaborate model.Thus, Grant and King (1982) opined that planning managers should divide the environmental assessment function into just two essential components:

- Techniques and devices for describing the *current* environment, both by diagnosing the present situation and by extending prevailing trends or patterns into the foreseeable future using data bases, trend analysis, and cross-impact matrices; and

- Techniques for evaluating *alternative futures*, including various forms of vulnerability analysis, Delphi forecasts of alternatives, dialectical analysis, and simulation models.

Narayanan and Fahey (1987) proposed that the EA process really needs to include only four sequential elements: broad environmental scanning; more focused monitoring of the most important factors discovered by scanning; forecasting those factors to which the firm is most sensitive; and perpetually reassessing outcomes of those three functions. Three years later, Ginter and Duncan (1990) came to a very similar conclusion.

Herring (1992) has proposed that the EA process may be incorporated into the strategy formulation process in six steps:

1. Describing the firm's competitive environment,

2. Forecasting variables to which the firm is sensitive,

3. Challenging assumptions on which forecasts are predicated,

4. Identifying vulnerabilities of the firm that would existwhen taking new strategic action,

5. Adjusting strategy to mitigate serious vulnerabilities or otherwise adapt to the environment, and

6. Determining when the prevailing strategy no longer is sustainable within present or anticipated environmental circumstances.

Exhibit 2.5
Environmental Assessment Functions for Strategic Planning

Summary

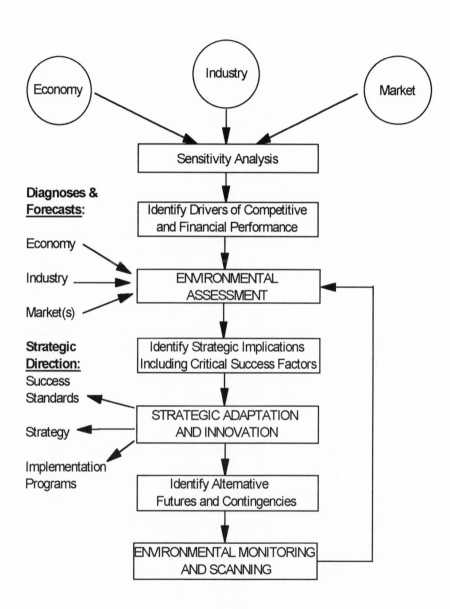

In these authors' opinions, environmental assessment processes should be so well-structured that they can be conducted and maintained efficiently. One means of accomplishing that procedural objective is to implement a comprehensive environmental scanning system wherein the EA function becomes an integral part of a firm's strategic management fabric. Guidelines for setting up such a system are provided in the following paragraphs.

Setting Up an EA Scanning System

Specifications and guidelines for setting up EA procedures and data bases are abundant in the literature of strategic management. King and Cleland (1974) offered some of the earliest guidelines, and they still are recommended reading for planning managers whose firms don't yet have EA data bases. However, even with such guidelines, the planning manager must exercise a great deal of discretion in deciding on the contents of an EA database, since interindustry differences are quite significant (Fahey and King, 1977), and the amount of available data may be overwhelming. The good news in getting started, however, is that plenty of information usually is readily available.

One of the best environmental data sources in terms of both quality and quantity is the U.S. Government which collects, maintains, and disseminates a huge amount of information relevant to commercial decision making. Recent advances in information technology also have provided planning managers with a large variety of online data bases. Firms of all sizes now can reach these with economies of time and expense. McGrane (1987) chronicled such benefits from the use of Lexis-Nexis and similar systems. Today, even planning managers in smaller firms can acquire a broad scope of business intelligence at much lower costs and with less difficulty than only a few years ago. Indeed, in the present age of information abundance, smaller firms enjoy some advantages over larger firms; they are much less visible than their larger competitors about whom they can obtain considerably more information electronically than large firms can obtain about them (Hershey, 1980).

In setting up and implementing an environmental assessment system and related procedures, pragmatism is important. Procedures should be as simple and results-oriented as possible, consisting of straightforward methods for collecting, evaluating, storing, analyzing, and disseminating refined information rather than raw data (Gilad and Gilad, 1985). In this age of electronic data profusion, it often is cheaper to purchase information gathered and refined by commercial services without delay than to perform that work internally, even if internalizing such functions is in the interest of propriety or confidentiality. Indeed, nearly two decades ago, Diffenbach's (1983) survey of 90 large industrial companies already had disclosed that even large corporations with well-developed EA functions found it difficult to comprehend and respond effectively to the massive environmental information they had accumulated.

Many volumes have been written about opportunities to exploit the abundance of electronic (and other) information available to support comprehensive business planning. (For example, see Reimann, 1988; J. L. Webster, Reif, and

Bracker, 1989; Mockler, 1991). While such sources indeed are abundant, the planning manager's challenge is to see that their usage is well directed. Above all, EA information must be relevant to strategic decision making. Thus, as managers consider the broad scope of economic, industry, and market information that they might gather and monitor, they should attach a high priority to collecting data from which management may draw consequential inferences.

CONCLUSION

Virtually every book regarding strategic management or comprehensive business planning prescribes some approach to environmental assessment functions. There is really no question of the vital role EA functions must play in strategic planning. However, as numerous academic studies and observations of practitioners will attest, environmental assessment functions have been remarkably unsuccessful in gaining widespread acceptance, let alone implementation, notwithstanding their substantial potential to enhance a firm's competitive capabilities. Typically, chief executives neither appreciate EA functions nor have implemented them proficiently. Herring (1992) drew the simple but alarming conclusion that very few firms actually are proficient at the competitive intelligence function, even though management can derive successful strategies only when it has good intelligence. It is, indeed, puzzling that U.S. management has not better appreciated or exploited this important function.

Fahey (1985) proposed that there are five alternative answers to the paradox mentioned above. First, some executives may not believe that it is possible to understand the nature of complex business environments well enough to enhance the quality of strategic planning. Second, the scope of assessment may be either too broad or too narrow, depending on complexity and the rate of change in both internal and external environments. Third, there is a tendency of executives to treat forecasts more like promises or *a priori* statements of fact than probable outcomes of stated assumptions—and to expect more than can be delivered. Fourth, there is a mistaken tendency of managers to work with data taken directly from the environment rather than analyses of such data, and only then to draw inferences regarding options for enhancing performance potential. Finally, planning professionals often fail to establish a sufficient link between the results of environmental analysis and strategic decision-making alternatives' potential outcomes.

In the light of EA functions' relative inability to gain widespread acceptance and the technical flaws with which environmental assessment functions often have been implemented, it is not difficult to conjecture on at least one major reason for comprehensive business planning functions' lack of success. When planning functions fail, it is often because planners have not anticipated foreseeable business conditions or prepared strategic responses in time to react effectively. However, when environmental analysis functions succeed empirical investigations and observations discussed in the previous paragraphs suggest that planners seem to meet one methodological requirement: they have a deliberate, systematic approach. They implement a formal procedure, if not a system, continuously. The scope of such a systematic procedure includes scanning the relevant environment, monitoring environmental forces that can influence performance potential, forecasting those forces and continuously evaluating their potential impacts on feasibility of existing strategy or appropriateness of new strategy (Exhibit 2.4). Rather than adopting such a systematic approach, however, management typically employs a much less deliberate approach to environmental analysis or lacks any formal approach at all.

We conclude this chapter with an axiom that successful strategic planning requires an effective environmental assessment function, conducted deliberately and regularly. In performing that function, management's challenge is to adopt methods and procedures at each stage that provide the most accurate and insightful results. The next five chapters will provide planning managers with guidance in selecting and applying such methods.

Part II

Evaluating the Present Situation

CHAPTER 3

Economic Analysis

Executives sometimes express impatience with economists and economic analysis functions, insisting that they have small relevance to the practicalities of doing business. These views are ill-founded. To the contrary, successful planning managers must have skills to employ a growing abundance of economic information that is available from public and private resources. Thereby, they may achieve insights into the firm's business conditions that would not be attainable otherwise.

Business planners can derive at least three kinds of benefit that from the skillful application of economic analysis. First, recalling Exhibit 2.1 in the previous chapter, a firm's economy really is an artifactual construct that provides a useful perspective from which to view relevant industries or markets. Thus, economic analysis provides a broad perspective of the whole environmental system in which a firm, its industry, and its markets exist. Often the economy is like a deep river with a strong current that carries along all firms in its path. Firms that produce commodities such as food, fuel, capital goods, and raw materials are especially sensitive to the general economy. Many service firms—such as those that distribute food and fuel, hotels, airlines, truckers, and builders—also are in this category of economically sensitive industries. Macroeconomic analysis can be very helpful in anticipating these industries' trends and cycles.

Firms in industries that add considerable value to their products (e.g., more technologically intensive industries versus commodity processors) also can benefit from economic analysis—not just to understand their own industries better, but to gain insights into the markets upon which sales of their products or services depend. In this latter context, few firms cannot benefit from economic analysis in preparing their business plans.

Macroeconomic forces can influence or even determine an industry's structure and performance potential through their impacts on market boundaries, supply and demand aggregates, and critical success factors (Narayanan, 1984). In short, sound economic analysis provides planning managers and top corporate executives with the big picture that is essential for a realistic perspective of their firms' and their customers' performance potential.

Consider, for instance, the long-term structural shifts in America's economy—from prior dominance by agrarian, to manufacturing, to service, and, most currently, to information industries. Figure 3.1 depicts dramatic shifts in the importance of the manufacturing and service sectors. Later in this chapter we explore the nature of these long-term shifts and ways in which business planners can benefit from their diagnosis.

Figure 3.1
Emergence of the Service Economy: 1960–1998

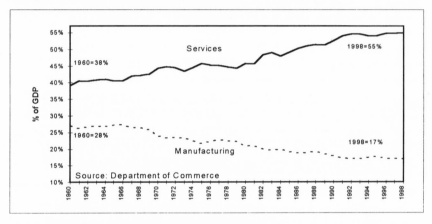

Source: Council of Economic Advisors, 1999. Tables B-8 and B-12

A second benefit of economic analysis for business planning derives from an understanding of fundamental mechanics that drive supply, demand, competition, pricing, and profitability of nearly all industries and markets. Illustrations of economic factors addressed by analyses of this type include demographics, employment and earnings, personal and industrial risk, the propensity to save (versus spend) incomes, capacity utilization, debt, and governmental monetary policy. The dynamics of these functions can have far-reaching impacts on industries' and markets' structures as well as their short term revenue and profit potentials.

Business planners may derive a third benefit of economic analysis by identifying economic precursors of industries' and markets' performance shifts. Economic analysis provides the planner with methods for selecting variables to use in forecasting an industry's output or a market's demand. As such, economic analysis typically is a fundamental prerequisite for effective industry/market forecasting.

GENERAL METHODOLOGY

For such a complex and broad scope of inquiry, fundamental economic analysis of the present environment is remarkably straightforward. Economic analysis for this purpose entails procedures of description and measurement using data available from public and private resources. Often, planning managers can obtain sufficient data with which to perform such functions from agencies of the U.S. government for well under $2,000 per year (see Appendix III). However, large corporations often spend many times that amount to obtain compilations or condensations of the same information from commercial reporting services that may add very little additional value.

With the advent of electronic access to large databases, planners can retrieve economic information almost as soon as it becomes available. Today, even small firms have an ability to gather relevant economic facts with facility no less than that of the largest corporations. Incidentally, planners also may obtain information of comparable or superior quality from the Canadian government. (Data from Mexico are less reliable.) Together these sources enable analysts to evaluate the business economy of North America as a whole. Planners also can find good quality in data distributed by the International Monetary Fund (IMF), the European Union (EU), and agencies of several foreign countries. Appendix III provides several devices for retrieving data that are readily available from such sources.

Economic analysis functions largely are addressed to taxonomy— measurement and monitoring of data that describe the relevant economy's structure and trends in its composition. However, the methodology of economic analysis also draws on theories that help to explain the environment more fundamentally. Such theories employ a variety of useful concepts—including firms' motives to pursue earnings at either maximum or only satisfactory levels; the influence of money supply on prices; impacts of demographics on employment; interrelationships of employment and inflation; impacts of consumer and business confidence or pessimism on risk-taking; relationships between debt and economic stability; the influence of capacity utilization on inflation; and the nature of business cycles. Because they may be useful to planning managers in evaluating the business situation, we will discuss several of those theoretical concepts in the rest of this chapter.

The Economic Aggregates

In its most basic form, we may divide the system that is used to account for purchases of goods and services in the U.S. economy into four sectors:

- Personal consumption;
- Private domestic investment;
- Government expenditures; and
- Foreign trade.

Two agencies of the U.S. Department of Commerce—the Economics and Statistics Administration and the Bureau of Economic Analysis (BEA)—jointly publish accounts of activity in those sectors and related analyses in considerable detail on both a monthly and quarterly basis.

The two pie charts in Figure 3.2, prepared by the BEA, demonstrate that proportionality of the four economic sectors has been changing over several years.

Figure 3.2
Shares of Gross Domestic Purchases: 1959, 1997

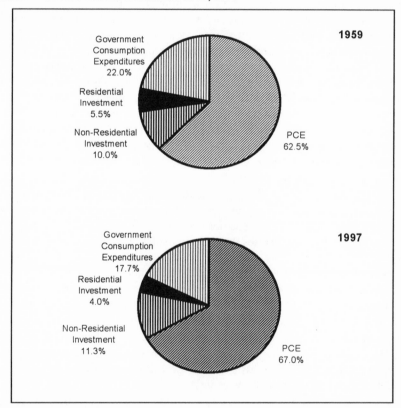

*Source:*U.S. Department of Commerce, Bureau of Economic Analysis, 1998

Those charts demonstrate that since 1959 the importance of consumer spending in the American economy has increased from about 62% to 67% (two-thirds) of all spending. On the other hand, government expenditures have decreased from about 22% to 18%. The importance of residential investment also has declined from about 5.5% to 4.0%, while the importance of nonresidential investment has remained at about 10%.

Later in this section, we will explain why these shifts represent fundamental changes in demographics and social preferences that planners must understand before they can anticipate future trends accurately. For the present, however, it is simply compelling to appreciate the overwhelming importance of personal consumption in America's economy and the changing mix of residential versus nonresidential investment in the construction sector.

Figure 3.3
Shares of National Income: 1959, 1997

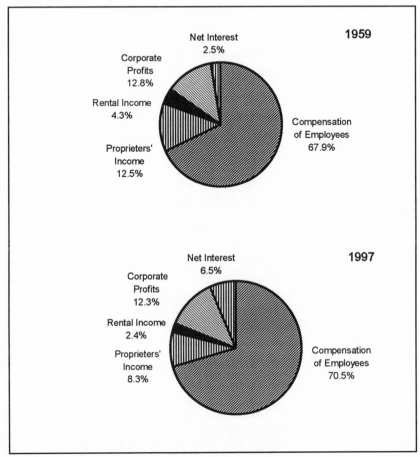

Source: U.S. Department of Commerce, Bureau of Economic Analysis, 1998

Expenditures are not the only frame of reference for evaluating the importance of economic sectors. Consider the two pie charts in Figure 3.3 (also prepared by BEA) that divide national income into its principal categories. In 1959, employees' incomes represented less than 69% of national income. By 1997, that proportion had grown to nearly 71%. Meanwhile, the total of corporate profits and proprietors' incomes dropped from just under 25% to less than 21%. Reflecting a dramatic increase in debt financing, net interest grew from 2.5% to almost 7% of national income while rental income dropped sharply from 4.4% to 2.4%. These trends reflect fundamental shifts in America's economy that planning managers should recognize before analyzing industries and markets in greater detail.

Inflation Adjustment and Chain Weighting

One problem that troubles economists in the computation and interpretation of data which purport to show trends in the economy's composition arises when they attempt to develop real (uninflated) measures of trends in economic activity. Typically, economists apply fixed weights to quantities and prices of goods and services in some base year. Then, they calculate subsequent years' measures, using the same set of volume weights over an entire time period. However, fixed-weighted measures of real Gross Domestic Product (GDP) for extended periods reflect a substitution bias that can cause significant errors in estimated growth rates.

Consider the impact of substitution bias on real output measures for fast growing industries versus mature industries. During 1982–1987, computer prices declined at an average annual rate of 17%, while computer shipments increased at a 34% annual rate. In 1977, a small mainframe computer might have cost $80,000, whereas a new single-family home might have cost $43,000. By 1987, the price of a computer with the same capacity probably dropped to about $30,000, while the price of the same-sized new home might have reached $125,000. (Those trends have continued, of course.) Without some adjustment, fixed weight computations of both industries' real output would be greatly misleading. Similar shifts have occurred in the prices of many products, even basic commodities such as fuel. For these and similar reasons, a new approach called *chain weighting* was devised.

Beginning in 1997, chain weighting procedures began to compute annual changes in quantities and prices together. This approach permits year-to-year effects of changes in relative prices and output to be reflected in economic time series without the need to make large revisions when base years are changed. The result is a more valid system of estimating real trends in industries' output and economic aggregates (Landefeld and Parker 1995, 1997).

Commercial Data Sources

The U.S. government is not the only source of good data for describing trends in important sectors of the U.S. economy (although it is by far the most important). Data that describe the U.S. economy and its various sectors are abundantly available from several firms that analyze and forecast economic industry and market trends. Several of these firms are listed in Appendix IV. Planning managers can gain considerable analytic insight from these firms often at a very reasonable cost.

For example, the National Planning Association (NPA), provides substantial data regarding economic, demographic, and residential building activity at the local level (cities and counties) throughout the United States. This information can be obtained through NPA Data Services, Inc., in Washington, D.C. NPA data are comprehensive and analytically insightful. Similar information is available from the FW Dodge division of McGraw-Hill and Co., albeit at greater expense. Dodge offers the most comprehensive source of nonresidential construction data available. Data sources for other industries include their trade associations and a multitude of commercial services.

Appendix IV contains a list of several well known professional firms that provide economic reporting and forecasting services. The two largest firms of their kind, DRI/McGraw Hill and the WEFA (previously, Wharton Economic Forecasting Associates) subsidiary of Primark Corporation, will be found on that list. Three banks also are listed in this section; each provides free access to its econometric forecasting model: these are extraordinarily valuable resources. Finally, we have included three well-known universities' econometric modeling services, including that of Yale University, which also provide free access.

ECONOMIC DRIVERS

Among the hundreds of variables reported and monitored by public and private agencies, a few can have particularly forceful impacts on the behavior of industries or entire sectors of the economy. These variables are *drivers*. It is important to appreciate that drivers are not to be confused with causes except in a general sense. Many economic drivers, themselves, are driven by others; and true cause-effect relationships rarely can be defined. It is better to think of drivers as precursors rather than causes. With that caveat, the following paragraphs address some of the driver variables that planning managers often find especially relevant.

Consumer Sector Drivers

Drivers of personal spending include demographics, consumer confidence, employment, personal income, and saving. While the complicity of those variables in determining consumer spending is generally accepted, the nature of such relationships is not always clear. Consider for instance the generally assumed relationship between unemployment and inflation. Theory long has held that there is an inverse relationship (the Phillips curve) between unemployment and inflation (Phillips, 1958). A recent interpretation of this theory is that inflation should accelerate or decelerate depending on whether unemployment is below or above a natural rate. Gordon (1996) opined that the natural rate is about 5.3%. Knowing the natural rate should enable business analysts to anticipate potential shifts in inflation based on actual unemployment trends. However, in the second half of the 1990s that theory was not upheld, since both unemployment and inflation rates declined. Thus, the "inflation puzzle" described by Lown and Rich (1997) remains to be solved.

Akerlof, Dickens, and Perry (1996), at the Brookings Institution recently demonstrated that the unemployment rate itself depends on the inflation rate and that a moderate, steady rate of inflation permits maximum employment and output. They proposed that the pursuit of very low inflation can increase unemployment and reduce the level of national output. In essence, therefore, it appears that the relationship between unemployment and prices is bidirectional; an increase or decrease in one variable beyond an equilibrium point can elicit an inverse reaction in the other. Consequently, if there is a mechanical relation-ship between unemployment and inflation, it is not unidirectional as theorists previously had supposed.

Studies of relationships between unemployment and prices clearly justify a healthy skepticism when economic theory has not been well confirmed by em-pirical research. As Schoeffler (1955) argued with eloquence over 40 years ago, a great deal of economic theory suffers from over reliance on logic without substantiation by evidence. Moreover, economists often must revert to the theories of other social sciences—including psychology and sociology—for possible explanations of economic phenomena such as consumption, saving, and risk-taking. Accordingly, business planners should not hesitate to draw upon those other behavioral disciplines if they help to explain how changes in economic drivers, such as the confidence of consumers and business leaders can elicit shifts in spending and saving behavior.

The U.S. Department of Commerce and the University of Michigan con-duct regular surveys of consumer confidence and buying anticipations. Al-though there is some skepticism regarding the predictive reliability of reported buying anticipations (which will be discussed later), trends in sentiment cer-tainly can be helpful in anticipating short-term (but not long-term) fluctuations in consumer spending and saving.

Consumer confidence (or, conversely, consumers' perceived risk) also can be viewed as a driver of economic activity. Since shortly after the 1981–1982 recession, the saving rate, expressed as a proportion of disposable income, has trended downward, reflecting consumers' lower perceived risk (Figure 3.4). At the same time, sentiment measures, such as the consumer confidence index, have trended upward (Figure 3.5), except during the 1991–1992 recession. Therefore, an inverse relationship between saving and confidence is suggested.

Figure 3.4
Long-Term Saving Trends: 1967–1998

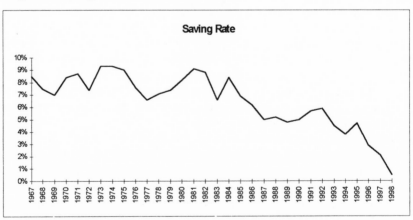

Source: Council of Economic Advisors, 1999. Table B-30

Figure 3.5
Consumer Confidence Trends: 1967–1999

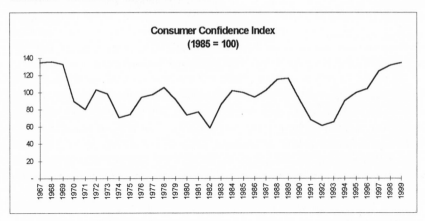

Source: The Conference Board (www.crc-conquest.org)

   Whenever consumer sentiment turns pessimistic, saving rates are likely to increase. The business press typically is focused on short-term dynamics of savings, which can fluctuate in either direction. However, planning managers should be more concerned with longer-term trends. During the 1980s and 1990s, the trend toward lower saving rates and slower formation of capital seems to have destabilized the economy. With less in reserve and higher levels of personal risk, consumers are more likely to respond in the extreme when economic conditions shift positively or negatively, thereby destabilizing the fundamental economy. This condition is evident in wide cyclical swings of rates at which consumers take on installment debt (see Figure 3.6).

Figure 3.6
Consumer Debt Trends: 1967–1998

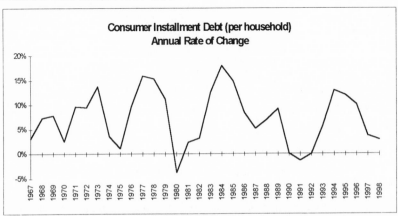

Sources: Council of Economic Advisors, 1999. Table B-77 (Consumer Installment Debt) and U.S. Bureau of the Census 1967–1998 (Households)

The long term decline in saving rates trouble economists who are concerned about the resulting fragility of consumer spending and low levels of investment in America's industrial capital base. Explanations for this problem certainly are not limited to consumers' increasing confidence. The ease with which consumers and firms can borrow, and high levels of government borrowing, also are among the most important explanations (Summers, 1987).

Bosworth (1991) conducted extensive statistical research in an attempt to confirm economical (versus behavioral) explanations for changes in saving rates. However, his results were disappointing. Neither demographic changes, income distribution shifts, nor capital gains in real estate and financial assets could explain declining U.S. saving rates.

Another driver of economic activity is the relative size of each sector in the economy. During the past 15 years, fundamental shifts have occurred in the proportions of consumer spending for services, nondurables, and durables (see Figure 3.7). Many business analysts don't appreciate that more than half of consumer spending now is for services related to housing, transportation, medical care, insurance, financial services, and so forth. According to the Bureau of Labor Statistics (BLS) that proportion will remain about the same through 2005. But, based on demographic and income trends, it is hard to believe that services will not grow even more important in the coming decade.

Figure 3.7
Trends in Consumer Purchases: Services, Nondurables, Durables: 1970 –1998

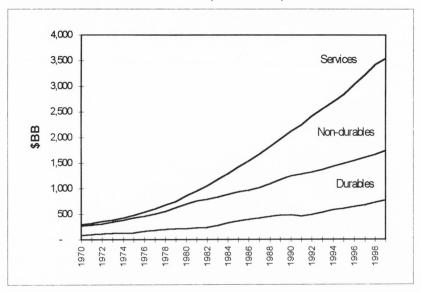

Source: Council of Economic Advisors, 1999. Table B-2

Because median incomes of consumers are rising, the mix of expenditures for nondurables and durables also has shifted significantly. In 1983, 34% of consumer spending was for nondurables—largely nondiscretionary items, such as food, fuel and clothing. Only 12% was for durables, cars, furniture, and appliances. However, by 1994 the share of spending for nondurables had dropped to 31%. BLS has estimated that this share will decline to 29% or less by 2005. At the same time, the share of consumers' discretionary expenditures for durables now exceeds 15% and is rising. Business planners who probe the details of such trends can obtain valuable insight into the changing nature of opportunities in consumer markets.

Industrial Sector Drivers

A large portion of the popular business press is devoted to anticipating changes in industrial output. Suppliers of producers' goods and services in particular need to know as much as possible about drivers of such changes in time to plan their production in keeping with demand. The National Association of Purchasing Managers and the National Federation of Independent Business publish indicators of businesses' purchasing expectations and small business optimism (Dunkelberg, 1996). Results of these surveys provide useful indicators of spending potentials in the Industrial Sector.

When forecasting capital spending for producers' machinery and equipment, business analysts often focus on two fundamental drivers of producers' expenditures. These are corporate profits and capacity utilization, both of which are reported regularly by the U.S. Department of Commerce. The Commerce Department also conducts and reports quarterly surveys of producers' capital spending expectations, six months foreword.

At a more fundamental level, economic theorists are concerned about slowing rates of capital formation in America's industrial sector and business investments in productivity-enhancing assets, including advanced technology. Bailey and Schultz (1990) recently argued at a Brookings Institute conference, that the U.S. economy's growth had faltered in previous years largely due to a shortfall in technological investment. In a rebuttal to that paper, Jorgenson (1990) responded that the Bailey-Schultz argument focused too much on issues of capital-labor substitution arguing that such substitutions already had largely run their course by 1990. Instead, substitutions of new capital for old capital and more sophisticated labor for less sophisticated labor—capital-capital substitution and labor-labor substitution—characterize the present industrial economy.

Capacity utilization may be a driver of industrial machinery and equipment purchases. But, inflation and employment are drivers of demand for producers' output and, thereby, of capacity utilization. So, here again, cause-effect relationships are hard to find. Researchers at the Federal Reserve Bank of San Francisco have demonstrated rather close relationships between capacity utilization, inflation and unemployment (Mattey, 1996). Figures 3.8 and 3.9 depict those relationships. Figure 3.8 demonstrates a close relationship between capacity utilization and the employment rate. (Perhaps this intervening variable of capacity utilization helps to explain the previously mentioned inconsistency in simple relationships between employment and inflation.)

Figure 3.8
Employment Rate vs. Capacity Utilization[1] : 1967–1996

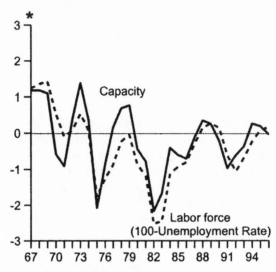

* Number of standard deviations from mean.

Source: Mattey, 1996.

Figure 3.9
Capacity Utilization vs. Core Inflation[2]: 1967–1996

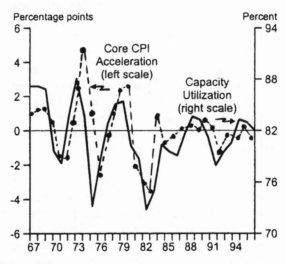

Source: Mattey, 1996.

[1, 2] Reprinted from the Federal Reserve Bank of San Francisco Economic Letter (Number 96-34, November 15, 1996). The opinions expressed do not necessarily reflect the views of the management of the Federal Reserve Bank of San Francisco, or of the Board of Governors of the Federal Reserve System.

Figure 3.9 demonstrates the relationship between capacity utilization and consumer prices. Thus, as an economy's physical and human resources approach full utilization, it is not surprising that prices tend to increase.

Even if the precise nature of relationships between capacity utilization, employment, and prices is not clear, as Akerlof, Dickens and Perry (1996) have shown, analysts should expect significant price increases to occur when capacity utilization *and* employment rates both approach their practical limits. At such times, conditions surely are conducive to extraordinary price increases.

However, analysts must take care to define the scope of relevant markets appropriately. For instance, concepts of employment and capacity utilization should not be limited to the domestic economy in commodity industries such as petro chemicals. If world prices of a commodity are weak, then high employment and capacity utilization in any single country may have only small impacts on domestic prices for that commodity.

Fiscal and Monetary Policies
of the Federal Government

An understanding of the Federal Reserve's current monetary policy and its targets for interest rates can give the industrial business analyst substantial insight into potential shifts in asset-intensive industries' activity. Unfortunately, the Federal Reserve's effectiveness in implementing policy is far from perfect. Problems in implementing policy probably stem from three sources: (1) the significant lag between Federal Reserve policy adjustments and actual industrial business spending decisions; (2) the Fed's inability to control long-term versus short-term interest rates; and (3) significant delays in measurements of policy decisions' impacts using conventional economic data (Walsh, 1994b). Although the Federal Reserve's direct influence is primarily on short-term interest rates, its actions can have indirect impacts on long-term rates as well. Long-term rates typically reflect a premium for inflation and uncertainty over short-term rates. Moreover, when observers believe that Federal Reserve policy is changing, that very expectation may heighten uncertainty and, therefore, cause an increase in long-term rates premiums for risk.

In the long run, federal monetary policy can affect inflation, but probably not employment. (Walsh, 1994a). Accordingly, the Federal Reserve's policy tends to focus on inflation control. Nevertheless, most analysts agree that the 1990–1991 recession was caused primarily by a restrictive federal monetary policy prior to 1990 (Walsh, 1993).

The federal government's fiscal policy also can have a significant impact on industrial activity both directly (for example, in the form of spending) and indirectly (for example, when the government competes with private investors for borrowed funds). During periods of high funding requirements, federal borrowing may compel the Treasury to engage in competition for credit with private businesses. Since the government's credit rating is superior to that of private borrowers, it obtains borrowed funds more easily than businesses, thereby crowding out private enterprise from credit markets because private borrowers are unwilling to pay higher premiums and interest rates. Conversely, reductions in federal spending and borrowing can make it much easier for private enterprise to obtain borrowed capital at favorable prices. Thus, business planners should pay close attention to trends in federal expenditures, receipts, financings and budgetary estimates. A summary of such trends that existed at the time of this draft (Bersani and Bilenki, 1999) is provided in Exhibit 3.1.

In the fiscal year ending October 1, 1999, the U.S. federal government expected to receive more than $1.8 trillion and spend more than $1.7 trillion. The largest categories of expenditure are for transfer payments ($1,087 billion), national defense ($277 billion) and interest on the national debt ($227 billion). The largest transfer payments are for Social Security ($393 billion), Income Security ($205 billion), Medicare ($205 billion); and other public health programs ($143 billion). In recent years, these categories' proportionate importances have shifted dramatically. Between FY1997 and FY2000 (preliminary estimate) alone, expenditures for defense will drop from 16.9% to 15.5% of the total budget and interest expenses will drop from 15.2% to 12.2%. Conversely, transfer payments' importance will increase from 62.6% to 64.7% and the importance of other government operations' expenses will increase from 5.3% to 7.6%. Such significant changes in just three years are quite remarkable when one remembers that these are portions of $1.8 trillion in total spending.

Exhibit 3.1
Receipts and Disbursements of the U.S. Government
Unified Budget: FY1997–FY2000   (FYE October 1): $ Billions

	FY1997	FY1998	FY1999B	FY2000E
Receipts	$1,579.3	$1,721.8	$1,806.3	$ 1,883.0
Less:				
Disbursements:				
Discretionary				
National Defense	270.5	268.5	276.7	274.1
Gov't Operations (Nondefense)	84.4	107.3	135.8	133.5
Subtotal, Discretionary	354.9	375.8	412.5	407.6
Transfer Payments:				
Social Security	365.3	379.2	392.6	408.6
Income Security	230.9	233.2	243.1	258.0
Medicare	190.0	192.9	205.0	216.6
Health	123.8	131.4	143.1	152.3
Other	92.3	96.7	103.6	107.4
Total Transfer Payments	1,002.3	1,033.4	1,087.4	1,142.9
Net Interest	244.0	243.4	227.2	215.2
Total Disbursements	1,601.2	1,652.6	1,727.1	1,765.7
Surplus (Deficit)	$ (21.9)	$ 69.2	$ 79.2	$ 117.3

Source: Bersani and Bilenki, 1999

Trends in U.S. population composition will compel significant changes in the composition of future federal budgets. For the next two decades, demographers expect growth of the American workforce to low and ultimately decline. But, they also anticipate significant increases in the numbers of teen-age children and senior citizens. Thus, federal disbursements for services to non-working adults and school-age children should increase, thereby also increasing demands on both the federal government and employed tax payers for the funds with which to make these payments. Since the number of working-age adults is expected to grow more slowly and even to decline for several years after 2005 (Cutler et al., 1990), this situation is especially alarming and has particular significance for long range planning in service industries such as insurance, finance, education, and health care.

BUSINESS CYCLES

It is easy to think of the business cycle as a periodic pendulum-like fluctuation in aggregate economy activity—first shifting positively, then negatively, and so on. However, aggregate economic cycles really represent the composite behavior of many industries, each with different cyclical characteristics. (See Exhibit 3.2.) For instance, near the lowest point of an aggregate cycle, interest rates may fall sufficiently to encourage investment in residential structures, perhaps encouraged further by government subsidies in the form of tax credits. Therefore, economists view residential construction as a leading sector of the U.S. economy because its expansion stimulates growth of employment in other industries that produce building components, as well as construction. Spending in those industries then can start a chain reaction of economic expansion.

Increased production, employment, and incomes in leading industries and markets stimulate higher output and expenditures in other industries. Eventually, asset-intensive industries experience rising capacity utilization rates. To meet growing demand, their managers must add new capacity. Of course, new capacity also will add overhead costs and/or capacity excesses that encourage price reductions and erosion of profit margins. Those diseconomies in turn encourage reductions in controllable expenditures, and ultimately, a reversal of the aggregate cycle.

In fact, there really is not one economic cycle. Rather, several cycles act concurrently, as Schumpeter (1939) demonstrated (pp. 173–176). Even the present business cycle of total economic output may be viewed as an aggregation of many industries' cycles. Exhibit 3.2 provides examples of four large industries' cyclical returns during the 1982–1991 cycle.

High technology is one sector of the U.S. economy whose cycle has attracted a great deal of attention (Mandel, 1997). Total U.S. expenditures for computers and communication equipment in 1996 were $420 billion. Purchases of information technology hardware alone exceeded $282 billion. That was 17% more than auto purchases, 49% more than investments in new homes and 168% more than commercial and industrial construction. In that year, high-technology contributed between 20% and 25% of the Nation's real wage growth. During 1964–1996, the high-tech sector contributed 20% of total economic growth, while only 14% was attributable to residential housing and 4% to the automotive industry. Obviously, as the current cycle matures, the high-technology sector warrants scrutiny by economic analysts, because a large portion of its output consists of discretionary goods and services that are especially cyclical.

Exhibit 3.2
Cyclical Patterns in Four U.S. Manufacturing Industries
Average Rate of Return on Equity (%): 1982–1991

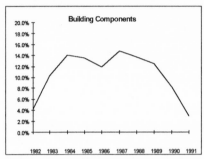
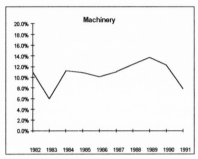
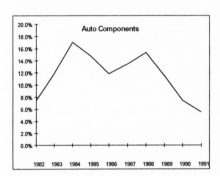
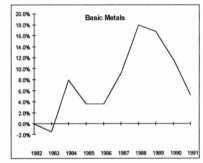

CONCLUSIONS

1. This decade began and ended with recessions, thereby defining a complete U. S. economic "cycle."

2. The building components cycle was typical of the general cycle.

3. But, some industries' cycles began earlier (e.g.,auto components) or later (e.g.,basic metals) than the general cycle. Other "cycles" were much less typical (e.g., machinery).

4. Not shown here, are many other important industries - processing, services, technology, among others.

5. But these examples demonstrate that individual industries follow their own "cycles" which, in the aggregate, comprise the general economic cycle to which most literature refers. Thus, there really is not just one economic cycle, there are many.

Source: The *Value Line Survey*, archives: 1982–1991

In the late 1990s, backlogs of unfilled orders for information technology equipment declined and demand for personal home computers decelerated. Since the high-technology sector contributes substantially to other industries through a very high multiplier effect reflecting extraordinary wages, any downturn could have severe implications for the economy as a whole. A comparison of the current expansion in high-technology industries to previous expansions of industries that at the time were high in technology (for example, railroads), discloses that long-term growth of these sectors indeed can be interrupted by sharp downturns during their long term expansions. (Such a reversal occurred in the railroad industry.) Some segments of the high-technology sector already may be faltering. For instance, semi-conductor chip sales in the United States recently seemed to be declining. Since purchases of computers and other high-tech equipment by both businesses and consumers are discretionary in nature, consumers or businesses well may defer such purchases should confidence turn downward. Impacts on the general economy then would be widespread. The point to be emphasized is that even high-technology industries eventually must mature at which point, they also will exhibit classically cyclical behavior (Mandel, 1997).

LONG WAVES

The typical business cycle lasts about 7 to 10 years. However, there may be another class of cycles that last considerably longer. The concept of *long waves* in economic activity first was proposed by Kondratiev (1926) in a paper delivered at the Economics Institute of the Russian Association of Social Science Research. Taking data from the economic records of France, England, and, to a somewhat lesser extent, the United States, his research approach employed statistical time series decomposition methods that still are in use today.

Kondratiev presented a fully developed body of empirical research complete with statistical analyses and theoretical explanations for certain long waves of economic expansion and contraction. His principal findings were as follows:

- Whereas, prevailing economic theory recognized business cycles of 7 to 11 years, he found cycles with durations of 48 to 55 years,

- During positive phases, intermediate recessions were mild; but they were especially severe during negative phases,

- Three socio-economic patterns occurred at different stages of the cycle: (1) profound changes in socio-economics, manifested by rapid technological change before and during the growth phase; (2) higher incidence of social upheavals during the positive phase and; (3) severe depressions in agriculture (commodity industries) during negative phases.

Kondratiev proposed an economic model to explain long-wave cycles. His model explained that technological innovation was most likely to occur in cycles' negative phases and subsequently to be followed by periods of capital formation. It is also noteworthy that Kondratiev presented this paper in Russia during 1926, only eight years after the Communist Revolution. Since then, Kondratiev's concepts have attracted some, but remarkably little, attention. His concepts are far from generally accepted and have been seriously questioned (Mansfield, 1983; Rosenberg and Frischtak, 1983). However, Modis (1992, 1998) argues strongly in the support of long waves, providing many examples. Snyder's (1984) analysis also supported Kondratiev's essential arguments, citing the work of several other researchers who have drawn similar conclusions. He also looked back into history and found 50-year cycles recorded by the Mayans in Central America as early as 1260 and, even before then, by the Romans.

Because they were inconsistent with classic Keynesian theory, cyclical theories such as Kondratiev's were not very welcome after World War II. Keynsian economists endorse policy mechanisms through which economic activity can be managed by government agencies. Thus Keynsians propose to counteract economic cycles. However, in the early 1970s and 1980s, economic management policies failed to avoid two severe recessions in 1974 and 1981. The similarity of those downturns to others in the 1810s, 1860s, 1920s, and 1970s stimulated new conjectures that cycles with durations of 50 to 60 years actually do exist, as Kondratiev had suggested.

Mansfield's (1983) research seems to support Kondratiev's theory regarding increases and decreases in technological innovation during downturns and expansions, respectively. He studied 175 innovations in three heavy industries during 1919–1958 investigating their relationships to capacity utilization (as a barometer of the cycle's stage). Up to the point of 70% utilization, there was a direct relationship between capacity utilization and innovation. But over 70%, the relationship turned inverse. Mansfield also observed that other researchers previously had obtained similar results. Thus, there is substantial evidence that depressions stimulate innovation and that good times witness the postponement of new designs simply because they are not needed as much. When economies turn negative, the economic need for innovation is strongest.

Notwithstanding the encouragement of findings such as those cited previously, Rosenberg and Frischtak (1983) challenged the long-wave theory by imposing tests of logic that valid economic theories allegedly must meet, including causality, timing, economy-wide repercussions and reliable reoccurrence. Employing these strict tests, the authors concluded that it was not possible to confirm the theory of long waves in economic activity. Certainly, experience in the 1990s also has undermined the validity of long waves since, according to Kondratiev's theory, a serious recession (at least) is overdue. Moreover, during the recent economic expansion, technological innovation has been quite remarkable. Thus, it is possible that recent efforts of national banks and central governments to moderate economic volatility through monetary and fiscal policy indeed have succeeded in extending the present cycle's positive phase.

Notwithstanding these theoretical conjectures, planning managers still should take a long view of the economy and their industries. At a minimum, they should attempt to identify the current stage of their industry's business cycle and, if it is helpful to do so, the current phase of longer cycles in relevant economic and industrial activity, such as products' life cycles.

LIMITATIONS OF ECONOMIC THEORY: DO ECONOMISTS REALLY KNOW WHAT'S HAPPENING?

This overview of economic analysis will conclude by raising two troubling issues. The first of these issues is a challenge to the very core of economic analysis. It questions whether economic theory is fundamentally valid. In a thought-provoking volume, nearly a half-century ago, Sidney Schoeffler (1955) made a convincing argument that much of economic theory really isn't valid or reliable. (Schoeffler later went on to develop the PIMS approach to industry analysis and found the Strategic Management Institute, which has provided the planning profession with many empirical foundations of generally accepted methodology.) Schoeffler pointed out that because they have borrowed their models and methods from other sciences and disciplines for which those models and methods were developed in the first place, economists cannot predict economic events very reliably. Thus, economic concepts of demand, risk, and resource allocation originally were the subjects of more fundamental disciplines, such as psychology and agriculture, where the statistical models used by economists (with questionable effectiveness) are more appropriate.

Sometimes economists propose theories that give the impression of determinism when, in fact, the phenomena they attempt to describe are not determinable at all. Schoeffler cited the example of an astronomer who predicts a solar eclipse. Because the model used by astronomers contains most, if not all, of the information required for a closed logical system, its prophecy is almost invariably borne out. Social scientists, including economists, never will enjoy such luxuries, and they should not pretend to do so.

Schoeffler humorously likened economists to studying the nucleus of an atom with a stethoscope. But, he was not entirely pessimistic about the discipline of economics. In the mid-1950s, economists were developing theories and tools unique to their discipline. Most encouraging were input-output models, the statistical inferences one can draw from empirical studies of cyclical economic activity and the descriptive benefits that can be obtained from using econometric models in simulation. Those developments, Schoeffler acknowledged, indeed are unique to the economics profession. Remarkably, those same three developments still are emerging. But, by no means had they been brought to fruition as this book was drafted, four and a half decades later.

Since Schoeffler's book (1955) was published, economists certainly have made great progress in describing economic phenomena and their interrelationships. However, for reasons that we will explore later, the predictive power of econometric models still leaves a great deal to be desired. Moreover, although input-output models are more widely available today, the potential of such models remains to be realized due to delays in obtaining necessary data. The federal government's present input-output tables are comprised of data collected during a census more than five years ago. Recently, private economic consulting firms have begun to update I-O tables on a limited basis much more frequently (annually, quarterly, and even monthly) depending on data availability. These firms' capabilities are discussed in Chapter 5 and Appendix IV.

LONG-TERM ECONOMIC THREATS
TO THE UNITED STATES

The second issue was raised in a report issued by the MIT Commission on Industrial Productivity in 1990. MIT based its report on a broad-scoped study of America's long-term economic problems and potential solutions. The study concluded that America's most pressing economic problems may be traced to two fundamental sources: (1) reliance on mass production of standard goods; and (2) an incorrect perception that the United States can continue to flourish as a private economic stronghold, relying on its own markets and technical expertise.

It is widely recognized that the technological shortsightedness of several American industries' managers during the 1960s and 1970s placed them at severe competitive disadvantages. Well-known examples include the automotive, basic steel and consumer electronics industries. In the 1990s, America's high-technology industries have made substantial recoveries; but the challenge remains in others. A well-educated workforce, able to employ more sophisticated technology in industrial processes is at least as important as progress in any single industry. But, the United States' educational system is falling further behind foreign educational systems each year.

American history manifests a cultural heritage—formed by the Industrial Revolution, its European ancestry, and the World Labor Movement—in which management and labor divide themselves into opposing camps, each with conflicting objectives. Of course, this conflict between Labor and Management also exists in other industrialized countries. But, in many of them, culture has permitted an accommodation of the common interest, whereas that is not yet the case in the United States. One probable reason why the post-war Japanese industrial system succeeded so well (until a recent debacle in its financial institutions) is the cultural ability of disparate groups to work toward common goals.

The MIT commission's report concluded that if America's economic future is to be as bright as its past, four fundamental flaws must be remedied:

1. Parochialism: we must correct historic over-reliance on our own markets and failure to understand competitive requirements in other economies;

2. Short-term bias: we must resist the temptation to pursue short-term gain and attractive quarterly earnings statements at the expense of long-term performance potential and American Industry's survival as a competitor in global markets;

3. Process weaknesses: America's technological emphasis has been on *product* design rather than *process* design, while the emphasis in other industrial countries has been just the reverse. Aggravating this imbalance of technological emphasis has been a scarcity of teamwork between designers and operators, failure of higher educational institutions to appreciate the need for better process engineering, an educational system that fails to prepare youth for technological employment, and a host of government policies that fail to encourage solutions to these problems,

4. Self-defeating conflicts: rivalries such as those that exist between labor and management, manufacturers and suppliers, suppliers and customers are detriments to the Nation's economic welfare. They must be resolved if the United States is to achieve a sustained competitive advantage in world markets.

The commission's report concluded that solutions to these problems are not infeasible, but will be very difficult to implement. The American people must be willing to make long-term investments in technology and fundamental improvements in U.S. educational systems. Most important is the need for cultural changes wherein labor, educational, political, and business leaders are willing to take a longer-term view. Surely the community of professional business planners also can contribute to such far-sighted corporate philosophies.

CHAPTER 4

Industry Analysis

From the broad perspective of economic analysis, we turn to the more specific environmental drivers of firms' performance potentials which are endemic to individual industries. Planning managers need to understand the structural anatomy of any industry in which strategy is to be implemented, for at least four reasons. First, some industries and segments simply are more attractive than others because they are characterized by higher rates of growth, return or cash-flow. Second, an industry may present unusual opportunities (or problems) for the firm to exploit proprietary resources. Third, competitive conditions—both existing and prospective—may present a firm with extraordinary problems or opportunities for return. Fourth, industry attractiveness is by no means static. If an industry segment is in its infancy, it may be much more or less attractive than a more mature one. For all of these reasons, industry attractiveness is directly relevant to the firm's performance potential.

Before taking a strategic direction, management must assess the chances for success when engaging other firms on the competitive battlefield. Therefore, this chapter provides guidelines for conducting such an evaluation by taking four approaches:

1. Analysis of industry performance norms: growth, costs, profitability, rates of return, and so on.;

2. Analysis of industry structure with respect to sources of competitive advantage and disadvantage;

3. Analysis of the industry's life-cycle stage, and

4. Analysis of individual competitors.

The following pages discuss each of these approaches in turn.

INDUSTRY DIFFERENCES IN
PERFORMANCE POTENTIAL

The importance of a thorough industry analysis was demonstrated by McGahan and Porter (1997) who, following a line of research initiated by Schmalensee (1985) and Roquebert et al. (1996), conducted extensive research to measure the separate influences of industry versus individual firm effects on operating income variability (see Table 4.1). Using Standard and Poor's Compustat data files, they studied more than 12,000 business units and 7,000 corporations in 628 industries over a 13-year term from 1982–1994. To measure the portion of variance in operating profit margins explained by industry and firm differences, a comprehensive multivariate statistical approach was employed. About 52% of the variance in profitability thus was explained. Of that amount, industry differences explained about 19%, and firm effects explained 32%. But these proportions varied drastically between industries.

Table 4.1
Inter-Industry Differences in
Operating Profit Margins: 1982–1984

	Industry	Firm
Percent of Variance Attributable to Industry and Firm		
Lodging/Enter.	64.30 %	19.41%
Services (other)	47.37	33.46
Wholesale/Retail	41.79	2.04
Transportation	39.50	9.72
Ag & Mining	29.35	5.02
Manufacturers	10.81	35.45
Average	18.68	31.71

Source: McGahan and Porter, 1997

Thus, industry-endemic factors are especially powerful influences on firms' performance potentials in the lodging, general services, transportation, and distribution industries, but less powerful in the more asset intensive manufacturing industries.

Rumelt's (1991) findings previously had differed from those described in Table 4.1 primarily because service industries had been excluded from his sample. But, his published report still has been interpreted widely as supporting a resource based view of firm versus industry factors' relative impacts on performance potential and strategic priorities. Due to limitations of the sample that he studied (principally manufacturers), Rumelt (1991) concluded that firm effects predominate—differing sharply from Schmalensee (1985) who had concluded that industry influences predominate. Finally, McGahan and Porter (1997) reconciled the two views by demonstrating that the balance of these two forces—industry and firm effects—differs between industries.

ANALYSIS OF INDUSTRY
PERFORMANCE NORMS

Firms often select financial and competitive objectives on the basis of industry performance norms. Thus, if a firm's management desires to achieve superior results in an industry, a thorough analysis of such norms, their trends and underlying drivers is mandatory. In a large study of 245 firms in 18 industries, over the 20 years of 1947–1966, Lev (1969) demonstrated that firms' financial ratios do seem to converge toward stable norms over time. Therefore, as an industry grows more mature, its performance norms are likely to become more reliable. A corollary to this conclusion is its inference that extraordinary results become increasingly difficult to achieve as industries mature.

To measure trends in an industry's revenues, cost, rates of return, capital composition and productivity of assets, analysts may employ any of several sources. The approach is essentially statistical and should employ one of two general methods. The first method entails constructing a representative sample and accounting for differences between segments, or effects of drivers, using inferential methods. For instance, one can use statistical sampling techniques to perform comparisons of especially successful and unsuccessful firms to identify critical success requirements and possible objectives of strategy. The second method is to establish norms by conducting a census, essentially accounting for all, or nearly all, of an industry's or segment's behavior. In industrial research, census methods often are feasible, especially when the industry under study is highly concentrated or regulated. Examples include automobile manufacturers, electric utilities, insurance firms, hospitals, airlines, banks.

Sources of data that may be used for trend and pattern analysis include much of the previously described economic information available through the U.S. Department of Commerce's Bureau of Economic Analysis. That agency distributes regular reports on individual industries' performance. Commercial services, including Standard and Poor's, Value-Line, and Moody's also sometimes can provide the business analyst with substantial historic information in a more readily usable form.

One problem with data available through public sources (including commercial services) is their reliance on disclosures by publicly-owned firms. Such data are significantly biased for at least two reasons. First, publicly-owned firms—especially those monitored by commercial services—tend to be much larger than average. Second, by their very nature, these firms have gained access to public sources of equity funding and, therefore, do not rely as much as privately owned firms on lending institutions to obtain capital. Privately owned companies tend to be smaller and more highly leveraged.

One of the few reliable sources of data describing privately-owned firms is Dun and Bradstreet's (D&B) on-line marketing information data-base. Analysts may use the D&B system to construct a sample of companies that are both publicly and privately owned in just about any industry and geographic market. One drawback of the D&B system is its lack of trend information for most companies. However, D&B staff personnel can create limited trend data at a significant additional expense. Another limitation is D&B's reliance on firms to report accurately (although some verification is done).

For each firm, D&B's on-line data-base contains industrial classification codes, numbers of employees, plant areas, sales, and various other financial data. Through careful sampling, and after elimination of unrepresentative observations, it often is possible to construct profiles of industries' productivity and capacity utilization by using those data, as Figure 4.1 illustrates.

Figure 4.1
Industry Analysis:
Productivity and Capacity Utilization (Example)

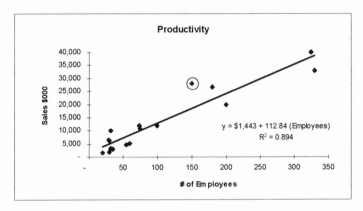

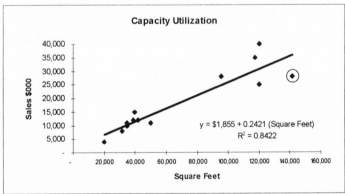

In Figure 4.1, which is derived from an actual case history, the subject firm (whose plot point is circled) enjoys high labor productivity but low capacity utilization. Its near-term operating strategy for improving profitability clearly should reflect more aggressive marketing. Compared to its peers, this firm probably has relatively low direct labor costs and high fixed overhead costs (due to under absorption). The sales objective apparently should be upwards of $32 million versus the present level of about $27 million. This firm's marketing strategy thus should be capable of generating about $5 million in additional sales; so, that might be one of its "strategic objectives." In setting objectives for improvement in sales and operations, such analyses can be very helpful. Thus, as in the example of Figure 4.1, if a firm has abnormally high labor productivity and low capacity utilization, opportunities for profit improvement probably are more likely to be found in an aggressive selling effort than in workforce cost reductions.

There are few other large-scale sources of information regarding performance norms of privately owned companies. One in particular is Robert Morris Associates (RMA), which conducts and publishes studies of financial statement norms for firms at specified levels of sales (from very small to very large) in a wide variety of industries. Since RMA conducts these statement studies every year, planners also can use its historic reports to assemble trend information.

A rarely employed approach, but one that nevertheless can have very satisfactory results, entails collecting annual reports of companies in industries of specific interest. By preparing one's own analytic data-base, rather than relying on data provided by commercial services, the analyst often can develop information that is much more relevant to the firm. Consider, for instance, the large number of companies engaged in multiple lines of business but which, by federal regulation, must report sales, operating profits, and net assets employed in separate lines of business. While a sufficiently motivated business analyst might go to the trouble of retrieving line-of-business data from historic annual reports, commercial services may not separate them in much detail. Since many large corporations engage in multiple lines of business, do-it-yourself methods of constructing industry norms often provide the only way to compile valid trends and patterns in specific industries and segments of interest.

STRUCTURAL ANALYSIS

In the following paragraphs, we review two very different approaches to evaluating the structure and nature of competition in an industry. One of these was conceived by Michael Porter (1979, 1980, 1985). Because of its very comprehensive and intrinsically rational nature, Porter's approach to evaluating an industry's competitive intensity has been extremely influential—it entails describing an industry's structure, following a general model of five forces that that determine the intensity of competition. The most notable potential flaw in Porter's approach is its reliance on *prima facie* logic. The five forces model takes its authority from little empirical justification and stems mainly from theory. Nevertheless, this model still has become a mainstay of industry analysis The five forces model will be explained later in greater detail.

An approach quite the opposite of Porter's is that of the PIMS[1] studies. Begun in the mid-1960s at the General Electric Company, under the direction of Sidney Schoeffler, a statistical model was compiled to describe influences of firms' operating characteristics and strategic decisions on their performance potential. In 1975, Schoeffler founded the Strategic Planning Institute that carried this line of research forward and eventually collected long-term financial and strategic histories for more than 4,000 businesses. Although a majority of these businesses are engaged in manufacturing, the data-base also includes information from a large number of service firms.

Through multivariate statistical inference, the PIMS studies developed several principles relating industry structure, competition and firm strategy to financial performance. The PIMS data-base is perhaps the most comprehensive of its kind in the world; and the PIMS concept of comparing firms' actual results to "par" performance for their industry segments is powerful. Buzzell and Gale (1987) most recently summarized the PIMS principles of industry structure and competition. Their findings will be discussed later in this chapter.

By becoming familiar with Porter's theoretical principles of industry structure and competition, on the one hand, and principles derived empirically by research such as the PIMS studies on the other, planning managers can obtain valuable tools with which to evaluate the attractiveness of their firms' competitive positions and the industries in which they participate.

In this book, it is not possible even to summarize adequately the wealth of information that one may obtain from Porter's two widely distributed volumes (1980, 1985) and that of Buzzell and Gale (1987). Accordingly, planning managers should consult those volumes for more detailed explanations. The following paragraphs provide an overview of the principles that those sources offer. Subsequently, a few other approaches to structural analysis of industries are discussed. They include Hambrick's (1983) typology of mature industrial manufacturers; the special case of industries serving territorial markets; input-output analysis; and metaphorical analysis.

Porter's Principles of Industry Competition

Porter (1980) opined that, in any industry five fundamental forces determine the intensity of competition:

1. Intensity of rivalry among existing competitors
2. Barriers to entry by new competitors
3. Availability of substitute products or services
4. Buyers' bargaining power
5. Suppliers' bargaining power.

According to Porter's theory, eight factors increase the *intensity of rivalry* among existing competitors:

1. The number of competitors
2. Slow industry growth
3. High fixed costs
4. Low customer switching costs
5. Lack of differentiation
6. Abundance of capacity
7. High exit barriers
8. Large consequences of winning and losing.

Any of the following seven factors can elevate *entry barriers*:

1. Scale economies
2. Product differentiation
3. Capital requirements
4. Customer switching costs
5. Limited access to distribution channels
6. Restrictive government policies
7. Cost advantages of incumbency, such as access to raw materials, favorable location, and proprietary technology.

In his second volume (1985) Porter delved most deeply into the nature of *substitution threats*. Although he acknowledged their importance in the first volume, Porter devoted an entire chapter to that subject in the second volume. The probability that a customer will substitute one product for another reflects the combined impacts of three factors according to Porter's model: (1) the relative value of alternatives, (2) the customer's switching costs, and (3) a buyer's satisfaction with the present product or service. Of course, these factors will change over time and differ between market segments; and they are consequences of complex microeconomics which Porter explains.

Impacts of substitutes on industry structure can be far-reaching. For instance, if the substitute product is more durable than its predecessor, total demand for the product or service in question may decline. Alternatively, if the product's performance is significantly superior to that of its predecessor, total demand for the product or service may increase. Firms that seek to substitute their products for competitors' can pursue a variety of strategies, including identification of customers with high propensities to switch—for instance, those presently redesigning their products or processes. By providing free training or money-back guarantees, they can help customers reduce switching costs or subsidize those costs. It is even possible, by intent or accident, to encourage backward integration of present customers' customers using your product, thereby engaging your present customers in competition. So, substitution may not be a desirable strategy in those cases.

Five factors enhance *buyers' bargaining power*:

1. Dependence of the firm on purchases in large volumes by a relatively small number of buyers
2. Standardization of products between competing suppliers, including the firm (thereby minimizing differentiation)
3. Low switching costs and, thereby, easy access to substitutes
4. Feasibility of backward integration (potentially eliminating the customer's need for a firm's products or services)

5.   Relative freedom from need for the firm's specific products or services
     (again referring to substitution potential).

Suppliers' bargaining power, conversely, is determined by the following
factors which essentially are contrapositives of those for buyers:

1.   Relatively few sources of concentrated supply

2.   A limited number of substitutes

3.   Relative importance of the supplier's product to the buyer rather than
     vice versa

4.   Product differentiation or high switching costs

5.   Feasibility of the supplier's forward integration (that is, by selling to
     the customer's customers).

In his first volume, Porter (1980) provides guidance to the analyst in selecting attractive industry targets for competition. He then provides guidelines for
competing in selected segments. Fundamental to these guidelines is a selection
from Porter's now-famous three "generic" competitive strategies"—cost leadership, differentiation and focus.

A least-cost competitor is able to earn acceptable rates of return after other
competitors have lost significant portions, if not all, of their profits through
rivalry. Low cost provides a perfect defense against powerful suppliers, because—at the end of competitive evolution—only the least-cost competitor may
remain as a customer of the supplier. Thereupon, the least-cost competitor may
regain bargaining leverage. A least-cost position also poses a substantial entry
barrier to potential new entrants who do not enjoy scale economies or benefits
of industry experience. Of course, to accomplish a least-cost position requires
some distinctive competence or competitive capability. Advantages of this nature might include favorable access to raw materials or proprietary technology.

In any given industry (or segment), there can be only one least-cost competitor. Competing firms often lose sight of this fundamental truth and delude
themselves into believing that, simply because they have low costs, they are
able to compete successfully with this strategy—a delusion that may prove fatal.
However, those firms that can make good their claims to the least-cost competitor's position are indeed hard to beat. Thus, one of the first steps in any industry analysis is to identify the least-cost competitor.

Porter's second generic strategy is differentiation, the process by which an
industry perceives a product or service as being unique in some valuable respect. Thus, both costs and prices may be higher than those of the least-cost
competitor. This is not to say that a differentiated firm ignores costs, but that
the strategic focus is on delivering greater value to customers by virtue of the
very nature of a product or service. By preserving margins, differentiation thus
provides an adequate defense against least-cost competitors. However, by developing unique features of its product or services, a firm may limit the number
of potential customers attracted to its offer of added value. Consequently, a differentiated competitor may not hold the largest share of its market. Another

early step in the analysis of an industry should be to identify competitors that are attempting to achieve segment-leadership via claims to adding customer value through differentiation.

Porter's third generic strategy is a combination of the first two—focusing on a limited segment of the market and developing either unique features (differentiation) or the lowest-cost product or service for customers in a particular segment. Porter calls such approaches to competition *focus* strategies. Simply because there are more possible combinations of cost and differentiation—and more segments—on which different competitors may concentrate, focused strategies typically are the most abundant.

To summarize, there can be just one least-cost competitor in any industry. There may be a few competitors, each of which has some unique claim to providing customers with added value that differentiates the competitor from all others and accordingly justifies higher prices than the least-cost competitor can command. More abundant still are the focused competitors, each of which attempts to select a specific market segment on which to concentrate with some combination of low cost and/or differentiation strategies.

Each of Porter's three generic strategies carries some level of risk. To maintain cost leadership, a competitor usually must conduct a never ending battle to maintain state-of-the-art operations, modern technology, scale economy, and proficient cost management. But, by concentrating intently on holding costs to a minimum, such competitors can fail to realize the emergence of altogether new product concepts, technologies, or changes in the availability of resources, any one of which ultimately can eliminate competitive advantages of currently least-cost competitors. Because a lower-cost competitor that may not be able to offer comparable features still may be able to "buy" business from customers of more differentiated competitors, the differentiated firm always is at risk. Moreover, if its approach to differentiation is highly successful, then the firm should expect competitors to imitate that approach so that it becomes less distinctive over time. Similarly, over time, buyers' needs for the differentiating factor may decline.

Competitors also can approach a focused firm's customers with their own specifically targeted appeals—perhaps by focusing on even more limited segments than the present supplier. Competitors with focused strategies are always at risk as well. The ultimate endpoint of such a process would have individual suppliers focused on individual customers' requirements, which indeed seems to be occurring in some industries already (Peppers and Rogers, 1997). Of course, to the extent that differences between the selected market segment and the market as a whole narrow, then the effectiveness of a focused strategy also will decline. As an industry matures, such homogenization becomes more and more likely. Thus, differentiation strategies effectiveness can decline with market maturity.

In Porter's first book (1980) analysts also will find a comprehensive approach to the analysis of industry segments: assessment of industry groups as a rational basis for industry segmentation (Chapter 7); industry evolution and the life-cycle concept as a means of testing the appropriateness or inappropriateness of strategy (Chapter 8); fragmented industries (Chapter 9); strategic characteristics of emerging industries (Chapter 10); mature industries (Chapter 11); and declining industries (Chapter 12). Porter's second book (1985) is particularly noteworthy for its introduction of the value chain concept. At one level, this is simply a conceptual model for classic incremental cost analysis of industry structures—identifying value added from production through distribution. However, the model can be used to identify points of competitive advantage— for instance, by defining the role of technology at alternative value chain levels.

One of Porter's students (Harrigan, 1980) wrote an entire text on the application of his theories to competition in declining industries where, quite remarkably, she found several opportunities to prosper. However, risks in mature and declining industries obviously can be especially high. It may become increasingly difficult to dispose of productive assets which are unique to a declining industry. So, as the "end game" draws to a close, exit barriers, in the form of high closure costs can grow severe.

Porter's views on structural industry assessment (1980, 1985) have provided planning managers with important perspectives on the nature of competitive advantage and its accomplishment which, of course, is the intent of business strategy. It is important to acknowledge that Porter succeeded singularly in demonstrating the vital interrelationship between structural diagnosis of industry competition and a correct prescription of strategy for the individual business.

The PIMS Principles

In seeking to discover critical success factors for an industry, planning professionals should consider the PIMS program's findings. As observed earlier, the PIMS program has accumulated data with which very extensive empirical investigation of relationships between firms' strategic positions and their financial performance can be conducted. Unlike the theory-centered, deductive approach of Porter (1980, 1985), the PIMS approach is almost exclusively inductive—predicting relationships between firms' industry positions and their financial performance potentials exclusively on the basis of large-sample statistical evidence. [2]

The PIMS model and data base provide substantial insights into variables that influence the firm's financial performance potential and are subject to management's influence or control. Such factors include market share, relative quality, proportionate sales from new products, relative R&D expense, marketing expense, added value, asset intensity, age of plant and equipment, labor productivity, inventory turnover, and capacity utilization. The PIMS model also includes several uncontrollable market/industry influences on performance potential, including industries' growth rates, stage of industry evolution, inflation and selling prices, concentration of suppliers, typical size of purchase, the importance of products to customers, unionization, exports, imports, and standardization of products. Table 4.2 summarizes some of those environmental factors' relative impacts on rates of return and profit margins.

Table 4.2
Market/Industry Influences on Profitability:
An Overview of Major Relationships

| | Impact on Profitability | |
| | ROI | ROS |
Market/Industry Profit Influences	+ = Positive	- = Negative
• Real Market Growth Rate (annual %)	+	+
• Stage of Market Evolution		
- Growth Stage	+	+
- Decline Stage	-	-
• Rate of Inflation in Selling Prices	+	+
• Concentration of Purchases with Few Suppliers	+	(+)[a]
• Typical Customer Purchase Amount		
- Small	+	+
- Large	-	-
• Importance of Product Purchase to Customer		
- Low	+	+
- High	-	-
• % of Employees Unionized	-	-
• Industry Exports	+	+
• Industry Imports	-	-
• Standardized Products (vs. Custom-Produced)	+	+

Note: [a]Relationship not statistically significant.

Source: Buzzell and Gale (1987: 47)

Most of the findings in Table 4.2 are not too surprising. Thus, we would expect that faster market growth would promote higher profit margins and rates of return. Similarly, markets in their growth stages should witness higher returns than those in declining stages. However, it is somewhat less self evident that when customers purchase relatively large amounts of a product, or the product is especially important to customers, profit margins, and rates of return typically are lower. Another important finding, not disclosed in that table, is the impact of an industry's asset intensity: as investments in fixed assets or working capital proportionate to sales increase, industries' profit margins, and rates of return typically decrease.

The PIMS program's finding agree with Porter's theories in a fundamental and important respect. That is, there are significant inter-industry differences in the competitive factors that affect performance potential. Even after adjusting their data for several intervening variables, Buzzell and Gale (1987) concluded that some industries simply are more profitable than others. Certainly, planning managers of firms engaged in more than one industry should take this fundamental fact of life into consideration. Two variables which can explain why industries differ in intrinsic profitability are their *maturity* and *growth* rate. The impact of industry growth on profitability is most apparent at the extremes. When real growth rates were 10% or more, rates of return were exceptionally high; but when industries declined, rates of return were characteristically quite low. In between those extremes, financial results did not differ much.

A particularly interesting finding from the PIMS studies pertains to the size of typical purchases in an industry. When the purchase size is quite large, profit margins tend to be characteristically small. Conversely, when the purchase amount is low, rates of return are higher. This finding has nothing to do with least-cost competition or anything of that sort. Rather, it represents the impact of more careful deliberation by customers in making buying decisions when their purchases are relatively consequential. Consider the purchase of a car versus laundry detergent. The former will have a significant impact on a customer's living standard, and its impacts will be long-standing. The latter purchase decision is of relative insignificance. Not surprisingly, profit margins realized by consumer nondurable manufacturers are much higher than those of consumer durables producers. In industrial commodity markets, this effect is especially pronounced.

Concentration of suppliers also is influential. However, in this case, financial results of industries where suppliers' concentration is neither exceptionally high nor exceptionally low tend to be best. Moreover, in industries with vertically integrated suppliers that can compete with their customers in the firm's industry, rates of return, and profit margins are characteristically lower than most others.

The PIMS studies disclosed that industries with high levels of unionization tend to have lower financial results than others for two principal reasons. First, highly unionized workers tend to be less productive in terms of value added per person than nonunionized workers. Second, their wage rates tend to rise more rapidly than others. Moreover, greater mechanization and higher technology usually accompany increasing levels of unionization, as employers attempt to offset rapidly rising wages. Unfortunately, the capital costs of such investments typically exceed their benefits.

The PIMS findings regarding asset intensity are especially important, albeit troublesome. To the extent that industries are more capital intensive than others, their profitability and rates of return are relatively low. High labor productivity can offset some of these industries' disadvantages, but not enough to pay for higher levels of investment. It is important to acknowledge here that, to avoid incomparability of firms with asset bases of different ages, one should measure capital intensity by the replacement costs of assets, rather than their net book values.

Intuitively, added capital somehow should produce added value—most likely in the form of greater efficiency. Thus, one would expect that profitability should *increase* with capital intensity. However, in the PIMS studies, the most capital-intensive businesses actually earned only about one-third of the margin required to exceed a 20% pretax rate of return on equity. By contrast, firms with relatively low asset intensity enjoyed profit margins more than twice the level required for a 20% return, as portrayed in Figure 4.2.

Figure 4.2
Asset Intensity and Productivity: Impacts on ROI

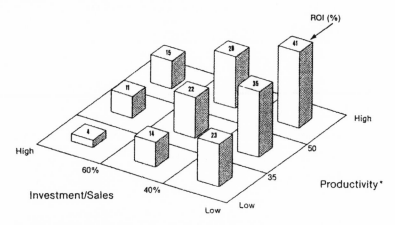

Heavy Investment to Sales Drags Profitability Down and High Productivity
Only Offsets Some of the Damage
*Value added per employee. 1980 U.S. ($000).

Source: Reprinted with the permission of The Free Press, a Division of Simon & Schuster,
Inc. from *The PIMS Principles: Linking Strategy to Performance* by Robert D. Buzzell and
Bradley T. Gale. Copyright © 1987 by The Free Press

Buzzell and Gale (1987) conjectured reasons for the depressing effect of
capital intensity on profitability disclosed by the PIMS data. Especially when
the business cycle is in a negative phase, and managers seek to keep capacity
utilization rates high, capital intensity leads to aggressive competition and relatively low prices. Moreover, heavy capital intensity acts as a barrier to exit that,
as Porter (1980) observed, tends to increase rivalry and price competition. Finally, managers in capital-intensive industries often simply fail to recognize the
increased margin requirements for acceptable rates of return. They set their
prices with the same margin objectives that exist in less capital-intensive industries, thereby condemning their firms to low rates of return. Unfortunately,
when such pricing behavior occurs industry-wide, it dooms that entire industry
to low returns. Of course, there are many good reasons to invest capital at high
levels. Unfortunately, however, the PIMS findings make it clear that many such
investments do not increase margins or returns commensurate with costs of
capital

Hambrick's Typology Approach

One researcher has attempted to find a middle ground between two extreme approaches to industry analysis for strategy making purposes. At one
extreme, firms try to match internal capabilities to an industry's unique requirements. At the other are generic approaches such as those discussed in the
previous two sections. Hambrick (1983) introduced the notion that, at various

stages of industry life cycles, there may be a parsimonious number of typologies for each of which a unique approach to strategy also is appropriate.

Using the PIMS data-base, Hambrick (1983) conducted a cluster analysis of environmental characteristics in 300 mature industrial products businesses with considerable success. He first identified nine critical environmental dimensions :

1. Industry concentration

2. Infrequency of customer purchases

3. Importance of sales from new products

4. The rate of increase in raw material prices

5. Product sophistication

6. Industry vulnerability

7. Exports

8. Demand instability

9. Market share instability.

Hambrick then identified eight unique industry clusters of those dimensions, each of which contained some of the 300 companies whose performance data this analysis employed. From a discriminant analysis of the eight clusters, he finally developed a model that accurately predicted over 90% of the members in each cluster. Those eight clusters were given unique names, as follows:

1. *Roller coaster commodities*—unstable markets for products with infrequent concept changes, i.e., dynamism

2. *Disciplined capital goods makers*—infrequently purchased products, above-average exports, stable market shares

3. *Aggressive makers of complex capital goods*—high product dynamism, unstable market shares, infrequently purchased products, high exports, high product sophistication, high vulnerability

4. *Closeted (localized) combatants*—low exports, low import vulnerability, intensely competitive

5. *Unruly mob*—low exports, stable demand, unstable market shares, high purchase frequencies, fragmentation, absence of strong leaders

6. *Passive crowd of provisioners*—low industry concentration, infrequency of purchased products, low vulnerability, low exports, stable market shares

7. *Aggressive marketers of stable feed stocks and supplies*—frequently purchased products, heavy exports, high concentration, stable demand, unstable market shares

8. *Orderly producers of mundane supplies*—high concentration, frequently purchased products, low product dynamism, stable market
shares.

This research demonstrated that a compromise between the two extremes
which historically have dominated structural industry studies may be possible.
At one extreme is the situational or contingency approach, wherein strategy
seeks to balance a firm's specific internal capabilities to specific environmental
circumstances. At the other extreme is the pursuit of universal laws, such as
those of Porter (1980, 1985), Buzzell and Gale (1987) and Henderson (1979).
Hambrick argues that a more effective approach would seek a parsimonious
definition of contingencies that are specific enough to permit strategic effectiveness, but few enough in number to be pragmatic. This demonstration of
cluster analysis as a tool for structural diagnosis of industries seems to be a step
in the right direction. Remarkably, however, not much further research along
these lines appears in the literature.

Analysis of Industries
Serving Territorial Markets

Most large industries serve very broad, multiple markets. But a few industries serve territorial markets; such industries include airlines, hotel chains,
thrift institutions and banks. These industries' *total* markets consist of many
smaller, geographic markets, which are susceptible to domination by a different
leader. Each territory also may be more or less important to competitors, in
terms of their proportionate revenues, earnings, or assets. Thus, a rival may be
the leader in one territory, but a follower in another, and markets will differ in
their importance to competitors.

Research recently has investigated the dynamics of *strategic deterrence*
that leaders of territorial markets can impose to control the aggressive inten-
tions of potential challengers. Gimeno (1997) demonstrated that airlines which
dominate route-markets protect their spheres of influence (where they often
have hubs) by establishing tactical positions in potential challengers' most important territorial markets, thereby posing a retaliatory threat. Dominant airlines hold prospective challengers in the leader's sphere of influence in check
by the prospect of a counter-strike in the challenger's own sphere. The resulting
mutual forbearance of competitors from making incursions into each others'
territorial strongholds can be beneficial to all, by reducing levels of rivalry
(thereby protecting market positions), lowering costs of competition and maintaining profit margins—in effect, providing the benefits of collusion to rivals
who honor these de facto nonaggression pacts. To understand such markets,
therefore, it is very helpful for planning managers to map industry leaders'
spheres of influence carefully.

Gimeno's (1997) study included 48 airlines on 14,121 routes in 2,898
markets during 1984–1988. His results demonstrated that airlines do forbear
from attacking competitors' spheres of influence when those competitors can
counter-strike in the aggressors' own spheres of influence, or in markets on

which the aggressors depend or where they have invested substantial resources. Conversely, competitive behavior was found to be more aggressive toward rivals who are less able to launch effective counter-strikes. Although Gimeno conducted this study solely in the airline industry, it promises broader application to other industries that serve territorial markets. To the extent that this is so, Gimeno and others who are studying territorial industries (Alexander, 1985; Mester, 1987; Chen and Miller, 1994; Baum and Korn, 1996) have begun to demonstrate that mutual forbearance of rivals in such industries depends on a system of checks and balances imposed by de facto nonaggression pacts. Thus, a protracted stalemate of deterrent warfare solidifies market structures after a few strong competitors achieve dominant positions in separate local markets or other spheres of influence.

Input-Output Analysis

Every five years, the U.S. Department of Commerce publishes a series of input-output tables that show the inter-relationships of about 500 different industries in great detail. These I-O tables demonstrate the proportionate inputs that each industry supplies to all others. Thus, they provide an industry-specific model of GDP. The tables also include measures of value-added by labor and profit. With the tables, one can derive any combination of industries or products mutual inputs and outputs—including individual industries contributions to the GDP.

Input-output tables permit analysts to measure impacts of both direct and indirect changes in production or consumption of commodities on the demand and supply of other commodities and industries. To illustrate, an increase in demand for automobiles will have a direct effect on auto manufacturers that, in turn, will have indirect effects on steel production. Changes in steel production will affect the demand for chemicals, iron ore, and electrical power as well as hundreds of other products used in steel production. Changes in their production will have still other effects on the demand for automobiles. Planners can use I-O tables to determine the end results of such chain reactions. They also can model industry-specific impacts of hypothetical fluctuations in aggregate economic activity (such as a recession). Alternatively, they can use the tables to measure potential impacts of hypothesized or actual shocks in major industries (such as a strike or natural disaster) on total economic output. In this sense, the input-output tables demonstrate definitively a principle developed at the outset of this text—namely, that an economy really is the sum of its industries inputs and outputs.

Analysts may encounter several problems in the use of input-output tables. Most important, preparation of the tables is very time consuming. The U.S. Department of Commerce derives input-output coefficients primarily from economic censuses conducted every five years. The resulting input-output tables and their mathematical models then become available five years later and within one year after release of all economic census data. (The Commerce Department began to publish I-O tables from the 1992 census late in 1997.)

Of course, a lot can change in a nation's economic structure during the five years between the taking of a census and publication of input-output tables. For instance, changing technology easily can invalidate the assumption of constant relationships between inter-industry inputs and outputs. So, for I-O tables' use to become widespread, some methodology to update and produce them more quickly is required. Commercial economics consulting firms, including the WEFA division of Primark Corp., have begun to address this requirement. WEFA's staff partially updates the tables annually, quarterly and monthly as industry data become available (see Appendix IV for economic forecasting firms' addresses and telephone numbers).

The potential usefulness of I-O tables when linked to econometric modeling systems, is nearly unlimited. In mature industries, the tables can be used to explain a great deal about inter-industry relationships and the chain reaction effects of nationwide or industry-specific economic trauma. Moreover, planners can augment the tables with regional data to reveal more localized impacts. For example, a state government agency has used regional input-output tables to estimate the economic effects of a high-speed inter-city rail project on that state's economy. In another application, input-output tables have been used to analyze the impact of a new sports stadium on the local economy (U.S. Department of Commerce, November 1994:M-12).

Non-Quantitative
Metaphorical Approaches

Using qualitative analogies to diagnose industries' structure is an altogether different approach. J.F. Moore (1996) employed a biological analogy, likening an industry or an economy to an ecosystem of interdependent participants. Like ecosystems, industries evolve over time. As they do so, their participants learn to interact with one another in a mutually supportive manner. In some cases, a company may have to become part of a successful ecosystem to survive. Otherwise, even though it is able to make products or deliver services of superior quality, it may not survive. For example, no matter how good its products or how efficiently it is run, a first-rate supplier to a collapsing retail chain is in danger. Firms can derive a competitive advantage from joining or building successful ecosystems. But, knowing how to join such a system requires an understanding of ecosystems' life cycle.

Moore proposes that business ecosystems evolve in four stages: pioneering, expansion, authority establishment, and renewal. In the third stage, a single company usually takes on a nuclear role through which it provides direction to the entire organism. As an illustration of the ecosystem analogy, Moore described Wal-Mart's development of interrelationships between nearly 3,000 stores and their suppliers—the largest discount retailing ecosystem in the United States. Much of Moore's discussion traces Wal-Mart's progression through the four stages of a business ecosystem's evolution. He also suggested that similar processes are unfolding in other industries, such as health care.

From Moore's ecological analogy, planning managers should be reminded that structural analysis of an industry or segment may not be as neat as conventional, quantitative models of relationships between customers, suppliers, and competitors might imply. Whether or not the ecosystem analogy becomes a useful one with which business planners can evaluate industry structures remains to be determined. However, it is interesting to conjecture on the similarities and differences between this ecosystem analogy and the structural model of industry competition advanced by Porter (1980) 16 years earlier. Analogies, such as the ecosystem, may perform some of the same integrative functions that more elaborately formalized micro-economic models perform.

LIFE-CYCLE ANALYSIS

The life-cycle concept describes a process in which firms introduce new products, services, or technologies; develop and grow them; fully commercialize them; and exploit them through their maturities until their decline and ultimate demise. In the strategy literature, this concept has become nearly axiomatic (Wasson, 1976; Allio and Pennington, 1979:15; Porter, 1980: 158–161; Rink and Swan, 1987). Although very little empirical verification of the life-cycle concept actually exists, statistical studies by Polli and Cook (1960) and Thorelli and Burnett (1981) have provided at least some confirmation of the concept's validity. In their study of mature firms in the PIMS data-base, Hambrick and Lei (1985) also found that—after controlling for economic sector and frequency of a product's purchase—the life-cycle stage influenced firms' earnings more than several other independent variables.

Figure 4.3
Three Phases of the Life Cycle

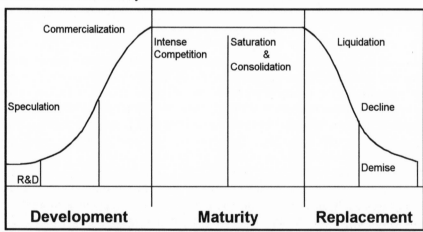

Source: Stages' concept: Wasson, 1976; Graphic representation: author

In fact, the life cycle may not be a single, continuous function as nearly always portrayed. Rather, there seem to be three distinct stages: an initial, sigmoidal growth curve, followed by a peak or plateau, and, finally, a decay function brought on by substitution of a replacement product or technology (see Figure 4.3).

For planning managers, accurate diagnosis of the present life-cycle stage can aid in: (1) assessing and forecasting likely competitive intensity, (2) selecting appropriate planning methods, and (3) formulating strategy. The life-cycle model also can aid planning managers in forecasting rates of growth in demand for a product, service, or technology. To use the model, an analyst must estimate likely durations of the current stage and the remaining stage(s). One approach to making that estimate is to use historic life-cycle analogies offered by comparable products, services, or technologies (Martino, 1972: 65–102). Another is to employ mathematical models of "growth curves": that approach is discussed briefly, below, and at greater length in Chapter 6.

Diagnosing and Forecasting Competitive Conditions

The sigmoidal (S-shaped) nature of the life cycle's *development* phase is fairly well understood and can be described mathematically by using curves first discovered by Gompertz (1820, 1825) and Pearl (1921, 1922). For guidance in applying such curves' mathematical models, planners may consult several authorities including Fisher and Pry, 1971; I.C. Hendry, 1972; Linstone and Sahal, 1976; Mead, 1984; Mahajahan and Muller, 1979; Martino, 1972: 103–127; and Modis, 1992, 1994, 1996). The development phase can be divided further into at least three stages: (1) initial conception, (2) entrepreneurial speculation, and (3) commercialization of concepts that survive in the previous stage (Wasson, 1976).

The second phase, *maturity*, may be short- or long-lived. As extremes, consider the most successful brands of household detergent (long-lived) versus the avalanche of new personal computing products conceived—and already replaced—in the current decade (short-lived). Early in this phase, competition intensifies as market growth and potential earnings attract new suppliers— especially if technology is still advancing at a rate that offsets incumbents' benefits of prior learning. However, as the demand for a new product, service, or technology becomes satisfied, drivers of competition shift from growth to efficiency and cost reduction. In this stage, many competitors are likely to withdraw, fail, or be acquired by more successful rivals.

Depending partly on industry incumbents' long range strategies, the product life cycle's third phase, *replacement*, may occur gradually or precipitately (Porter, 1980: 254–274; Harrigan, 1980). To resist replacement, manufacturers and suppliers may form alliances for their mutual benefit, whereas—in the previous phase—suppliers and producers may have pursued conflicting objectives. Ultimately, however, more advanced substitutes replace most products, and their cycles end. It is noteworthy that this last phase of the life-cycle concept is especially hypothetical. A terminal stage can occur much more abruptly than conventional wisdom suggests: for example, when a replacement product or technology virtually eclipses its predecessor. Such phenomena can occur as a result of regulation; for example, when bans were placed on environmentally hazardous refrigerants used in air conditioning systems, their use ended abruptly. Alternatively, a product or brand may remain popular for decades—as in the case of some household detergents and cleaning products.

Fitting Planning Methods and Strategy to the Life-Cycle Stage

The life-cycle model can be useful in diagnosing priorities for planning methodology (Mullick, et al., 1982; Smith, K.G. Mitchell and Summer, 1985; Rink and Swan, 1987); and strategy (Wasson, 1976). Table 4.3 illustrates how, as the life cycle emerges, planning priorities are likely to shift.

Table 4.3
Matching Planning Priorities to the Life-Cycle Stage

Stage	Planning Priorities
Brainstorming	Product feasibility studies, R&D
Entrepreneurial	Product design, market research
Early Growth	Marketing strategy, financing
Commercialization	Production requirements planning Investment planning, marketing programs, production planning
Maturity	Cost reduction, promotion, pricing Financial planning
Replacement	Cash management, phase out, liquidation planning

Source: Wasson, 1976

Wasson (1976: 299–308) observed that the nature of competitive rivalry and strategic priorities both change with the life cycle. At the outset, competition is not intense. But as a new product, service or technology emerges, new competitors probably will copy or imitate it. Later, only a few competitors will accomplish the scale of market participation, production and long-term technical resources required for sustained competition. Other firms then must withdraw, fail, or be acquired by survivors. Strategic objectives evolve accordingly. Initially, an objective is to minimize the time and cost of learning. Later, the objective is to gain recognition, promote increased demand and establish a strong market position. Later still, the objective is to maintain and defend profitable market positions. Finally, in an attempt to maximize cash-flow, the objective is to strike a profitable balance between costs and declining revenues. Different approaches to product design, pricing, operations, promotion, and distribution can be taken to pursue each of those objectives.

Allio and Pennington (1979: 15) have observed that each life-cycle stage also has unique needs for financial planning and management styles. Early in the cycle, an entrepreneurial style is appropriate. Later, planners and managers will need more sophisticated methods. Later still, they will require a higher degree of administrative control. Finally, to exploit short-lived possibilities of an end-game, a more opportunistic style is appropriate.

Hypothetical Example

Consumer products marketers, especially, are sensitive to financial concomitants of product life-cycle stages. Consider, for instance, the hypothetical hair products manufacturer that discovers a dramatically new formula to retard hair loss. Initially, substantial costs will be incurred for research, formula development, laboratory trials, FDA approvals, patent applications, and market research; there will be only investment and no return. If the initial stage is successful, market testing and early production planning will begin—still, no profit. Again, assuming no mishaps, commercialization will begin with costly marketing initiatives, investment in a production process, and further investment in working capital. At this stage, significant negative cash-flows are typical. But, with marketing success, earnings should grow with sales. Investment requirements still will increase, but sales and earnings may grow faster.

Figure 4.4
Hypothetical Product Evolution
on a Growth-Share Matrix

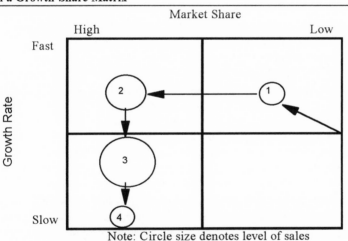

Note: Circle size denotes level of sales

1. *Innovation* leads to an embryonic product, service or technology.

2. *Commercialization*—substantial investment, fast growth, high return.

3. *Maturity*—intensified competition, slower growth, lower rates of investment, elimination of weaker competitors, positive cash-flow.

4. *Replacement* by new innovations, declining sales and earnings. Positive cash-flow still is possible until liquidation.

Source: author

Eventually, competitors will attempt to duplicate or imitate the successful innovation; so, margins may narrow as pricing pressures mount. Here is where the strategist must decide either to compete on the basis of cost and accumulated competitive advantage or to employ tactics of line extensions—shampoos, rinses, conditioners, and so forth—always staying one step ahead of the competition, thereby gaining or maintaining a high market share.

Within a short time—probably just a few years—the innovation no longer will be new. Then it is time to reverse direction: drastically reduce advertising and promotion expenditures; streamline the product line and production resources; and consolidate physical distribution. If costs drop faster than revenues, which may be sustained for a considerable time, positive cash-flows will be substantial, and the product will have been a financial success. Figure 4.4 depicts this process, portrayed on a classic growth-share matrix.

ANALYSIS OF
INDIVIDUAL COMPETITORS

Ultimately, analysis of an industry requires the planning manager or business analyst to obtain an understanding of its immediate competition. There is no better way to accomplish that objective, of course, than to study individual competitors in very specific terms.

Porter's text on competitive strategy and analysis (1980) contains two chapters on individual competitor analysis. According to his approach, an analyst first should inquire into the competitor's apparent goals. It may be obvious, for instance, that the competitor is more highly motivated by earnings than growth, or vice versa. By observing behavior of the top management organization and inquiring into its incentive structures, one may also draw conclusions regarding competing firms' motives. For instance, individuals on the board and their backgrounds may indicate the competitor's leanings in one direction or another. Often, this information is public knowledge. Simply by inquiring into the nature of its large contracts or regulatory filings, one also may infer a competitor's strategic priorities and limitations .

By composing a few test questions, it may be possible to assemble an appropriate profile of the competitor's strategic capabilities. For instance, have there been any noteworthy successes or failures in attempting different kinds of marketing strategy? Has the competitor been developing or losing competence in technical, operating, marketing or other critical functions? Has the competitor recently manifested widespread reductions in normal operating expenses, suggesting that financial results have weakened?

If a parent company owns the competitor, one should ask many of the foregoing questions about that company as well. What are the parent's manifest goals? More important, how important is the competitor's business to the parent company's portfolio? Why is the parent company engaged in this industry? Has it made a substantial commitment? Is the parent's strategy one of diversification or industry concentration? Has its senior management team formed any kind of emotional attachment to this particular business or industry? Is the parent pursuing an obvious generic strategy? What is the role of the competitor firm in the parent company's growth-share matrix?

Assuming that the competitor or its parent have the capability to engage in this industry for a prolonged period of time and have made commitments to doing so, then one must ask a further question: Is it possible that the competitors' goals and those of the planner's firm are compatible? For instance, is one comfortable in the role of a leader and the other in the role of a follower? Is one a least-cost competitor and the other highly differentiated? Are the two firms seeking success in different industry segments? If there is such a compatibility of goals, then a state of coexistence can exist. But if compatibility of goals is unlikely, then a direct adversarial relationship exists.

Ultimately, a complete assessment of any competitor should result in a competitive response profile that identifies the competitor's likely behavior in either an offensive or defensive mode. Knowing the competitor's goals and fundamental strategy should disclose the nature of its likely offensive behaviors.

Defensive behaviors should stem from the competitor's points of vulnerability, which it will seek to protect. In this respect, analysts may inquire as to the specific nature of their own firms' offensive behavior that will provoke competitors to retaliate. More importantly, perhaps, the analyst should form a judgment with regard to each competitor's retaliatory capability.

Competitors often make assumptions about each other's motives, market positions, or functional capabilities that—due either to wishful thinking or to inadequate information—are inaccurate. When a firm makes an incorrect assumption about such matters, it becomes vulnerable on those same points. Moreover, firms often draw incorrect judgments with regard to their own technological capabilities, relative costs, and customer loyalties. Misperceptions in any of these respects can provide competitors with opportunities to take the offensive on a favorable basis because the firm, in its ignorance, is not adequately prepared for an attack.

To avoid such miscalculations, competitors may send signals to each other. A firm may announce that it intends to add significant new capacity or to introduce a new product shortly, thereby warning competitors that it has seized the initiative. Of course, such announcements may be truthful or they may be bluffs intended to forestall similar moves by competitors. However, when such signals are truthful, a company may avoid unnecessarily intense competition by declaring that it (or a competitor) has won the present round. On other occasions, senior executives may engage in public discussions with the media to signal their willingness to see prices rise or competitive conditions change in some particular way. A sufficient number of such public discussions by competitors executives may facilitate more orderly marketing conditions than otherwise would be possible. Disclosures of important information to customers known to have relationships with both sides may serve similar purposes. Companies can conduct all of these market signaling activities without violating antitrust laws, but they should take care not to overstep the bounds of prudence, just the same.

Numerous authors and researchers have proposed ways in which to assess competitors' capabilities. Some of these techniques are quite straightforward.

They include obtaining financial records from publicly-owned competitors' regulatory disclosures or from Dun and Bradstreet reports if the competitor is privately owned. Several guidelines for evaluating competitors' financial condition are available (see Fifer, 1984a).

Guidelines for evaluating competitors' functional strategies, other than Porter's, also are available. Rothchild (1986) observed that evaluation of a competitor's manifest strategy really aims at finding inconsistencies—for instance, between product position, product development, funding capabilities, and marketing resource requirements. If product development, marketing tactics, production and financial strategies are not consistent, the analyst may find fatal flaws that aggressors can exploit. To conduct such an analysis, it will help to have a systematic procedure for doing so. One may use Fifer's (1985) checklist for this purpose. Another approach is to compare a target competitor to others in a winners and losers analysis (Rothschild, 1984). A similar approach might be to evaluate the competitor's relationships with its suppliers in search of potential strengths or weaknesses either in materials sources or credit capacity (Isenman, 1986).

Often, knowing the competitor's financial, physical, and marketing capabilities still may not provide sufficient information for making a correct competitive decision. The human element of top management also must be considered. Indeed, without an assessment of its top management team, no analysis of an important competitor would be complete (Ball 1987). This requires profiling individual executives skills, working history, style of management in different situations, and so forth. Sometimes, these individuals deliver speeches, give interviews, or publish articles that can be highly informative regarding their strategic aptitudes and inclinations.

It also will be useful to prepare a profile of the executive team. Knowing something about how the team works as a group can be especially enlightening. In some firms, the team functions smoothly, but perhaps without much imagination. Other teams may be more chaotic, but adventuresome. Management teams whose senior officers have long service records are likely to be more conservative than those comprised of younger, mobile professionals. Autocracies may be incapable of prompt response to competitive initiative when their CEOs are not available to approve the actions of line executives. Thus, it may be possible to arrive at a cultural assessment of the competitor; to form a conclusion with regard to its appetite for risks; and to foretell its willingness or ability to act quickly in response to competitors' initiatives. Of course, if the planning manager is contemplating an aggressive strategy, conservative unresponsive, and/or tolerant competitors certainly are preferable targets. On the other hand, to prepare properly, even firms whose interests are more defensive than aggressive will wish to identify potential new aggressors and market segments where entry barriers are the least forbidding to intruders. Fahey (1984) has offered guidelines for such analysis.

Assuming that the firm has established criteria for evaluating individual competitors, it still must obtain the necessary data—not all of which will be readily available. In response to the need for more comprehensive and accurate competitive intelligence, an entire profession seems to be emerging, and a professional society (The Society for Competitive Intelligence Professionals) now exists to represent persons who have chosen that field. The result, from time to time, has been heightened concern among senior executives with regard to corporate espionage.

Wall's survey (1974) disclosed that senior managers most often wish to obtain information about their competitors' pricing, expansion plans, promotions, sales, costs and research programs. Much of this information can be acquired by following a disciplined approach to memorializing disclosure remarks made to the firm's sales personnel, buyers, engineers, and other professional contacts. Additional sources include public financial disclosures of large corporations, reporting services such as Dun and Bradstreet, and industry surveys. To fill in the voids, a firm can conduct its own market and industry surveys. Moreover, the recent increases in on-line information sources including commercial research services now can provide planning managers substantial additional information (McGrane, 1987).

Competition now is so intense that many firms need some kind of systematic approach to obtaining and maintaining information about competitors. Fuld (1991) has provided guidelines for setting up such a system. He explains that the nature of a business intelligence function is to gather small pieces of information routinely and then fit them together into more meaningful patterns. But, when viewed individually by line managers gathering individual bits of intelligence may not seem to have much purpose. So, the competitive intelligence manager requires support from top management to implement the intelligence-gathering function effectively. The process can be a simple one, consisting of scanning publicly available information; or it can be more elaborate, requiring the services of a specialist trained to penetrate competitors' defenses.

Only a very small portion of American corporations probably know how to conduct sophisticated competitive intelligence gathering and processing functions to support strategic planning. Ettorre (1995) explains that American firms' naiveté about competitive intelligence may reflect the fact that America never has been in a war for its survival as have Japan, Israel, and France, all of whose commercial communities' intelligence practices are further advanced than those in the United States. A survey of recent competitive intelligence practices by Gelb et al. (1991) would seem to confirm that generalization; the typical approaches used by even large U.S. corporations for gathering competitive intelligence seemed to be fairly rudimentary.

Simply because worldwide competition is growing more intense, the need for competitive information also has increased and formalized competitive intelligence functions are increasing in number and size (Crock et al., 1996). A text on this subject and its methodology by Kahaner (1996) allegedly sold out its entire 20,000 volume initial edition in six weeks. Thus, interest in this new corporate function also seems to be increasing.

Gilad et al. (1993) have provided an approach to determine "gaps and blind spots in competitive intelligence." Their approach is directed toward: (1) identifying critical decisions that must be made; (2) identifying key individuals involved in making each decision; and (3) identifying questions that must be answered by decision makers before they can take competitively secure actions. Of course, significant ethical issues must be considered, and it is not clear that U.S. business students have been trained adequately to make appropriate judgments in this respect.

To conclude this section on competitive intelligence, it is fair to say that skills for evaluating direct competitors' strategic capabilities are not formally or well-developed in most firms. Impacts of such omissions on earnings can be substantial. For instance, Jones (1988) reported a recent case involving the Caterpillar Corporation. Specific estimates of competitors' product costs and substantial insights into their strategies were obtained from analyses of those firms' public documents regarding process controls, product costs, and other information that could be obtained through legal means. The result allegedly was a substantial (20%) saving in the cost of Caterpillar's factory modernization program.

NOTES

1.   Originally, PIMS was an acronym for "profit-impact of marketing strategy," the name of Schoeffler's program when it was transferred from General Electric to the Strategic Planning Institute. Today, the term refers to a diagnostic system comprised of a large data-base describing strategic variables of over 4,000 business units and a mathematic model used to evaluate those units' performance potentials.

2.   Buzzell and Gale (1987) prepared a compendium of results from the PIMS program in the form of several "principles" of competition. The following discussion relies substantially, but not exclusively, on that source. See also Schoeffler et al. 1974 and Schoeffler, 1977.

CHAPTER 5

Market Analysis

This chapter explores methods which the planning manager can use to evaluate a firm's relationships with communities of present and potential customers. These communities comprise the firm's markets. We begin by defining the scope of consumer and producer markets which are addressed at greater lengths in the following pages. Following that introductory section, five subsequent sections are addressed to methods for market segmentation (and market share calculation); a cyclical model for analysis of markets' timing; drivers of consumer markets' demand; drivers of industrial markets' demand; and approaches to the assessment of international markets. Thus, planning managers should be able to employ the principles of analysis discussed in this chapter to the broad spectrum of market assessments that must be performed in assembling evidence on which selections of strategy are based.

SCOPE OF ANALYSIS

At the broadest level, we may say that there are three fundamental market sectors—comprised of individual consumers, industrial firms and governmental agencies. In this chapter, we will be concerned primarily with the consumer and industrial segments and much less, the government sector. Marketing to government customers entails special political and regulatory considerations that this book will not explore. While markets comprised of government agencies are certainly important, they respond to driving forces that are peculiar to the public sector; and they often require an approach that differs significantly from those which apply to private-sector markets.

When discussing consumer market segments, that is, individual end-users, it is convenient to divide the scope of deliverables into nondurables, durables, and services. The term, *nondurable* is applicable to expendable goods with short life expectancies (certainly no more than three years). Moreover, based on the discretionary or nondiscretionary nature of such goods, this subsegment is capable of further division. Some segments of the most basic markets for food, clothing, and shelter are largely nondiscretionary in nature. However, beyond the level of subsistence, those segments also contain substantial discretionary subsegments.

To a significant extent, purchases of *consumer durable goods* are considered to be discretionary in nature. However, in the United States at least, the head of any suburban household with children will quickly point out that an automobile, lawnmower, washing machine and dryer, (and probably a television set), now are considered essentials. The point is that designations (and analyses) of discretionary and nondiscretionary purchasing behaviors may be more difficult to make than they seem to be, at first. Similarly, consumer services typically are viewed as discretionary in nature. However, as America's population ages, a large portion of the population perceives medical services as anything but discretionary. Here again it can be difficult to make distinctions between the discretionary and nondiscretionary nature of consumers purchasing decisions.

The industrial segment of markets consists of enterprises that consume the firm's goods or services in order to produce other goods or services, which subsequently are destined to their ultimate (or intermediate) users. Subsegments include expendable goods purchased for inventory and production, capital goods (machinery and equipment), property, and services. In general, industrial goods and services also may be discretionary or nondiscretionary in nature. However, it is usually (but not necessarily correctly) assumed that—inasmuch as they are subject to management's formal evaluation of costs and benefits— industrial enterprises' purchases of goods and services are primarily nondiscretionary in nature. In this respect, because they are subjected to intense public scrutiny, budgetary reviews, and regulation, governments and government agencies purchases of expendable goods, capital goods, and services also are perceived as nondiscretionary in nature .

Producer goods (and services) by definition are delivered to specific industries. Markets for such goods often can be segmented in terms of industries' structures, following principles discussed in the previous chapter. A structural analysis of the industries where specific goods and services are consumed or distributed will provide considerable insight into drivers of demand for goods or services offered to producers. To illustrate, a structural analysis of the automotive industry (supplemented by economic analysis of demand for consumer durables) will help market analysts understand changing demand for automotive components. Similarly, analysis of demand for machinery and equipment used in chemical plants, refineries, and steel mills, requires structural analyses of those industries, supplemented by economic assessments of relevant factors related to capital formation, including the business cycle, interest rates, and regulatory policy—all of which were addressed in Chapters 3 and 4.

MARKET SEGMENTS AND SHARES

If you consider the most frequently employed matrix methods of assembling a corporation's portfolio of businesses or products, it will become apparent that these generally accepted approaches to formulating business strategy essentially begin with market segmentation. Thus, some market segments are likely to grow faster than others; and this is an important consideration in creating the widely used growth-share matrix. Alternatively, the analyst may describe segments' attractiveness in terms of their profitability, risk levels, asset intensity and degree of competitive rivalry, among others. In any event, market segmentation within such dimensions is an essential precursor to the formulation of commercial strategies. Comprehensive guidelines that the business analyst may follow in dividing markets into segments will be found in very few texts, such as Weinstein's (1987).

Uses of Segmentation

Segmentation helps to define the fundamental structure for market analysis. As a general matter, segmentation usually proceeds by dividing a community of customers into subsegments that reflect variations in their needs (and, therefore, their demand) for products' or services' benefits. For example, one may divide markets based on consumers' age, income, other personal attributes, geography, topography, product features, and so forth. Thus, it is well-known that demographic characteristics vary substantially between regions and metropolitan areas of the United States. Similarly, country-markets' demographics differ substantially (see Appendix I). By identifying significant differences in the nature of demand between geographic markets, management may adapt strategies accordingly or choose to concentrate on some segments to the exclusion of others.

Effective market share measurement typically requires valid market segmentation. Consider, for instance, the market for residential windows. One may define important segments of this large market in terms of: (1) material (wood, vinyl, aluminum), (2) application (new construction versus renovation); (3) economic sector (residential, commercial, industrial, government); (4) single-family versus multifamily versus institutional residences; (5) standard sizes versus architectural shapes; and (6) geographic regions. Some producers offer relatively full lines nationwide; others are specialists. Some are least-cost competitors; others are highly differentiated. What good does it do for a regional institutional window specialist to compute its share of the total U.S. window market? Probably none.

The complexity of market segmentation can increase further if important drivers are in a state of change. Consider the difference between metropolitan and rural markets where demographic characteristics are stable versus those that are more dynamic—for instance, where there are military bases. Communities where residents are highly transient will witness larger demand for home furnishings and mortgage loan services than very stable communities. However, when defense budgets are cut and bases are closed, reductions in

spending power and demand for goods and services have devastated several
metropolitan and rural markets (Terleckyj, 1995).

Measuring Market Share

Since the subject of market share has arisen, a brief comment is in order.
Typically, strategic plans and top management view commercial success from
only a few basic perspectives. Thus, the firm's strategic objectives and/or goals
may be expressed in financial and competitive terms—as a rate of return on
shareholders' equity, perhaps, or as a market share. Measurements of financial
performance are not necessarily simple; but management often has much more
difficulty in measuring and monitoring the firm's share of markets, and market
segments, in which it competes. More difficult still is measuring and monitoring competitors' shares, since competitors rarely provide each other with the
data for doing so. But, if market shares must be calculated, it usually is worth-
while to define the segment of interest before going to all that trouble.

Consider Figure 5.1, which depicts trends in output of light trucks and
conventional automobiles in several size categories. Emergence of the light
truck segment is evident. Moreover, as Figure 5.1 also shows, producers' shares
of those two segments are quite different.

Figure 5.1
North American Automotive Industry Segments and Producers' Shares:
1995–1997 (Basis: Production)

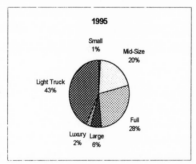
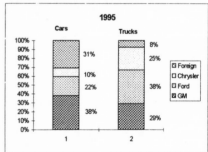
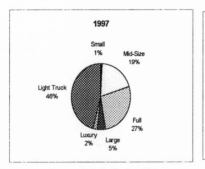
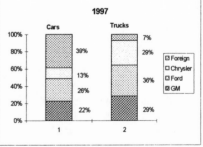

Source: Pugliese and McCulloch, 1997

While the information depicted in Figure 5.1 certainly demonstrates the importance of segmenting markets before calculating shares, and conveys considerable information, it sometimes is important for producers to study segment shares of an entire industry simultaneously in order to appreciate problems or opportunities to be anticipated from extending into new segments and/or adding new product lines. For example, consider the second portrayal of producers' shares in Figure 5.2. In that illustration, we examine the industry from Ford's point of view. While it has been very successful in the light utility truck segment, Ford may need to develop a more competitive sport utility vehicle. Similarly, Ford's small car segment share is high but its shares of the full-size and mid-size segments are low.

Figure 5.2
North American Automotive Industry Producers' Shares by Segment:
Light Vehicles (Basis: 1997 Production)

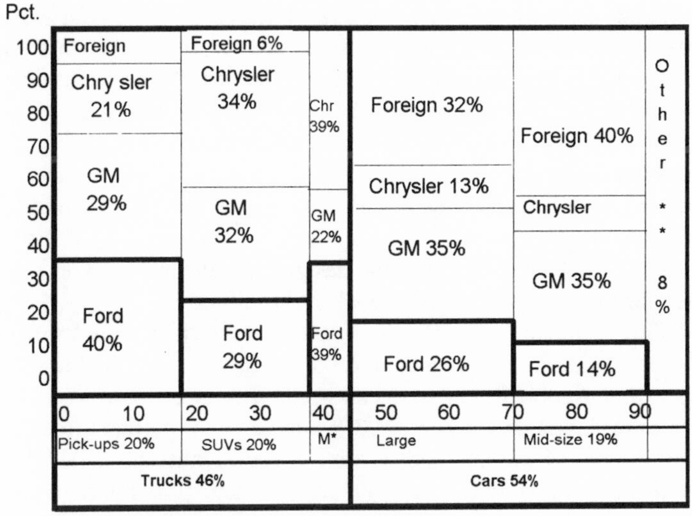

* M: Multi-purpose vehicles (vans)
** Luxury, near luxury, small and sport cars.

Source: Pugliese and McCulloch, 1997

Each of those low-share segments is a candidate for a segment-growth strategy. The choice of opportunities to pursue would depend on competitors' relative positions as well as Ford's internal design engineering and production capabilities. Judging from importers' large share of the mid-size segment, a nationalistic theme of promotion and advertising might be used to support the launch of a new domestic model in that segment.

Similarly, suppliers of related components for just about any family of products (or services) can use the approach in Figure 5.2 to examine market extension/incursion opportunities and/or threats. Some other industry examples might include suppliers of component parts for automotive transmissions,

HVAC systems, and building components, among others. But, the technique is not limited to the manufacturers. Service markets, such as the rapidly growing financial services industry, food service, lodging, and so on, all can employ it. Similarly, retail and wholesale merchandising industries offer several segmentation possibilities.

Impending Replacement of the
SIC System by NAICS

The Standard Industrial Classification (SIC) system is a basic resource for classifying and segmenting industrial markets. In the first quarter of 1997, the federal government announced that the SIC system will be replaced by the North American Industry Classification System (NAICS) beginning in 2000. Unlike the product and market-based categories that characterize SIC codes, NAICS will classify firms on the basis of their production activities.

NAICS' replacement of the SIC system reflects emergence of increasingly complex industry structures, especially in the service sector, throughout North America. Contributions to the new systems were received from Canada's and Mexico's counterparts of the U.S. Economic Classification Policy Committee. Thus, NAICS will be a mutual-use, standardized tool for all three North American Free Trade Agreement (NAFTA) group of countries.

Compared to the SIC system, NAICS greatly increases the number of classifications into which firms may be placed. Six—rather than four—digits of code will accommodate the increase in the structural complexity of North America's industries and provide subsector designation flexibility. The sixth digit is provided for unique needs in individual countries.

While providing a much more efficient and comprehensive basis for market and industry segmentation, implementation of NAICS may be troublesome. The good news is that users will be able to cross-reference more than two-thirds of all SIC code information directly to NAICS and segment markets in much more detail than before. The bad news is that changes inherent in NAICS' configuration will cause some time series data breaks where cross referencing is imperfect or impossible (see Appendix IV).

The creators of NAICS recognized a need to reclassify existing data in order to repair data breaks as quickly as possible. To that end, the Census Bureau designed the 1997 economic census questionnaire to provide dual SIC/NAICS establishment classifications. As a result, according to Zeissert and Wallace (1997), two methods will be available for collecting comparable data:

1.   *Comparative Statistics Tables* that present new industry data according to both systems, along with data from one or more earlier censuses based on the same system for comparison, and;

2.   *Bridge Tables*, that present new data cross-tabulated by both old and new classification systems identifying the lowest common denominator between the two systems.

Plans call for a staged implementation of NAICS to be complete by 2004. This would be a significant accomplishment in light of federal budget limitations.

One benefit of NAICS should be an increased capability to assess long-term impacts of NAFTA. Another will be the emergence of specific data describing industry sectors that previously were not disclosed by SIC codes. Illustrative NAICS/SIC cross-reference tables are provided in Appendix VI along with instructions for obtaining complete cross reference tables.

Dimensions of Consumer Market Segmentation

Unquestionably, demographics have provided one of the most fruitful disciplines for segmenting consumer markets. Fluctuations in numbers of children and the elderly stimulate demand for medical services. Increases in numbers of teenagers stimulate demand for educational services and fad products. Increases in young adults stimulate demand for homes, home furnishings, and appliances, while increases of senior-aged adults stimulate demand for financial services. These age-income dynamics are widely recognized. They have been described well by demographers and are monitored closely. (See the recent text by Pol and Thomas, 1997.) The planning manager will have no difficulty in identifying demographic market segments pertaining to age, sex, race, nationality, social class, type of employment, and so forth, which are relevant to the firm's marketing opportunities. Many sources of data are available to define differences in those demographic variables at the micro level of geographic detail and at any level of aggregation—nations, regions, countries, states and cities.

Demographics, of course, are not the only source of rationale for defining consumer market segments. There are many other bases upon which consumer markets may be segmented to understand sources of demand more accurately. Some important illustrations follow.

Psychographic and lifestyle studies attempt to identify consumers' personal characteristics that determine differences in their preference for products and services. Some of these characteristics may have relative permanence; for instance, attitudes about politics, the family, and personal health. Others may be only short-term in nature; for instance, shifts in fashion preferences. Notwithstanding their potential impermanence, cultural trends in attitudes regarding health, fitness, and so forth still can be important bases upon which to distinguish differences in consumers' priorities for making purchasing decisions.

Some approaches to segmentation focus on the product rather than the consumer. Frequency of products' use, for instance, might be just as important as the product's durability. Understanding such differences may be helpful in determining the relative advantage of products' durability versus convenience features or price. Thus, a spare tire in the trunk of a new car probably will be judged by consumers based on ease of installation rather than mileage, but replacement tires' durability claims are fundamental selling points.

Distribution channels may be at least as useful for market segmentation as demographics, psychographics, and product features. In an age of time compression, consumers often place great value on proximity to employment in making buying decisions. Moreover, some recent studies seem to be disclosing that the type of buying environment—the shopping experience—is at least as important as any other variable in the retail marketing equation. So, retailing themes also may be fruitful bases for segmenting consumer product markets.

Dimensions of Industrial Market Segmentation

Bonoma and Shapiro (1983) devised a "nested" approach to the segmentation of industrial markets based on a hierarchy of purchasing decision drivers. According to this model, there are five levels of progressively less visible but more basic sources of motivation for making industrial purchases. Each level provides a basis for segmentation, and will be discussed in the following paragraphs. At the outermost level are *demographic characteristics*, including the buying firm's size and location. These characteristics are easily discernible from outside the firm. Slightly less recognizable are *operating variables*, which include functional capabilities as well as technology and financial resources. Whether or not the target company presently is a user or non-user of the product or brand in question also is considered an operating variable.

The target company's *purchasing approach*—the third dimension of industrial market segmentation—is more difficult to diagnose. To classify a prospective customer on this level correctly, the analyst should consider five dimensions of a firm's buying behavior: (1) centralized versus decentralized buying responsibility; (2) locus of authority to make purchasing decisions (engineering, marketing, manufacturing, finance, or purchasing department); (3) existing relationships between suppliers and customers; (4) the customer's formal purchasing policies; and (5) qualifying criteria that the supplier's product or service must meet. Usually, only the latter two dimensions are apparent to a prospective supplier; but the first three probably are just as important.

The fourth level of this segmentation scheme consists of *situational factors*. These factors define benefits that the buying company requires from the present transaction. The same requirements may not affect future purchasing decisions. In each new requisition, even a qualified supplier must deliver these benefits, or it won't receive an order. Illustrations of such benefits include: (1) urgency; (2) functional accessories; and (3) order size. Suppliers that respond to customers' urgent orders most promptly may have different resources than those which are set up to produce very large orders and deliver them, on schedule, in complete shipments. Haley (1968) argued that such situational benefits can be powerful criteria for segmentation of industrial markets.

The fifth and final level of industrial market segmentation consists of decision-makers *personal characteristics*. These characteristics divide further into four sublevels: (1) buyer-seller similarity; (2) individual buyer perceptions; (3) buyer motivation; and (4) the buyer's approach to risk management.

Although each of these segmentation levels comprises a different dimension of industrial purchasing dynamics, Bonoma and Shapiro (1983) emphasize that they are not independent of each other. One level of segmentation does not preclude entry into another level. So, there is no particular reason why a firm's purchasing policies and its situational needs for particular transaction benefits should depend upon one another. Moreover, interactions of these dimensions can produce more effective bases for segmentation than any one level by itself. As an example, the authors discuss a manufacturing firm's decision to supply large versus small pipe fittings to distribution firms some of which require urgent delivery, while others are stocking distributors that do not require very fast delivery. This information is sufficient to form a two-by-two matrix (order size versus delivery speed) of four strategic alternatives. A supplier probably can select only one of those alternatives if it intends to focus its resources effectively.

The analyst can contrast competitors' positions within a particular industry or industry segment by using a benefits protocol. First, a list of potential benefits (need satisfactions) is prepared for each market segment. Then, the analyst can compare competitors on the basis of their ability to fulfill the needs of alternative segments, as Table 5.1 demonstrates:

Table 5.1
Profile of Market Segment Benefits for Competitive Analysis

	Requirements		Capabilities	
Benefits (examples):	Segment A	Segment B	Competitor 1	Competitor 2
Custom Design		♦	♦	
Delivery Reliability	♦			♦
Quick Delivery	♦		♦	
Response				
Product Line Breadth	♦		♦	
Quality		♦		♦
Price				

Source: Bonoma and Shapiro, 1983

Alternative Segmentation Approaches

While customer traits provide the bases for most segmentation approaches, that is not necessarily the only dimension available. Datta (1996) makes a strong case for segmenting markets based on product, rather than customer, characteristics.

Differences in buyers' criteria for initial versus replacement purchases also may provide an effective segmentation rationale. Thus, original equipment manufacturing (OEM) versus aftermarket segments often place much different priorities on product and service characteristics. Similarly, products that will be rented may be sold much differently than those to be purchased as installed equipment.

Peppers and Rogers (1997) have offered a very interesting new approach to characterizing markets based on customers' strategic value to suppliers and the extent to which suppliers must customize versus standardize their products or services. They construct a customer differentiation matrix using two dimensions: (1) customer needs differentiation versus standardization; and (2) the value of individual customers to the supplier. For example, management services firms often are able to distinguish sharp differences between customers' values. Moreover, each client's requirements tend to differ substantially from others'. In such situations, marketing strategy necessarily must be highly individualized. On the other hand, the typical gas station probably recognizes very little difference between customers' needs or values. Thus, there is not much opportunity for product customization. In the latter type of business, one basis for successful competition may be the provision of value-added services— for example, offering fast food at gas stations—in order to gain differentiation which cannot be achieved in the core business.

Conclusion

We may conclude this discussion of market segmentation by observing that in all but a very few markets and industries, segmentation is a necessary prerequisite for valid market share measurement and effective strategy formulation. Segmentation is essential because it describes natural divisions in the structure of markets and sources of demand. It often helps the business analyst to identify parts of markets that behave differently from others and, therefore, to select a strategy that is most responsive to market segment drivers.

A CYCLICAL MODEL FOR MARKET ANALYSIS: THE ABILITY/WILLINGNESS PARADIGM

Nearly all markets have cyclical characteristics, they rise and fall in response to ebbs and flows in their fundamental economic drivers. Thus, consider the hypothetical diagram in Figure 5.3 that depicts a simplified business cycle. This cycle conveniently divides into four equal quadrants. (Actually, there is evidence that phases of cycles are not equal in duration. Rather, in the United States, negative phases are becoming shorter and positive phases are growing longer.) In each quadrant, we assume that customers willingness and ability to purchase the goods or services in question will vary as indicated at the bottom of Figure 5.3.

Initially, the cycle may begin slowly, emerging from a prior cycle's recession. At this point, customers' willingness and ability to purchase goods and services both are at very low points. As a new cycle progresses, the second stage begins and customers' economic conditions improve. Whether based on personal or business incomes, savings, debt, or net worth, the ability to make purchases also improves. However, early in this second stage, customers aren't initially willing to employ their new purchasing power, for very understandable economic and psychological reasons. In the case of the consumer, until sufficient confidence of financial security returns, there is a natural reluctance to make substantial purchases—especially if debt must be taken. In the case of industrial customers, before increasing demand encourages the acquisition of new capacity, businesses first must utilize existing, surplus capacity.

Figure 5.3
The Cycle of Ability/Willingness to Consume

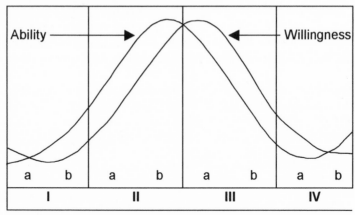

	Ia	Ib	IIa	IIb	IIIa	IIIb	IVa	IVb
Ability to Consume	Low	Low	Rising	High	High	De-clining	Low	Low
Willingness to Consume	Low	Low	Low	Rising	High	High	De-clining	Low

Concept: author

As this hypothetical cycle matures, consumption of goods and services accelerates as both consumers' ability and willingness to make purchases reach high levels. But, at some time after arriving at peak levels, customers' abilities to purchase goods or services eventually recede. It is an interesting phenomenon of economic nature that the full appreciation of such declining purchasing abilities may be substantially delayed. Similarly, industrial concerns often make decisions to add capacity late in the business cycle. By the time new capacity becomes available, demand already may have begun to subside. Inventory-building practices also may fail to appreciate the cycle's impending recession. Consumers similarly resist the reality of economic recession, preferring instead to persist in the most agreeable lifestyle for as long as possible. Thus, the *ability* to purchase goods and services (whether in consumer or industrial markets) often falls before *willingness* to consume incurs the necessary adjustment. Indeed, a generalization, at both extremes of the business cycle, may be that economic *ability precedes willingness* to consume and that the lag between these two forces depends on the extent of discretion and proportionate cost of the purchase in question.

The foregoing hypothetical model of demand is consistent with the research and theoretical writings of Katona (1951, 1960, 1975), Pickering (1975, 1981), and Winer (1985a, 1985b). However, none of those authors appears to have fully contemplated the *interactive* effects of willingness and ability.

Rather, they considered those individual demand components separately. If, however, one considers the interacting effects of these variables, ebbing and flowing as depicted in Figure 5.3, some intriguing possibilities for market analysis and forecasting emerge. Consider the diagram in Figure 5.4. Purchases should be at about the same level in Stages 2 and 4, but the marketing strategy that is appropriate to each differs quite fundamentally.

Figure 5.4
Interacting Sequential Effects of Cyclicality
in Ability and Willingness to Buy

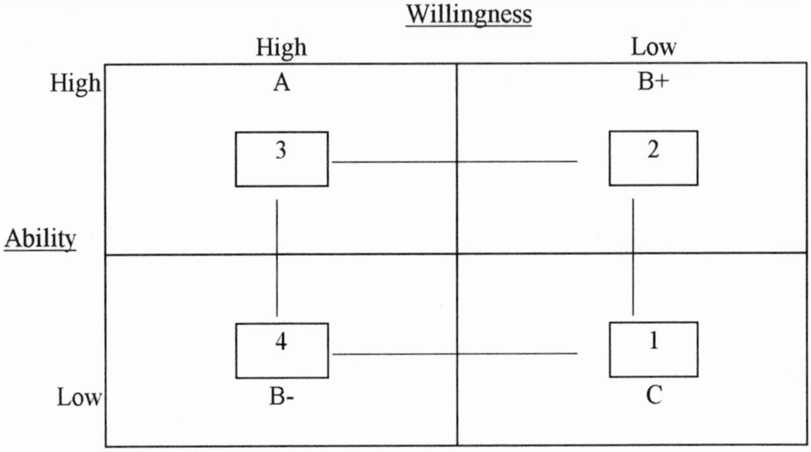

Legend A: demand is highest; **B+, B-:** demand is moderate, but either rising (+) or falling (-); C: demand is lowest.

Concept: author

The first quadrant represents market conditions when ability and willingness both are low. Hypothesizing a few economic variables may help to clarify such a situation. In this case, consumers' real disposable personal income, saving rates, debt levels, average employment hours, and weekly wages all would be at unfavorable levels. Similarly, indicators of willingness to consume would be reflected in low measures of consumer sentiment, employment rates, help-wanted advertising and actual consumption trends. In industrial markets, capacity utilization and purchasing managers survey results should be low.

Moving to the second quadrant, willingness indicators still would be low at the outset, but indications of purchasing ability would begin to strengthen. For instance, earnings may begin to increase. But, sentiment measures still would be low. In our market studies, we often find such situations. This is when we advise our clients to dispatch their sales forces to the markets in question and initiate more aggressive solicitations. The objective of marketing strategy at this stage is to benefit from competitive initiative before it becomes more obvious that customers' willingness to buy is catching up with ability—at which time rival suppliers will rush into the same market segments.

In the third quadrant, demand is strong, reflecting high levels of both willingness and ability to consume. But competitive rivalry also grows intense;. price discounting may begin. As competitive rivalry intensifies, consumers' (and producers') abilities to purchase goods and services eventually wane—perhaps due to rising prices, perhaps due to saturation of demand. Thus, the fourth quadrant is entered.

As supply overtakes demand, profit-eroding price promotions characterize marketing tactics in Quadrant 4. Customers may respond favorably to such promotions, as they struggle to sustain prosperity. When it is possible to move from this quadrant into markets with Quadrant 2 characteristics (perhaps, in another geographic region), we advise our clients to do so. It is remarkable that marketing managers rarely perceive the benefits of withdrawing resources from Quadrant 4 markets in time to avoid unnecessary losses. Some of the reasons will be explored later in this chapter.

Ultimately, all cyclical markets return to Quadrant 1, where willingness and ability again are depleted. In this quadrant, business conditions are more difficult. However, in the initial stages, markets in Quadrant 4 may not witness the full-scale reductions in consumption which are likely to occur later because, as noted previously, both industrial producers and ultimate consumers (for completely different reasons) are likely to defer reductions in purchases consistently with their reduced abilities. Recognizing this economic fact of life, managers who make correct diagnoses of their markets' ebb toward or into Quadrant 1 at least may avoid the mistakes of over-commitment and, instead, realign their resources to market realities—while competitors incur the adverse consequences of their failure to diagnose demand and risk more accurately.

ANALYSIS OF CONSUMER MARKET DRIVERS

We now turn to a consideration of factors that influence consumers' demand for goods and services. To place this discussion in context, we will begin with a brief review of theories regarding the nature of consumer purchasing decisions as they have evolved since the Second World War.

The Decision to Buy

Zaichowsky (1991) has written an overview of those theories' history, beginning with rationality models in the 1940s, which suggest that consumers decide to purchase goods and services depending on trade-offs of the satisfaction they receive versus the prices they must pay. Thus, rationality models essentially contemplate consumers engaging in fairly elaborate intellectual trade-offs of costs and benefits. Such models didn't explain how consumers actually make choices; rather, they proposed how consumers *should* make choices.

By the 1950s, theorists largely had rejected the notion of rationality as an explanation of decision-making by consumers, at least in most situations. Instead, theorists viewed consumers' decisions from the standpoint of less rational, psychological predeterminations. Thus, consumers often may not know why they make choices, but marketers presumably can anticipate, if not influence, them. However, both the rational and psychological approaches to explaining purchasing decisions have been disappointing. While each provides a useful perspective, neither has been very fruitful for predictive purposes .   ..

By the 1960s, psychological theories of consumer choices had been supplemented by more complex problem-solving models. The most influential versions of problem solving/information models characterize consumers as attempting to satisfy multiple demands and needs in making satisficing decisions (Simon, 1957; March and Simon, 1958; Cyert and March, 1963). In the 1970s, and subsequently, additional concepts regarding consumers' use of information, supplemented those models. Theorists then viewed consumers almost as complex computers, making choices based on availability and content of information in the marketplace. The consumer was perceived constantly to be gathering (or absorbing) data and thereby making more or less intelligent choices. Such cognitive models strongly influenced modern consumption theory; but research in grocery stores, for instance, seems to demonstrate that buying behaviors don't conform well to these models, either (Hoyer, 1984; Dickson and Sawyer, 1990).

Presumably, the parade of buying decision models will continue. It is somewhat remarkable that such models rarely reflect empirical evidence. Often, this is because it is too difficult to subject consumers to controlled observations. Moreover, laboratory experimentation may not provide results which can be generalized to the real marketplace. Therefore, to the extent that such models are hypothetical in nature, they may not do planning managers much good in defining driver variables that determine the demand for goods and services or segmenting markets.

In the absence of an empirically grounded theory that predicts, or at least explains, consumers' demand for goods and services—and how purchasing decisions actually are made in specific settings—planning managers are left to search among the hard data of empirical research and collect the facts that can be known separately about each market/industry interaction of interest; and then to apply what they find. In the next three sections, therefore, an overview of empirical data regarding environmental factors that influence consumer purchases of durables and nondurables is provided.

Using Demographics in
Consumer Market Analysis

Measurements of consumer markets' demographic composition often provide the single most powerful tools available to the planning manager or business analyst for explaining and forecasting demand. One can derive demographic variables' trends and patterns in the United States with considerable precision and reliability. Thus, it is possible to know how population groups are structured presently, how they have been changing, and how they are likely to change in the future.

The remarkable thing about projections of population groups' sizes, well into the future, is their high level of accuracy. To a large extent, the population groups of future years already have been born, and—with exception of structural abnormalities, such as dramatic shifts in immigration, war, or disease—their numbers are completely predictable. Less certain but still highly predictable, is the rate at which families will form and births occur (fertility). It is only in predictions of fertility and immigration that demographic forecasts are subject to significant error.

Some rather important shifts are occurring in segments of the U.S. population. Teenagers and senior adults who have not yet retired are increasing in numbers. However, the number of middle-aged (35–44) adults many of whom are mid-level managers and household heads, is expected to peak soon and begin to decline. Similarly, the number of infants will decline soon. To illustrate the value of such forecasts, consider that these last two shifts have ominous implications for the residential construction and home products industries as well as for manufacturers of products for infants and child care. In those industries, demographic analyses and forecasts are vital planning tools.

Another important trend is the pending decline of young (20–34) adults. The reduction in their numbers indicates that there will be a growing shortage of work force entrants. Impacts of this trend will be far-reaching. Illustrations include increasing competition for, and incomes of, young employees; higher incentives for industry to develop automation; and reduction in demand for starter homes.

Demographic trends have a great deal to say about future workforce composition. Clearly, the numbers of junior professionals as well as entrants into the workforce will decrease soon. These trends have the makings of significant social discomfort. With so many senior employees, opportunities for promotion through the ranks will be less available to middle managers, notwithstanding their growing seniority. At the same time, young adults will be more inclined toward entrepreneurial pursuits, because their avenues to advancement in corporate organizations may be blocked by layers of more senior managers. These trends also suggest that cultural strains between generations will increase due to conflicts of economic interests.

Cutler et al. (1990) conducted an extensive evaluation of imbalances between working-age groups and dendendant-age groups (children and seniors) in the United States (see Figure 5.5). Their findings regarding dependency trends will be surprising to many. It is commonly lamented that increasing numbers of persons over the retirement age relative to numbers of persons in the workforce will create a growing burden on future employees. In fact, trends in the elderly dependency ratio, which expresses the proportion of persons over 65 years old versus those of working ages between 20 and 64 years old, substantiate this concern. That ratio rose from 17% in 1960 to 22% in 1995. However, these researchers' computations indicate that the ratio should stabilize and even decline somewhat through the year 2010 (after which it will begin to rise again).

More important is the total dependency ratio that reflects persons under 20 years and those over 65 as a proportion of the total workforce. In 1965, this ratio was about 95%, but, it had dropped to 70% by 1995. This favorable trend will continue at least through the year 2010, when it is projected to reach 65%. Hence, the important driver of living standards actually exhibits a very favorable trend—contrary to the conventional wisdom.

Figure 5.5
Actual and Projected Growth Rate of Labor Force:
United States and Non-U.S.: 1960–2050

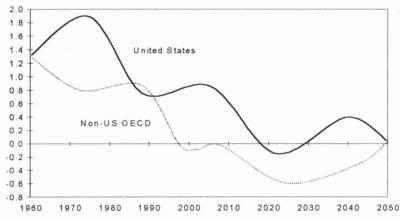

Source: Cutler et al. 1990

Reasons for the previously mentioned trends in dependency ratios include decreased fertility during the 1960s and 1970s, and a nearly assured reduction in growth rates of the labor force well below those of nonworking groups. Annual labor force growth rates during the past quarter-century averaged 1.7% during the 1970s, 1.3% during the 1980s, and 0.8% in the current decade. In the next decade, this rate actually may turn negative and continue downward through the first half of the next century. In fact, the workforce in other industrialized nations already has stopped growing, and further declines are projected through 2050.

Markets served by many industries already are experiencing the impacts of these, and similar, demographic shifts, which are the subjects of frequent articles in the business press. For instance, one writer pointed out that increasing numbers of senior working individuals are likely to have substantial impacts on the demand for leisure products, entertainment, home furnishings, financial assets and financial services (Schonfeld, 1995).

Cohort Analysis

From demographic analysis, it is possible to identify trends in age-income groups' sizes and migration patterns that can influence the potential demand for an industry's goods or services. Such groups are called cohorts. After likely shifts of important cohorts have been detected, marketing strategists typically try to understand cohort members' motivations to make purchasing decisions well enough to gain favorable market positions. Two members of the well-known Yankelovich market research firm recently demonstrated how market planners can use demographic analysis and identify motives that drive cohort members' purchasing decisions.

Smith and Clurman (1997) defined three generational cohorts with dramatically different buying tendencies. These three generations' differences in attitudes about what is important in life present significant problems and opportunities to firms that offer products or services to consumers. Smith and Clurman defined such implications based on several years of results from the Yankelovich Monitor, a research program aimed at defining trends in demographic groups' buying tendencies.

Matures (born during 1909–1945) are archetypical conservatives. They value discipline, hard work, and self denial, believe in sacrifice to reach goals, respect authority, and judge their success based on the success of their children. To a large extent, these persons either have retired or are preparing to do so. They grew up during World War II and its aftermath, the outcome of which justified their belief that the common good benefits individuals. They respect authority figures, including presidents, generals, institutions, and established brands.

Boomers (born during 1946–1964) are the children of matures. They grew up without fear of wars or concerns about potential economic hardship. Unlike their parents and grandparents, they cannot appreciate the concept of economic depression in real-life terms. Unworried about their economic futures, they developed early habits of self-indulgence and liberal attitudes about social entitlement. However, as one recession after another occurred, Boomers grew disenchanted. They turned to their jobs as sources of the rewards to which they felt entitled but had been denied. If and when successful, to convince themselves as much as others that they really had made it, they engage in conspicuous consumption. Now, whether successful in their jobs or not, Boomers still seek the gratification to which they feel entitled. They are more likely than conservatives to be self-centered and less likely to be brand-loyal. They will maintain these attitudes and buying habits throughout their lives. But without the financial wherewithal to realize satisfaction of their needs and gratification of their wants, many will be in need of financial services and products that give them some sense of security and support as they approach retirement years.

X-ers (born after 1965) are the Boomers' children. Whereas their parents were idealists and self-indulgent, X-ers are realists. They have been disenchanted by their parents' divorces, recessions, AIDS, high costs of homes, and the failure of government to provide orderliness, let alone higher standards of living. Believing that their seniors' institutions and philosophies of life haven't worked well, this generation is pragmatic to a fault, willing to work hard, not because of any intrinsic values associated with hard work (such as the matures), but simply because they know that, ultimately, they are their own sole sources of support. They have very limited allegiance to their employers and are more likely than any other group in U.S. history to strike off on their own by starting independent businesses. Their strongest affiliations are with persons of their own age, college class, work group, and so forth, rather than even their parents. Thus, they are cohort-oriented much more than they are family-oriented.

The reasonableness of Smith and Clurman's proposal that X-ers tend to be more strongly affiliated with persons of their own age, rather than their families, receives support from statistics in a 1994 report by the Carnegie Corporation that describes deterioration of the nuclear family in modern U.S. history (Table 5.2).

Table 5.2
Deterioration of the Nuclear Family: 1960–1990

	Percent	
	1960	1990
Children born to unwed mothers	5%	28%
Children under 3 living with one parent	7	27
Children under 3 living with both parents	90	71
Children under 18 living in a one-parent family	10	25
Married women with children under 6 who are in the work force	19	60
Children under 18 experiencing parents' divorce	<1	49

Source: Carnegie Task Force on Meeting the Needs of Young Children, 1994

These statistics tell a compelling story of the circumstances in which X-ers are growing up. Many were raised in a single-parent family or a family in which both parents work. Figure 5.6 demonstrates the number of "latch-key kids" who cared for themselves in 1991 while their parents were working.

Figure 5.6
Latch-Key Kids in America

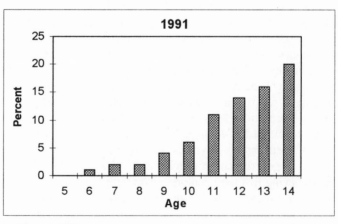

Source: U.S. Census Bureau, 1991

X-ers have been forced to rely on themselves for amenities that previous generations took for granted. In this less supportive environment, X-ers form strong values of survival and self-reliance differing sharply from their parents. Instead of the family, they often are more likely to bond with people in their own generation who also face stresses engendered by deterioration of traditional nuclear families.

Geo-demographics

Demographic analysis also may be conducted from a geographic perspective. Thus, Terleckyj (1995) has defined impacts of declining defense industries on metropolitan and rural population centers employment (See Table 5.3).

Table 5.3
The 20 Most Vulnerable U.S.
Metropolitan and Rural Markets

The 10 metropolitan areas and 10 nonmetropolitan counties with largest proportions of defense employment in 1992:		
	Defense Jobs as a Percentage of Total Employment, 1992	Projected Defense Job Reduction 1992 - 1999
Metro Area:		
Jacksonville, NC	65.23%	-13.77%
Fayetteville, NC	46.78%	-11.87%
Lawton, OH	46.67%	-10.33%
Fort Walton Beach, FL	42.93%	-11.08%
Clarksville-Hopkinsville, TN-KY	42.07%	-9.2%
Killeen-Temple, TX	39.46%	2.05%
Bremerton, WA	29.81%	-4.26%
Savannah, GA	26.57%	-6.03%
Biloxi-Gulfport-Pascagooula,	25.58%	-8.64%
Colorado Springs, CO	23.74%	-3.93%
County:		
Sierra, CA	98.77%	-10.38%
Alcona, MI	98.76%	-19.34%
Wakulla, FL	97.59%	-40.16%
Red River, TX	86.08%	-0.63%
Tooele, UT	80.81%	-25.84%
Martin, IN	72.5%	-20.92%
Pulaski, MO	71.98%	15.26%
Elmore, ID	71.43%	-31.09%
Riley, KS	89.28%	-13.53%
Sagadahoc, ME	68.42%	-26.78%

Source: Terelckyj, 1995

Between 1995 and 1999 the number of defense jobs is expected to decline by about 15% reflecting significant cuts in defense spending. Consequently, cities where large portions of employment are dependent on defense industries are especially vulnerable. Such cities include Biloxi, Gulfport, Savannah, Fort Walton Beach, and Fayetteville, North Carolina, among others. More vulnerable still, are several rural counties where more than two-thirds of all jobs are defense-related and subject to defense cuts recently enacted into law.

As opposed to the locations in Table 5.3, several other geographic markets have fared much better during the past five years. Metropolitan markets with the fastest recent employment growth rates include Atlanta, Houston, Los Angeles, the Washington D.C. area, and Dallas. Each of those markets also is expected to enjoy sustained growth through 2005.

Note of Caution: Make Few Assumptions

From time to time, conventional wisdom about demographics may not be correct. Consider, for instance, the phenomenon of a "shrinking middle class." In fact, the middle class has been shrinking in recent years (Daly, 1997). However, the reason is contrary to a common belief that there has been an increase in the number of lower income persons. Instead, during the 1980s, a significant portion of persons who previously were in the middle class actually moved into higher-income brackets. The point is that with available data, demographic assumptions usually are fairly easy to confirm or refute. One can obtain a great deal of such information inexpensively from the U.S. Census Bureau. Other sources include the National Planning Association and commercial monitoring services, such as the Yankelovich Monitor and A.C. Neilson Company's Homescan Research Service. So, demographic analysts may not need to make many assumptions. The fewer, the better!

Drivers of Demand for Consumer Durables

Certainly, if the notion of rational purchasing decisions were applicable in the consumer sector, it would apply best to the acquisition of big ticket items. Pickering (1975, 1978, 1981, 1984) developed several of the concepts discussed earlier in this chapter regarding willingness and ability to explain such purchases. Following the path of Katona (1951, 1960), Pickering addressed his research to the impacts of consumers' expectations, confidence and financial capabilities on purchases of durable goods. His initial research (1975) included a survey of 610 households during 1972 and 1973. Pickering's findings demonstrated that consumers' decisions to purchase durables for the first time differ fundamentally from decisions to make replacement purchases.

To establish relationships between general economic circumstances and consumer confidence, Winer (1985a) elaborated on Pickering's (1981) model. He clarified the nature of product-specific utility values in determining expectations that consumers will purchase durables. In a separate paper (1985b), he explored several economic variables related to durables demand and differentiated between those variables and initial purchases of durables versus replacement purchases. In that same discussion, he developed the concept of desired versus actual stocks of durables. Subsequently, stock models of durables purchases have gained a great deal of theoretical importance. Durables demand, then, is a two-fold function of initial purchases and replacements. Purchasing decisions are quite different in each of those cases.

More recently, Cripps (1994) tested theories about replacement purchases and found that they tend to occur at a slower rate than prevailing theories predicted. Those findings were explained by proposing that there is a tendency of consumers to trade off opportunity costs arising from obsolescence against the utility cost of product deterioration. ("Even if this car isn't the latest model, what will I lose by driving it another year?")

Returning to Winer's (1985b) research, he proposed the existence of *a hierarchy of needs* that determines the order in which initial purchases of specific durables occur—one before the other. However, demand for those same items' replacement is based on their ages and relative usefulness. Other driver factors that Winer's model included are family wealth, confidence, stage of the family's life cycle and, of course, price. Of those variables, the consumer's life-cycle stage (a demographic concept) was most influential in determining various items' initial purchases. Effects of family incomes on durables purchase decisions also were discerned; and Winer described a positively decelerating curvilinear relationship that stabilizes at the high end of the income spectrum. Prices' impacts on consumer durables purchases were described by four groups of variables: (1) expectations of future prices; (2) uncertainty of price expectations; (3) unanticipated increases in prices (sticker shock); and (4) the consumer's reservation price, at which an item must leave the family's budget.

To test his model, Winer (1985b) obtained data from the University of Michigan's 1977 survey of 2,563 households, obtaining 1,567 useful records. More than 1,000 variables' impacts on purchasing decisions were tested for the years of 1976 and 1977. A statistical model was fitted to the results. Unfortunately, its confidence level was low. Nevertheless, this research did succeed in demonstrating a workable method for studying drivers of durables purchases. Moreover, several previously accepted hypotheses were rejected. Among those is the notion that working wives increased the probability of durables purchases; that factor was inconsequential. Since Winer's research, theorists have refined models of durables purchases, but they continue to focus attention on the differences between drivers of initial purchases and replacements.

To explain and predict demand for consumer durables purchased initially and as replacements, analysts typically use stock adjustment models. To the extent that replacements are involved, consumers must make decisions about the utilities of presently owned products versus the values of new cars, stoves, washers, dryers, and so forth. Hymans (1970) wrote an extensive paper to describe how such a model may be constructed, using multiple linear regression analysis. His models explained automobile industry sales as well as purchases of other durables. Inclusion of the consumer sentiment index improved on a model containing conventional components of other stock adjustment models: disposable personal income, the unemployment rate, auto price increases, auto industry strikes, personal consumption expenditures (PCE) inflation rates, and industry inventory levels. Before statistical significance could be derived from its use, the consumer sentiment index first had to be filtered for large changes. However, when that variable was filtered and then entered into Hymans' model, the proportion of variance explained was improved substantially ($r^2 = .965$). Curiously, the consumer sentiment index only improved the model for auto purchases; but not for other consumer durables.

In the same paper, Hymans developed a regression model to explain the consumer sentiment index using disposable personal income, a stock market index, the PCE deflator, and the previous period's consumer sentiment index as independent variables. Remarkably, unemployment rates did not improve the explanatory power of this model.

One of the panelists (Juster) reviewing Hymans' paper opined that the consumer sentiment index did not help to explain purchases of household durables other than autos—such as washing machines—because purchases of those items tend to act more like nondiscretionary than discretionary decisions. Juster also remarked that a better model, still, would separate consumption of auto parts from purchases of new cars; and that purchases of new cars should be segmented into the portion purchased by businesses rather than consumers, because the former portion has become quite large. Thus, segmentation can play an important role in econometric research, just as it does in industrial market research.

Since Hymans' research, several other factors have been found to influence consumer durables purchases reliably. Mannering (1991) explored the causes and effects of shifts in brand loyalty on automobile manufacturers' market shares. Similarly, Arguea (1994) investigated consumer preferences' impacts on durables' price elasticity. Cripps (1994) explored impacts of perceived differences between obsolescence and product deterioration, discovering that subjects in a simulation experiment made replacement purchases at a slower rate than one would predict when assuming adherence to the principles of optimal replacement. So, some unexplained variable must have been at work. Putsis and Srinivasan (1994) may have contributed a partial answer to this puzzle by exploring deliberation and delay in purchases as a function of the amount of relevant information consumers receive, and several other more conventional variables, such as price expectations versus quotations, intrinsic motivation, and even marital status.

We conclude this brief discussion of consumers' decisions to purchase durable goods first by acknowledging the complexity of such decisions. However, the literature makes clear at least a few generalities. First, decisions to purchase items for the first time are substantially different than replacement decisions. Second, it is important to segment markets at least on the basis of benefits anticipated by customers—for instance, separating purchases of cars by businesses and consumers; for commuting to work versus leisure travel, and so forth. Moreover, the distinction between product deterioration and obsolescence adds an important refinement to the classic stock replacement model. Finally, as Hymans (1970) demonstrated more than a quarter century ago, consumers' sentiment (willingness) can be just as significant as their economic abilities to acquire big ticket items in determining their ultimate purchase decisions. Although statistically less rigorous, the findings of Katona (1951, 1960) and Pickering (1975, 1981) would support that conclusion.

Drivers of Demand for Consumer Nondurables

When consumers purchase durables, they well may take a rational approach to such decision making simply because the amount invested can represent a significant portion of the buyer's wealth. But, purchase decisions may not be so rational in the case of nondurable goods and services. Economic variables, including consumers' incomes, debt, and savings relative to products or services' prices, probably still enter into the decision process. But, because purchases of nondurables may be either discretionary or nondiscretionary, decisions to purchase them are even more difficult to understand. Factors that can influence discretion in decision making are primarily psychological in nature. They include cultural variables, tastes, sentiment regarding future economic prospects and habit, among others. On the other hand, absolute needs have greater impacts on nondiscretionary buying decisions.

The nature of psychological determinants of discretionary purchasing decisions is beyond the scope of this book. (We have observed earlier how such variables may differ substantially between demographic cohorts such as age generations.) For purposes of this discussion, therefore, we will focus on the somewhat less complex process by which nondiscretionary consumer purchasing decisions are made. Admittedly, this artificially limits the scope of discussion. However, it does make the subject matter more manageable, and will enable essential methods of analysis to be demonstrated.

To a significant extent, nondiscretionary consumer purchasing decisions involve rational choices based on need. Theories of such decisions may reflect assumptions that some kind of a deliberate decision process is involved. Olshavsky (1979) classified such rational decision making concepts into four categories: (1) budget allocation; (2) generic decisions to buy for specific products and services; (3) store patronage habits; and (4) brand selections. However, he also concluded that a rational decision making process does not necessarily precede these purchases. Instead, nondiscretionary purchases may reflect subconscious desires to conform to group norms regarding the brand purchased, for instance; or, product choices simply may occur at random after the need to acquire a nondiscretionary good or service is perceived.

Using a controlled laboratory experiment with 120 subjects, Moore (1980) studied consumers' search for information regarding purchasing decisions. The commodity in question (bread) was of small significance to the consumer's budget. The results of this research demonstrated that several situational variables can influence buyers' search behavior greatly. Time pressure, the number of purchases in the same shopping trip, and repeat purchases of the same commodity all seemed to reduce external search behavior. However, the product's health impact (perceived effect on obesity), risk of a bad choice, and the buyer's intelligence level seemed to encourage more extensive search behavior. Finally, this study discovered that there were significant differences in shopping styles, depending on time pressures, habit, and product claims. Thus, consumers seem to exercise considerable discretion in making nondiscretionary purchases! Such discretion is largely situational rather than product-engendered. Therefore, retail marketers' strategy must focus on the shopping situation at least as much as the product(s) offered.

Hoyer (1984) conducted in-store research, including 120 grocery shoppers. Again, the product (laundry detergent) was not significant to the family budget. The typical purchase in this study took only 13 seconds, including time to approach the product. Usually, subjects considered only one brand. This report concluded that—by applying psychological models involving considerable cognitive effort and deliberation immediately prior to making a selection—consumer decision theories have erred. In this study's observations, there was no time for elaborate contemplation. Instead, consumers often purchase in a repetitive fashion, benefiting from choice rules and decision criteria accumulated over successive shopping experiences. Inasmuch as they tend to minimize the time and effort of making relatively unimportant decisions, one benefit of such behaviors is their efficiency.

To investigate the price knowledge and search behaviors of supermarket shoppers, Dickson and Sawyer (1990) conducted another grocery store study. Their purpose was to examine several established theories of how consumers make purchasing decisions based on price promotions, frequency of shopping, advertisements, brand image, information recall, and inter-store price shopping. The products studied included coffee, toothpaste, margarine, and cereal. Fifty interviews conducted in each of four stores for each product brought the total to 802 interviews. The statistical rigor of this study was considerable and its results were remarkable:

- Less than half of 802 shoppers could recall the price of an item just placed in their baskets;
- Many price promotions in the store weren't noticed at all;
- Only 58% of these shoppers even checked the price; and
- Only 42% of those who bought store specials even estimated the price reduction they had realized.

However, price promotions did tend to increase consumers' notice of advertisements, increased the probability that shoppers would check the price, increased the probability that shoppers would compare brands and encouraged inter-store shopping. Therefore, price promotions may increase exploratory behavior, but not necessarily consumers' propensity to buy the brand being promoted.

These researchers also discovered a separate segment of their population—about 22% of the shoppers studied—that compared prices more carefully than the others. They conjectured that there must be a separate market segment of careful shoppers, who are more rational in their selections than others. On balance, however, this study seems to have cast a great deal of doubt on the effectiveness of promotion-oriented marketing methods. Instead, the primary environmental variables of strategic significance seem to have been situational.

A recent survey of promotional practices by Donnelly Marketing Inc. (Schermach, 1995) drew a somewhat complementary conclusion. It identified couponing (rather than price discounting) as the most frequently employed promotional device that nondurable consumer products manufacturers use to generate consumer trials and to leverage other retail support approaches. Coupons avoid the risk of impulse buying by consumers because they require that a specific brand be selected before the shopping situation is entered. Thus, couponing forces consumers to make more rational choices.

In recent years, the consumer's shopping experience itself has become a focus of research, as explained earlier in this chapter. Market research studies are discovering that effective retail marketing usually requires merchandisers to create a distinctively satisfying shopping experience. Thus, increasing attention has been directed to the importance of creating enjoyable shopping experiences to supplement product-oriented marketing strategies. Neither the product nor the situation, by itself, is sufficient any longer. Thus, planning managers in a retailing firm that supplies consumer nondurables now must be as concerned with slow check-out lines and pleasant shopping experiences as with the products or services offered. (Discount Store News, 1995; Rigney, 1995).

ANALYSIS OF INDUSTRIAL MARKET DRIVERS

The scope of industrial purchases is essentially the same as that for consumer purchases: expendable goods, durable goods, and services. However, unlike consumer markets, industrial markets are believed to be primarily rational in nature, reflecting a universal assumption that managers' motives in making purchases for industrial enterprises reflect consideration of their profit impacts. Nevertheless, as successful industrial sales persons know, industrial purchasing decisions often are not nearly as rational as one might suspect, and psychological determinants of discretionary purchasing decisions frequently come into play. But, simply because the amounts of money involved and the degree of formality can be substantial, rationality of purchasing decisions probably is much more important in the industrial marketplace than the consumer marketplace.

For the purpose of taxonomy, a strategic analysis of industrial customers' purchasing decisions, and the drivers that influence them, may take any or all of four perspectives:

- Rational/transactional
- Cyclical/ market timing
- Industry-specific
- Psychological

The following paragraphs explore each of these perspectives.

Rational Approaches

The rational industrial purchasing manager approaches acquisition of products and services primarily to satisfy financial motives. Purchasing managers may measure the financial outcomes of buying decisions by conventional financial indicators, including incremental costs, profit margins, rates of return and discounted cash flows. However, they also may make rational industrial purchasing decisions for nonfinancial reasons, such as insulation of the firm from potential impacts of materials shortages and work stoppages. To maintain or attain a technological parity with competitors—if not a competitive advantage— the general manager may feel compelled to acquire capital assets, notwithstanding their cost. Another nonfinancial rationale for acquiring capital goods may be the code of regulatory requirements to maintain or remediate the environment so that pollution is minimized, albeit at the lowest possible cost. Obviously, the business analyst, strategist, or planning manager must attempt to understand which of these factors are most important in driving industrial customers' buying decisions.

Cyclical Approaches

The business cycle significantly impacts nearly all industrial markets. Therefore, purchases of industrial machinery and equipment are especially cyclical. We observed earlier that purchases of industrial fixed assets often occur late in the business cycle as capacity limits are approached. However, additions to capacity late in the business cycle may add disproportionately to fixed costs of operations, thereby impacting financial results adversely. Consequently, the same manufacturers may be compelled to reduce their operating expenses and capital expenditures, thereby producing the pronounced reactions of capital goods markets that typically occur when business cycles recede. Indeed, relationships between economic and industrial market cycles are so close that analysis of the two often may be performed together comfortably. Hence, industrial business planning managers frequently evaluate their markets' potentials effectively by employing economic analysis techniques—especially those addressed to diagnosing and forecasting stages of the business cycle.

Industry-Specific Approaches

The goods and services that many suppliers offer in industrial markets may be intended for very specific applications. Thus, some industries use a limited scope of materials (basic metals, lumber, concrete, chemicals, grains, and so forth). Marketing managers of firms that supply such materials often become experts in the supply and demand dynamics of their customers' industries. Similarly, fabricating firms' purchasing managers may become experts in the technology and economics of industries that supply the materials and equipment which they buy. Since a majority of industrial markets are so product/service specific, the industry analysis chapter in this book also should be consulted for guidelines on analyzing industrial markets' structures.

Because industrial purchasing decisions tend to be fairly rational, industrial marketers must understand the critical success factors that drive buyers' willingness and abilities to transact purchases. Industrial marketing managers often become virtual experts in their customers' industries, able to anticipate trends and patterns in demand for customers' products as well as their customers. Indeed, by developing core competences to solve customers' product or process problems with superior materials, machines, systems, distribution, and so on, successful industrial marketers can achieve competitive advantage. For instance, the successful auto parts manufacturer's product engineers may be just as knowledgeable about an automotive performance problem as they are about the metallurgical, forging, stamping, or casting processes employed to make the products that solve those problems.

Psychological Approaches

Notwithstanding the fundamentally rational elements of industrial market analysis, there also are substantial psychological dimensions of industrial purchasing decisions. However, psychological aspects of industrial buying decisions are less well understood than they are in consumer markets. Katona (1951, 1960, 1975) made one of the earliest attempts to understand psychological drivers of industrial purchase decisions. In the first of three works on psychological analysis of economic behavior (1951), he devoted three chapters to motivation of industrial production, pricing, and investment decisions. Most of the principles articulated in that volume remain valid today, and some of them are discussed in the following paragraphs.

In making nontrivial purchasing decisions, the industrial manager must formulate expectations regarding future business conditions. Of course, significant uncertainty pervades such matters. Managers differ in their tolerances for risk, and they may exchange large but uncertain potential profits for more modest but less uncertain profits, and vice versa. Such trade-offs lend themselves to psychological analysis, and the industrial marketer may be able to evaluate customers on that basis. Simply due to their substantial size, some industrial customers will not be nearly as motivated to avoid risk as their smaller, less resilient competitors.

To the extent that risk minimization is a motive, managers likely will select profit objectives on the basis of satisficing criteria rather than maximization criteria. The analyst may discover differences in firms' risk tolerance from a study of their financial statements, strategic positions, top executives' background and track records, trends in policies and recent purchasing decisions. From such studies, the industrial market analyst also should be able to gain insight into intersections of target firm managers' strategic and psychological needs. Then they can offer products or services which are most responsive to the buyer's motives.

Economic theories may prescribe ways in which businesses *should* attempt to maximize profits, but how businesses actually behave may be quite different. In fact, it is this disparity between reality and theory that often reduces the value of economic theories to business executives in decision making.

Consider what happens when customers notice that prices are increasing. Economic theory would hold that customers will purchase less when prices rise. In fact, common experience demonstrates that consumption actually may increase substantially in anticipation of further increases. On the other hand, customers could view the same price increase as unsustainable or temporary, in which case they indeed will defer purchases. In this case, customers' pricing expectations, rather than actual price levels at the moment, will drive their purchasing decisions. Such expectations, of course, are psychological phenomena.

Katona's (1951) surveys of industrial managers at the University of Michigan disclosed that his subjects exhibited two types of motive in weak markets. First, they were reluctant to give up volume, and might attempt to hold customers by discounting prices even to unprofitable levels. Theories of the firm typically envision firms' motives as profit maximizing. But, that kind of price cutting is hardly profit maximizing behavior. Alternatively, when managers feared industry-wide chain reactions of price cutting they implemented more rational downsizing and other cost reduction measures.

Katona proposed that industrial managers are strongly motivated to avoid risk and uncertainty. Accordingly, downsizing and cost reduction should be likely to occur when markets weaken, simply because the outcome of cost reducing actions is more certain than that of price reductions to which both customers or competitors may react either favorably or unfavorably. Katona acknowledged the inadequacy of theory to reconcile these motives, and pleaded for empirical investigations to develop theories that describe trade-offs of uncertainty avoidance and price cutting tactics.

Reactions of producers to materials cost reductions may differ dramatically, again for psychological reasons. If a reduction is due to lower commodity prices on an industry-wide basis, a producer may have no choice other than to pass the savings along to customers. But, if the cost reduction is proprietary, a more rational choice may be to offer quality improvements or simply not pass through the saving. Nevertheless, Katona's surveys seemed to indicate that if they do not pass through savings some executives feel guilty. Similarly, if they raise prices even when costs increase, some executives again feel guilty. In the latter cases, there usually is an attempt first to offset increasing costs by raising volumes and gaining scale economies. But, if prices are cut and margins squeezed in the process, such efforts usually do not succeed in the long run.

Some industrial behaviors can become quite habitual, at which times rational processes may not prevail (Katona, 1951: 230). Examples of habitual rules of thumb may be found in industry-wide pricing conventions, preferences for high rates of capacity utilization even when they are not economical and preferences for high liquidity even when capital is not used productively. Another interesting example of habitually irrational industrial decision making occurs when competitors follow the leader. Thus, firms throughout an industry may purchase a particular type of equipment, simply because a large competitor has done so, and competitors don't want to be left behind (236). In such situations, companies tend to take action relatively quickly, because there is no doubt that the firm is at risk of a competitive disadvantage and uncertainty is not a problem.

One of the most interesting psychological influences in industrial decision making is found in capital expenditure justification procedures. Habitual approaches to such decisions may include prohibitions on replacement of assets until they are fully depreciated. Thus, if assets have seven-year accounting lives, it may be mandatory that they remain in use for at least that length of time, even if they become technologically obsolete. Another habitual impediment to rational decision making may occur when top management imposes short payoff criteria. Accordingly, new machines must pay for themselves within three years or some other brief period when, in fact, the machine simply is vital for the company's competitive viability, and/or has a much longer product life. By deferring capital investments when assets cannot meet short payoff criteria, firms may deny themselves needed asset replacements and, consequently, become uncompetitive.

How Industrial Firms Make Purchasing Decisions

In devising an industrial marketing approach, it can be very helpful to know whether purchasing decisions by customers are most likely to be centralized or decentralized. To make such a diagnosis, the analyst can evaluate several dimensions of a firm's or industry's purchasing practices. Bonoma and Shapiro (1983) proposed the evaluation of six dimensions, each of which encourage centralization:

1. Large size of the typical contract or order
2. Standardization (versus diversification) of the purchaser's requirements among multiple operating sites
3. Availability of scale economies and learning benefits
4. Influence of engineering staff on purchasing decisions
5. Concentration of the supplier-industry
6. Breadth of suppliers' distribution (large producers with many sites versus small producers with single sites).

The purchasing function's stage of evolution and sophistication also may be a basis upon which to characterize prospective customers' likely purchasing practices. (Risley, 1972: 79, 80). According to this construct, firms' purchasing practices evolve through four stages of maturity: (1) simple buying practices that involve primarily clerical procedures; (2) classical purchasing disciplines that entail greater administrative sophistication, usually including a department consisting of buyers supervised by a purchasing manager; (3) supervision of the procurement function by a higher-level manager with technical skills to conduct make versus buy decisions, evaluate vendors, and negotiate more complex contracts; and (4) modern materials management, which includes inventory control, value analysis, and participation in product development decisions. Each level of sophistication usually encompasses preceding levels within the next most senior manager's scope of responsibility and authority. Thus, a modern materials manager would be responsible for procurement, purchasing, and buying functions as well as inventory control and, perhaps, physical distribution—each of which probably is directed by a different manager.

It also is important to diagnose the prospective customer's point of buying authority. Purchasing managers tend to rate themselves as being more important to their firms' purchasing process than other executives perceive them to be (Weigand, 1966). Research conducted by Cooley et. al. (1977) demonstrated that purchasing departments' power tends to be greater when decisions regarding supplier selection are to be made than when decisions involve product selection. As a general rule, when the purchasing function is relatively powerful in a company versus other functions (such as engineering or operations) pricing will be the most important criterion in selecting a vendor.

Of course, the personal relationships between buyers and sellers also can influence buying decisions. Thus, several studies have demonstrated that vendors' approaches to prospective customers will be most successful when there are close similarities between the buyer and the seller's representative (Evans, 1963; Gadel, 1964; Brock, 1965). Especially important, perhaps, was Brock's (1965) experiment in which sales persons who recommended paint based on their experience in a similar job had higher closing rates than sales people who recommended the same paint based on experience with a dissimilar job. Studies by Evans (1963) and Gadel (1964), in the insurance industry, also demonstrated that the level of similarity between personal characteristics of agents and customers was closely correlated to closing rates.

The buyer's motivation of course is an equally important consideration, as observed in the previous section. Whereas generally accepted buying criteria include price, quality, service, availability of goods, and transactions' reliability (Hill, Alexander, and Cross, 1975), less rational motives also may determine buyers' purchasing decisions. Thus, Webster (1968) demonstrated that purchasing managers exhibit both professional career aspirations and needs to be accepted by other managers in the organization when making buying decisions.

The buyer's risk tolerance is another critical determinant. Wilson (1971) demonstrated that most buyers exhibit risk-aversion in making buying decisions. About 30% of the managers he studied attempted to maximize expected value from purchasing decisions—he called this the normative group. A second category of conservative purchasing managers attempted to avoid uncertainty and large negative outcomes; they comprised about 55% of the sample. Therefore, risk-avoiders greatly outnumbered risk takers. (A third group of 15% vacillated between the two extremes.)

Wilson, Matthews, and Sweeny (1973) studied 130 purchasing managers and identified four different patterns of risk avoidance. These patterns responded to combinations of risk sources on two scales. Each scale's extremes represented internal or external sources of risk or consequences (see Figure 5.7)

External uncertainty reduction motivates the first group of purchasing managers. These managers' approaches included first-hand evaluation of qualified bidders' plants and obtaining delivery assurances from successful bidders before placing orders. *Internal uncertainty* reduction motivated purchasing managers in the second group. That group tended to rely on suppliers' published records, other buyers' opinions of prospective vendors, and so forth Thus, the second group conducted indirect investigations using reference checks, but did not conduct investigations of prospective vendors directly. Within each of the first two groups, there were two subgroups. *External consequences* reduction motivated purchasing managers in the first subgroup. This group engaged in direct price negotiation and, if necessary, split orders between suppliers to maximize leverage in negotiating prices. *Internal consequences* motivated managers in the second subgroup. They tended to consult with peers and higher level managers before placing orders.

Figure 5.7
Purchasing Managers' Risk Avoidance Strategy Options

Sources of Uncertainty

	External	Internal
External	Evaluate bidders, first hand Divide the order	Check the bidders' references Divide the order
Internal	Evaluate bidders, first hand Obtain consensus to buy	Check the bidders' references Obtain consensus to buy

(Sources of Consequences — left axis)

(Concept adopted by author: Wilson, Mattews & Sweeny, 1971)

Cardozo (1968) further classified purchasing managers' behavior as either evaluating alternative vendors simultaneously (to select the best) or in a sequential fashion (choosing the first one that is satisfactory). If the size of purchase, price variability, and doubt about vendors' abilities to perform all are high, purchasing managers typically evaluate several vendors simultaneously. But if price variability and vendor performance risks all are low, then purchasing managers tend to take a sequential approach. Even the vendor's *relative* ability to deliver doesn't matter much in that case. Cardozo further proposed that six factors contribute to the risk of a purchasing decision:

1. Expenditure size,
2. Transaction complexity,
3. Value added to the end product,
4. Probability of an unsatisfactory choice,
5. Visibility of an unsatisfactory choice's consequences, and
6. Probability that the purchasing decision will influence the market significantly.

These characteristics of purchasing decisions and their risks demonstrate that industrial purchasing decisions may not be entirely rational exercises. However, to the extent that industrial marketers are able to segment markets and classify buying motivations of purchasing managers correctly, the probability of a marketing strategy's success should be enhanced.

Conclusion

We may conclude this discussion of industrial market drivers by observing that commercial purchasing decisions are more likely to be rational than consumers' purchasing decisions. In part, this is because business buying decisions are subject to close scrutiny according to rational criteria, such as cost, profit, and return on investment. Consequently, purchasing managers tend to employ rational processes of evaluation. However, industrial purchasing decisions do not always reflect rational processes. Therefore, industrial market analysts may find opportunities to perform more subtle and potentially more rewarding evaluations of habitual behaviors manifested by individual executives or even entire industries (Hambrick, 1983). Such opportunities often are not very hard to find and may provide avenues to competitive advantage.

ANALYSIS OF
INTERNATIONAL MARKETS

We close this discussion of market analysis methods by observing the extent to which markets differ between countries of the world. When evaluating consumer and industrial markets of foreign nations, one can apply the principles contained in each of the preceding sections of this chapter, to some extent at least. However, dramatic differences between countries' markets make the task of foreign market analysis immensely more difficult than analysis of domestic markets.

Simply because of the extensive interrelationships that now occur between country-markets, focusing on an individual country's economy, industries, or markets individually may not provide reliable forecasts of demand for goods or services in that country alone. To illustrate, Brazilian assembly plants extensively consume auto parts made in North America and Europe. Then, they ship their output to customers throughout South America and the world. Therefore, even when those plants are active, their nations' economies may not be. Hence, forecasts of some industries' production must be based on global market conditions.

Although there is substantial interest in the emergence of global markets, this alleged phenomenon often is more concept than reality. To the extent that significant differences in market dynamics of separate countries exist, the multinational corporation is unable to conduct business uniformly on a worldwide basis. Accordingly, global marketing strategists still must evaluate competitive requisites of each country-market separately.

Population, Wealth, and Infrastructure

Graphic exhibits in Appendix II demonstrate some dramatic differences between economies of many nations and most world regions. Depending on the product or service in question, consumer marketing opportunities in various nations will stem from diverse, but often measurable, sources. For example, country-markets' relative economic development, and, more importantly, standards of living are reflected in measures of wealth such as real GDP per capita and employment. Demographic analysis of different country markets also is imperative. The age compositions of most countries differ dramatically from that of the United States. Another important demographic variable to consider is simply the density of population; many nations' populations are much more dense than the United States'. Accordingly, tastes and needs for both discretionary and nondiscretionary products differ substantially from those in the United States.

Related to the issue of population density is that of a nation's infrastructure. One convenient indication of a nation's internal development is its highway system, which can be defined both in terms of paved and unpaved road miles proportionate to population, land area and—more interestingly, perhaps—the number of registered automobiles. Obviously, the maturity of infrastructure development will have a profound impact on demand for building components, automobiles, auto parts, and travel-related goods or services. Too little and too much infrastructure maturity can characterize unattractive markets—or, at least those which are not likely to provide inherent opportunities for growth. The best growth markets are neither too early or too late in their growth curves.

In some nations, single industries, or just a few industries, may have determining impacts on the level of economic activity or, more precisely, the level of employment. These nations are recognizable for their substantial dependence on exports and fluctuating trade balances. But they often can be important (albeit insecure) producers of natural resources for—example, petroleum.

Managing Risk

In many respects, domestic firms' analysis of foreign markets must be focused on the relative risk that nonpatriot investors are likely to incur. Thus, numerous authors have cautioned U.S. investors to evaluate foreign markets in terms of risk as well as return (for example, Stobaugh, 1969; Bradley, 1977; Rummel and Heenan, 1978; and Desta, 1985). In lesser developed regions, the most significant risk of all must be the likelihood of expropriation. Bradley (1977) advised that, before focusing on a specific country, analysts first should examine historical patterns of expropriation in entire regions. Only if regional risks are acceptable should an analysis consider the country and industry of interest as an investment domain. In emerging regions of the world, risk analysis should focus on governments' aspirations for economic development, the credibility of governments' guarantees to foreign investors, and legal/regulatory provisions for foreign investment and repatriation of profits.

Rummel and Heenan (1978) provided a comprehensive review of strategies for minimizing risk in international commerce. For instance, a corporation may retain proprietary intangible assets, including research and development skills at the corporate headquarters and centralize worldwide brand management. Of course, maintaining control over supplies of essential materials, technology or talent also will provide significant insulation from expropriation. Thus, before undertaking significant foreign investments, business planners should evaluate their firms' abilities to accomplish such safeguards.

Consider also the disparate impacts of oil prices on nations' economies. Simos (1990) prepared simulations of economic reactions to increases in oil prices from about $20 per barrel to about $28 per barrel. The result was a decline of economic growth in all industrial countries by nearly a full percentage point. The simulations' wholesale prices in major industrial nations rose about 4%, while consumer prices rose about 1.5%. Short term U.S. interest rates rose and then stabilized in the 7.8–8.0% range. Rates went higher than that in Germany and Japan. However, due to their proprietary oil sources, England and Canada experienced less inflationary pressure.

Analytic Sources

Fortunately, as a result of recent improvements in the quality of international market data, foreign market analysts' tasks are growing somewhat less difficult. In the United States and other nations, there is a growing abundance of commercial information that can be obtained from readily available sources. So, the resourceful foreign market analyst should have a reasonably good chance of describing general market conditions wherever in the world a firm seeks to do business. Worldwide electronic information exchange systems, in particular, have enhanced the availability of information, if not its quality; and there is a growing abundance of data from agencies such as the International Monetary Fund (IMF). The IMF's bi-annual world economic report provides thorough statistical and qualitative evaluations of nearly all significant nations' economies, industry conditions, and financial markets.

Another excellent source is the Economist Intelligence Unit (EIU), a separate division of the U.K. company that publishes *The Economist*, a widely respected economics and business journal. The EIU collects and analyzes market and industry data from many countries and prepares numerous reports—including in depth analyses and forecasts—which it offers for sale. The EIU accepts commissions to do special studies.

The U.S. Government also provides several excellent sources. For instance, most U.S. embassies around the world issue country background notes and make them available to business analysts through both the U.S. Department of State and the U.S. Department of Commerce. Less well-known is a series of reports on countries' economies maintained by the U.S. Central Intelligence Agency. The U.S. Census Department also maintains extensive population data for several countries of the industrialized world.

Although many nations have made recent improvements in gathering and providing economic, industry, and market data, it still may be very difficult to evaluate countrymarkets using data expressed in different currencies. Simply translating foreign currencies into their U.S. equivalents using common exchange rates can be very misleading. A dollar may buy both a cup of coffee in the United States and 130 yen in Japan. But, 130 yen may not buy a cup of coffee in Japan. The Penn World tables provide international business analysts with an invaluable tool for comparing and consolidating nations economies and market sectors on a currency-consistent basis (Summers and Heston, 1991; Heston and Summers, 1996).

Using a simple exchange rate translation process, the analyst wishing to perform comparisons and consolidations of international economies and markets typically will convert one nation's income accounts into another's currency. Since the same commodities are more or less expensive in different countries, this procedure can produce substantial errors. Thus, a U.S. dollar's worth of local currency won't buy the same amount of gasoline, food, transport, or shelter, in one country as it will in another. Consequently, purchasing power parity (PPP) differs both between nations, generally, and between commodities within nations. Valid comparisons and consolidations of nations' wealth are possible only after PPP adjustments have been made.

Figure 5.8
National Wealth vs. Average Price Levels

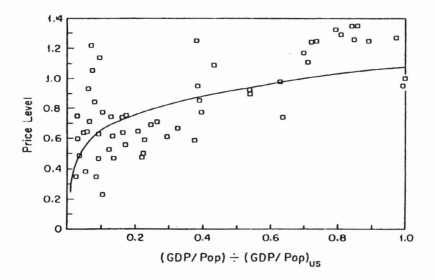

Source: Robert Summers and Alan Heston, "The Penn World Table (Mark 5): An Expanded Set of International Comparisons, 1950–1988," *The Quarterly Journal of Economics*, 106:2 (May, 1991), pp. 327–368. © 1991 by the President and Fellows of Harvard College and the Massachusetts Institute of Technology

The Penn World Tables enable international business analysts to make PPP translations fairly easily. The National Bureau of Economic Research makes the tables available on computer disks. They contain PPP-adjusted data for 138 nations. The tables provide PPP factors constructed from periodic surveys of 1,500 commodities, many (but by no means all) of which are conducted in the field by the UN's International Comparison Program. (Participating nations report other commodities' prices without U.N. verification.)

Conventional exchange rates and PPP conversion factors can differ quite significantly. So, the common practice of comparing nations' exchange rate trends as barometers of shifts in inflation rates is both invalid and risky. However, after PPP adjustment, there is an exponential relationship between nations' living standards (GDP per capita) and their price levels, as depicted in Figure 5.8.

By grouping nations based on their wealth, one can test a large number of hypotheses using the Penn World Tables. For instance:

- In poor nations, the average share of GDP represented by domestic investment is much higher in national currency than in PPP- adjusted international currency (about 21% versus 13%) Thus, capital goods are disproportionately costly in poor nations. This differential narrows steadily as national wealth increases;

- As national wealth (GDP per capita) increases, the portion of GDP consumed by expenditures for food decreases; and

- The values of services and construction labor are fairly constant proportions of GDP regardless of national wealth. This finding is contrary to conventional wisdom.

As the world's economies interact with greater frequency, and country-markets begin to merge, the Penn World Tables' (or their successors') importance surely will grow. Without such a device, suppliers' abilities to compare and consolidate the demand for specified goods or services in different countries and regional markets may be severely limited, if not impossible.

Part III

Forecasting

Part III

CHAPTER 6

Conventional Forecasting Methods

In the previous chapters, three dimensions of the business environment—economy, industry, and market—were explored. In particular, Chapters 3, 4, and 5 reviewed methods and procedures for discovering the nature of economic, industry, and market factors which can influence a firm's performance potential. Those factors that can be significantly influential often are called performance drivers. This section discusses methods and procedures that planning managers may employ to anticipate changes in driver variables and their impacts on a firm's performance.

SCOPE OF FORECASTING METHODS

Environmental forecasting methods have not changed a great deal for many years. To describe the scope of alternatives, a classification framework employed by Makridakis and Wheelwright (1979a) is probably just as useful today as it was 20 years ago. According to that framework, forecasting methods may be descried within two dimensions:

- *Systemic*: either historic patterns will persist, or factors external to a system of relationships between a firm and its environment will cause changes in the firm's performance potential; and

- *Nature of information*: data on which forecasts will be based are either qualitative or quantitative.

A basic framework for classifying forecasting methods can be obtained by constructing a simple 2x2 table using these two dimensions. Such a table is provided in Figure 6.1. Forecasting methods that assume the persistence of historic relationships between quantitative variables include growth curves, decomposition, and time series approaches. The latter range from very simple, such as moving averages and exponential smoothing, to very complex auto-regressive inductive moving averages (ARIMA). Methods that assume the persistence of relationships between qualitative variables include formal analogies and life-cycle models. Thus, if some new technology seems likely to replace an earlier technology, then diffusion of the new technology may follow a course from introduction to acceptance like its predecessor's. The most widely acknowledged analogy of products' emergence and maturation is the product life cycle.

Figure 6.1
Scope of Forecasting Methodologies

	Quantitative	Qualitative
Historic Relationships Persist	Time Series Decomposition of trend, season and cycle Growth Curves	Analogies - life cycles - predecessor products Industry research Expert panels
Exogenously Driven Relationships	Econometric models Input-output tables Multiple regression Factor analysis	Expert panels - Delphi - Cross-impact analysis Market research

Source: Adapted from Makridakis and Wheelwright, 1979a, p. 2

While historic relationships and patterns such as seasons and cycles can be both pervasive and resilient, they seem to have become less reliable in recent years. For instance, it would appear that business cycles' expansion phases are lengthening, and recession phases are becoming shorter. Moreover, as technology crosses borders, third-world economies emerge, and the world's demographic composition shifts, it is hard to believe that historic relationships between firms and their international markets will persist. Thus, evolving systems of historic relationships between external drivers and firms' operating results are likely to alter many firms' long term performance potentials. Models that assume persistent relationships of environmental variables have a great deal of difficulty dealing with such discontinuities.

Forecasters also may employ several quantitative methods to construct predictive models of external business conditions that do not assume persistent relationships. Such methods include multiple linear regression analysis, non-linear curve-fitting techniques, factor analysis methods for defining clusters of correlated structural variables, and input/output tables expressing relationships between industries' consumption of each others' goods and services. These multivariate techniques enable the forecaster to consider impacts of simultaneous changes in several driver variables on the firm's performance potential. One problem here is that a planner first must forecast—or at least hypothesize—how driver variables will change. Moreover, still other variables probably drive those driver variables. So the process goes in what Collis (1994) has called a system of "infinite regress," where no root cause can be found.

Impacts of shifts in multiple qualitative drivers also may be estimated by using expert panels such as Delphi forecasting and cross-impact methods. Less elaborate, but more pragmatic, methods include definitive market research studies. Each approach may be effective. For instance, either type of study might be aimed at evaluating how new life styles and/or tastes will affect opportunities of consumer products suppliers to serve emerging markets.

At a minimum, taxonomies of forecasting methodologies must distinguish between those that deal with qualitative, and those that deal with quantitative information (Chambers, J., Mullick, and Smith, 1971; Gross and Peterson, 1979; Makridakis and Wheelwright, 1979a). While classification schemes nearly always acknowledge methods that use qualitative information, those methods rarely receive the same amount of attention as that given to quantitative methods. This is probably because it can be somewhat more difficult to reduce qualitative methods to repeatable procedures and, thereby, evaluate them in terms of reliability or accuracy. Nevertheless, judgmental methods such as Delphi forecasting and the use of scenarios in developing forecasts of driver variables seem to have attracted increasing attention in recent years—perhaps because they do not impose requirements for artificially precise measurement or technical rigor on either the forecast or the forecaster.

Makridakis and Wheelwright (1979a) also acknowledged that the foregoing "2x2" framework doesn't provide for a wide-enough range of methodological variations. They suggested that a more comprehensive, albeit complex, framework should include the following additional dimensions:

- *Time horizon*—short (1–3 months), medium (3–24 months), long (2+ years);

- *Type of pattern*—horizontal, trend, seasonal, cyclical; and

- *Basic methodology*—time series, explanatory, subjective, technological.

In classifying quantitative forecasting methods, it may be useful to divide them even further, according to computational complexity. Surveys of sample populations and compilations of survey findings probably are at the lowest end of this spectrum. Simple trend analysis then might be followed by more complex time series methods that recognize and isolate trend, seasonal, and cyclical components. More sophisticated models of learned behavior, such as Markoff chains and auto regressive integrated moving averages (ARIMA), subsequently might follow correlative and regression methods. Complex econometric methods would be placed at the highest end of this spectrum.

Planning managers should recognize that expert forecasters rarely use just one method to the exclusion of all others. Instead, their challenge is to find a combination of methods that is sufficiently valid, pragmatic, and cost-effective for the situation at hand. Nevertheless, with so many alternatives from which to choose, making this selection can be a challenging task. Accordingly, the following paragraphs provide a few selection criteria which may be helpful.

FORECASTING METHOD
SELECTION CRITERIA

The forecasting literature contains remarkably few guidelines for planning managers to use in selecting a forecasting method. The literature that does exist on this subject seems to suggest that there are four types of selection criteria, based on the firm's life-cycle stage, industry-specific requirements, forecasting horizon and accuracy requirements. Some other approaches ("hybrids") employ multiple criteria. Each category is explored in the following paragraphs.

Life-Cycle Criteria

Chambers, Mullick, and Smith (1971) suggest that firms' forecasting needs are likely to differ between stages of an industry's life cycle. They evaluated 18 different methods with regard to forecasting accuracy, methods' abilities to identify turning points, typical applications, data requirements, cost, and the time required to construct a forecast. A large, fold-out table, which makes this article still one of the most useful of basic references for planning professionals, provides an evaluation of each method. The 18 forecasting methods are divided into three broad categories: qualitative methods, time series, and causal models.

The authors judged time series to be poor predictors of turning points and causal models (econometrics) best for that purpose. They also judged ARIMA and time series techniques to be the most accurate among short-term forecasting methods; and they judged econometric techniques the most accurate mid-term and long-term methodologies as well as the best at identifying turning points. However, their judgment regarding methods for identifying turning points has been questioned by subsequent empirical research (Makridakis and Hibon, 1979; Fildes, 1982).

Early in an industry's or a product's life cycle, when product development functions are important, planners may use analogies as forecasting devices provided that both the proxy and current markets are well-defined. In such circumstances, the analogy employed may be either qualitative (based on comparable cases) or quantitative (employing logarithmic or S-shaped curves, for instance). Later on in the life cycle, planners won't need such conjectural techniques. Instead, econometric models that are able to anticipate rates of growth in demand for established products or services with established relationships to environmental drivers will be more helpful—for instance, in anticipating production requirements. Later still, short interval forecasting techniques, including time series methods, will be useful for balancing inventory requirements to fluctuations in demand and predicting cost variables that drive pricing decisions.

Lebel and Krasner (1977) also recommended selecting forecasting techniques based on an industry's stage of maturity, because the behaviors of forecast drivers typically differ from stage to stage. Thus, appropriate methods for anticipating diffusion of product technology, capital resource requirements, diversification requirements, production and distribution volumes, competitors' strategy and impacts of sociopolitical forces on strategic options may differ between stages. The authors evaluated nine forecasting techniques' applicability to long-range strategic planning, program planning, and operational planning applications. Their evaluation demonstrates the importance of selecting a forecasting method to fit the firm's planning requirements—which are likely to differ between life-cycle stages.

Inter-Industry Differences

Forecasting methodologies also may differ necessarily between industries. Drivers of demand for consumer versus industrial products or services, and durables versus nondurables, for example, naturally will vary for indigenous reasons. Therefore, planning managers must identify industry-specific drivers of the results to be forecasted before attempting projections. If such drivers are not known, diagnostic research requiring extensive statistical analysis may be required before a valid forecasting model is obtained.

For example, Jun and Peterson (1991) compared forecasting requirements of firms in a mature, low technology industry to those in a faster-growing, high technology industry—the paint industry and the computer industry, respectively. These researchers also distinguished between large and small companies in each industry. They found that larger companies were more likely than smaller companies in both industries to construct mid-range and long-range forecasts. This was especially true in the computing industry. Larger firms in both industries tended to use four-year horizons, while smaller firms typically chose two-year horizons. Computer manufactures used mid-range forecasts mostly for production planning, while paint manufacturers used them mainly for market and financial planning.

In this study, Jun and Peterson evaluated nine types of forecasting inputs: historical demand, marketing plans, technological data, competitors' activities, economic data, political data, demographic data, product life cycle, and customer preferences. Historical data, of course, were used most frequently. However, small computer companies were more likely to employ technological, life-cycle and competitor information—apparently finding these types of information most useful in developing new-product strategies. Large paint companies used analytical (versus subjective) forecasting methods more often than large computer companies. Small firms in each industry tended not to use analytical techniques. Rather, small firms were far more likely to employ subjective forecasting methods. Large computer companies used subjective techniques more often than large paint companies. Small paint companies were more likely to use subjective techniques than small computer companies. But, twice as many large paint companies as smaller ones used combination methods. Half of the computer firms (small and large) used a combination of subjective and analytical methods.

While this study addressed forecasting methods in only two industries, it did succeed in demonstrating that substantial differences can exist between methods that fit small versus large firms in stable versus dynamic markets.

The Planning Horizon

Selecting appropriate planning and forecasting horizons is a perennial problem, and the variance in forecasting terms is broad. In 1967, Denning and Lehr (1971) conducted a survey of 300 British companies listed in *The Times*: 75 of 98 respondents planned for at least three years; 59 planned for at least five years, and 12 planned for at least ten years. Boulton et al. (1982) conducted a survey of 142 North American firms' planning practices in 1979: 78% of all respondents reported planning terms in the range of 3 to 5 years. In a similar survey five years earlier, that proportion had been 5 points higher: 83%. The difference was attributable to a shift toward longer horizons. After conducting research into planning practices of small firms, Robinson and Pearce (1984) concluded that for small firms, the planning horizon should be no more than two years. Capon et al., (1987) found that 60% of 113 large industrial firms which they studied employed 5-year planning horizons and that 23% had 3-year horizons.

Since that last report, not much further empirical inquiry has been made into the length of firms' planning horizons. However, in previously unpublished research, Commercial Planning Consultants investigated the planning horizons during 1994 and 1995 of 322 companies listed by the Value Line Survey in ten cyclical industries: auto components, building components, basic metals, chemicals, machinery, petroleum, engineering and construction, environmental services, banking, and electric utilities (Table 6.1). More than half (59%) of these large, public corporations had planning horizons of five years or longer. In general, more asset-intensive industries, with their extended payback periods, tended to have longer forecasting terms than less-asset-intensive industries. Thus, planning horizons were five years or longer in 75% of electric utilities (at one extreme) but only 33% of banking firms (at the other).

To summarize, a majority of large publicly owned industrial goods and services suppliers seem to prepare plans with forecasting horizons of at least five years. Smaller firms' forecasting terms tend to be shorter. The longest horizons tend to be found in the most asset intensive industries. But this is not to say that companies necessarily choose their planning and forecasting horizons solely based on asset intensity and payback periods. Rather, it is just as likely that managers follow a sort of conventional wisdom on this subject—i.e., adopting the same horizon as other participants in the same industry. Some of the other criteria that are employed for selecting planning and forecasting horizons are discussed in the following paragraphs.

I. H. Wilson, (1973: 69) proposed that the planning term should be based, in part, on turbulence in the competitive environment. He argued that the horizon should be shortened when turbulence increases and lengthened during calmer periods. Moreover, he proposed that there usually is a very small number of strategic issues around which a firm's planning efforts revolve; these issues' horizons may dictate the forecasting term. A forecasting system, like a radar screen, thus should scan the future at a distance which is appropriate to deal with strategic issues, rather than simply matching assets' payback periods. Moreover, from a pragmatic point of view, the number of available projects will decline during recessions as should the planning horizon. But the number of possible projects (and planning horizon) will increase with the size (and complexity) of an organization.

Table 6.1
Planning Horizons in Ten Industries: 1994–1995 (N = 323)

	No.	Under 5 Yrs.		5 Yrs. or more	
		No.	Pct.	No.	Pct.
Electric Utilities	72	18	25%	54	75%
Petroleum	52	14	27%	38	73%
Bldg. Components	21	8	38%	13	62%
Basic Metals	27	11	41%	16	59%
Chemicals	28	12	43%	16	57%
Construction	16	7	44%	9	56%
Environ. Services	11	5	45%	6	55%
Auto Parts	20	10	50%	10	50%
Machinery	34	20	59%	14	41%
Banking	42	28	67%	14	33%
Totals	323	133	41%	190	59%

Source: Commercial Planning Consultants Survey

These views were corroborated by Kukalis (1991) who studied 115 large manufacturers and found that the planning horizon's length was significantly correlated to environmental complexity. In more complex markets and industries, planning horizons typically were longer. However, Kukalis' findings must be tempered by those of Lindsay and Rue (1976),who previously found that environmental turbulence (versus complexity) was inversely correlated to the planning term's length. Therefore, the implications of complexity and volatility of business conditions for an appropriate choice of planning and forecasting horizons, seem to be opposites.

Whereas, the foregoing viewpoints on flexibility of planning terms makes intuitive sense, Friedman, J. and Segev (1976) offered a more doctrinaire approach to selecting a forecast's term. They argued that there is a point on the planning horizon of every firm beyond which effectiveness of the strategic plan will not be improved by a longer forecasting term. Forecasting and planning beyond that point is fruitless because projections further into the future are irrelevant to performance potential. Criteria for selecting the planning horizon's limit accordingly include:

- The ROI payback period;
- The point where cash flows' present values reach zero;
- Length of the product life cycle;
- The relative permanence of goals; and
- The lead time from formulation of strategy until its realization.

Thus, notwithstanding asset intensity, firms with short product life cycles also should have short planning horizons, just as short payback periods should be accompanied by shorter planning horizons and vice versa.

The type of strategic planning to be practiced also can influence selection of a forecasting method. Edmunds (1982) distinguishes between four types of simultaneous planning and forecasting requirements: extrapolation; product substitution or market displacement; contingency planning; and adjustments of the firm's mission (which Edmunds calls "goal displacement"). When the planning approach is extrapolative, conventional forecasting methods including those examined in this chapter, may be employed. Product substitutions and market displacement strategies may require formal analogies such as life cycles and growth curves or anecdotal historic precedents, all of which are discussed later in this chapter. Contingency planning—the examination of alternative outlooks—is discussed in the chapter following this one. Methods of forecasting socio-cultural changes that may compel firms to alter their fundamental economic purposes (missions) are not explored at very great length in this book because they are the least formal and may extend well beyond the current business planning horizon. However, forecasts which are products of futurists' studies is discussed briefly in Chapter 7.

Forecasting Accuracy Versus Cost

Armstrong (1978) studied the accuracy of econometric forecasting methods. He surveyed 21 econometrics experts and obtained near unanimous (95%) opinions that, for short-range forecasting, econometric methods are more accurate than simpler methods. 72% of these experts also believed that complex models are more accurate than simpler models. Their confidence in that belief was high. However, when Armstrong analyzed data collected by other researchers, he actually found a negative correlation between econometric models' complexity and their predictive accuracy. Certainly, econometric models' complexity did not add to their accuracy, as the "experts" had opined.

Makridakis and Hibon (1979) studied 111 time series' accuracy. Like Armstrong, they also found that simpler forecasting methods worked as well as more sophisticated models. In this study, exponential smoothing adjusted for seasonality actually obtained the best results. After considering similar results of other studies, these researchers concluded that simple exponential smoothing methods may be just as successful as more elaborate methods.

Ultimately, forecasting methods' selection must address alternatives' potential accuracy. Fildes (1979) evaluated five causal methods: single equation regression methods, simultaneous models, simulation, cross-impact analysis, and input-output tables. The problem with regression methods, mentioned earlier, is that someone must forecast their independent variables. However, one can conduct a regression analysis fairly quickly and easily with minimal expense. Other quantitative techniques can be more complicated and expensive. Among them, input-output models are the most valid of all but their input parameters typically reflect data collected several years previously.

Fildes (1979) also evaluated the most frequently used extrapolative methods, comparing trend analysis, ARIMA, Bayesian, and other adaptive methods with lead times of one and twelve periods. The study used several available data sets. In all cases, a Bayesian model seemed to perform best. These results were discussed in light of two prior studies by other researchers that found the Box-Jenkins (1962) ARIMA model and a simple exponential smoothing approach to be most accurate (Makridakis and Hibon, 1979; Newbold and Granger, 1974). Since the three studies each gave a different conclusion, it was impossible to confirm a single best approach; nor was it possible for Fildes to conclude that one extrapolative technique is more accurate than any other.

Fildes (1982) also addressed the trade-offs of forecasting accuracy versus costs of judgmental, extrapolative, and causal methods. He found judgmental methods the least expensive and the most prone to error. Among extrapolative methods, he compared five approaches: simple trend analysis, decomposition (of trend, season, and cycle), exponential smoothing, auto-regressive moving average, and Bayesian methods. The study found decomposition methods to be superior in several respects: they are both well understood and valid. Unlike simpler trend analysis and more complex exponential smoothing methods, decomposition methods may be successful in anticipating turning points. ARIMA methods' primary benefit is their ability to adapt to shifts in time series quickly. However, they are costly, complex, and difficult to interpret. Bayesian methods are less expensive and quite versatile. However, they also are very complex; and, in Fildes' view, it is difficult to evaluate their accuracy.

It is important not to be too impressed by the presence of good statistical fit of inductively derived forecasting models to historic data. Makridakis and Wheelwright (1979b) demonstrated that a regression model could be made to fit historic data so tightly that it masked the effects of independent variables, which later would become more important for predictive purposes. Thus, forecasters must avoid the temptation to develop extremely tight historic models and then assume that those models necessarily have predictive power, without confirmation in subsequent periods of time.

Chambers (1990) demonstrated superior predictive power of a linear model, dynamically adjusted for habit formation, in predicting demand for consumer nondurables and energy (both, nondiscretionary purchases) four years forward on a quarterly basis. Chambers' data were drawn from 1956–1982 and his projection horizon extended to 1986. His dependent variables were shares of consumers' budgets for each of four groups of commodities. Previously, a similar method which applied exponential smoothing to regression models' coefficients was reported by Bonini and Freeland (1979).

Hogarth and Makridakis (1981) evaluated the entire domain of forecasting techniques. They drew several disturbing conclusions regarding forecasts' accuracy, concluding that long-range forecasts are notoriously inaccurate and that even forecasts of population, economic aggregates, energy, transportation, and technology tend to suffer from substantial errors. However, when compared to the simple judgmental forecasts of executives, any formal forecasting method will improve accuracy.

We may conclude that the planning manager must adopt at least some formalized (but not too complex) forecasting method. When the planning horizon is short, relatively simple time series techniques can be at least as effective as more elaborate methods. When the horizon is longer, time series decomposition methods may work best. Elaborate econometric models are valuable aids to explaining drivers' potential impacts and implications of alternative assumptions. But, they rarely improve forecasts' accuracy.

Limits of Feasibility

In the 1960s and early 1970s, forecasting technicians acquired a false sense of security during that period of relatively orderly business conditions. However, in the early 1970s, formation of the Oil Producing and Exporting Countries (OPEC) cartel and curtailment of low-cost energy supplies shattered established environmental assumptions. Critics then proclaimed the failure of conventional planning and forecasting when, in fact, they probably expected more than either discipline can deliver. Observing that forecasting methodology typically is unable to anticipate such turning points in the environment, Makridakis (1981) asked a rhetorical question: "If we cannot forecast, how can we plan?" His purpose was to confirm that, if corporate managers equate forecasting or planning with perfect prescience, they surely will be disappointed.

It is beyond the capability of most forecasting methodologies to anticipate nonseasonal turning points and fundamental discontinuities in the environment. The best defense against such surprises consists of: (1) continuous monitoring in order to detect the emergence of irregularities as early as possible; and (2) preparing for more than one scenario of environmental futures (contingency planning). Planners should use forecasts to appreciate the future implications of their present planning assumptions. But, executives should not require forecasts to be infallible predictions of the future. Rather, they should use forecasts to understand both the implications and limitations of environmental drivers' perceived impacts on the firm's performance potential.

STATE OF THE ART

Most professional business planners and senior executives do not understand forecasting methods very well. From their survey of U.S. corporations' forecasting techniques, Wheelwright and Clarke (1976) concluded that companies typically have poor technical forecasting skills and suffer from inadequate communication between forecasters and the line executives who make use of forecasts. Moreover, those authors observed that companies in their survey typically did not have programs for continually improving their forecasting methods. Although no one appears to have reported a comparable survey in the last 20 years, there certainly are no indications that the situation has improved since then. If that is so, then firms with sound forecasting capabilities well may enjoy a significant competitive advantage.

Methodological inadequacies that still seem to occur in forecasting procedures most often reflect management's failure to diagnose driver variables correctly and thereby to employ valid forecasting assumptions. For instance, statistical models that fit historic data may be inappropriate for detection of trend violations. Hogarth and Makridakis (1981) also observed that some managers bias their forecasts by seeking (not just receiving) information that confirms their expectations. When they achieve such biased confirmations and neglect contradictions, these managers attain a false sense of forecasts' accuracy. For reasons such as these, the authors concluded that managers must be skeptical about the accuracy of long-range forecasts that are based on historic induction and that the specificity of goals and forecasts should be inversely related to the length of their horizons.

To avoid invalidation of forecasts' assumptions, Capon and Hulbert (1985) recommended implementation of forecasting systems that monitor and project relevant environmental conditions in a perpetual, rather than ad hoc, fashion— a decided departure from prevailing once-a-year practices.

A Forecasting Exactness/Horizon Methodology Matrix

So far, in this chapter, we have summarized the broad scope of forecasting methods that are available to planning managers and criteria that may be employed to make appropriate selections. Now, a more specific and comprehensive architecture of forecasting methods can be constructed by considering possible interactions of two forecasting dimensions: (1) the exactness of forecasting logic—judgmental, extrapolative or explanatory; and (2) length of the forecasting horizon. Using these two dimensions, Table 6.2 portrays the scope of forecasting methodologies that presently are available to planning managers. The following paragraphs will explore these dimensions (which already have been discussed to some extent in the preceding pages) somewhat further, in this new context.

Judgmental Methods

As Table 6.2 demonstrates, judgmental methods almost invariably are qualitative in nature. There is one short-term exception, however; that is the Bayesian approach to formulating decision rules using conditional probabilities. As explained earlier, some research has indicated that this technique actually

Table 6.2
Forecasting Exactness/Horizon Matrix

--------------------Planning Horizon--------------------

Logic	Short <1yr	Medium (1-3 yrs)	Long (>3yrs)
Judgmental (Mainly qualitative)	Market Research Expert Panels Decision Mapping	Market Research Bayesian Delphi Analogy PERT	Visionary Delphi Analogy Cross impact studies
Extrapolation (Pattern persistence)	Moving Average Exponential smoothing Markov chain ARIMA Leading indicators	Decomposition - trend - season - cycle ARIMA	Decomposition Business Cycle Kondratiev Cycle Growth curves
Explanatory (Structural/Causal)	Econometric models Simple correlation and regression	Regression Econometric Models I-O simulation models	Econometric models I-O tables Life-cycle simulation

Source: author

can outperform other quantitative techniques (Fildes, 1979). However, it is very rigorous, difficult for most analysts to employ, and more difficult, still for managers to understand. Another midterm exception is the program evaluation and review technique (PERT), which employs subjective probability estimates in complex activity networks. PERT's accuracy in forecasting the time and cost to complete large, extended projects and its efficiency as a program control device generally are well regarded.

More typical judgmental methods include market research, expert panels, analogies, and Delphi forecasting procedures. Longer-range judgmental methods may be as simple as drawing on the vision of experienced executives or as rigorous as cross-impact analysis, in which Delphi panels evaluate impacts of some variables on the influences of others in determining the outcome ultimately to be forecasted (Helmer, 1977, 1979).

Delphi procedures unquestionably are the most frequently used of all judgmental forecasting techniques. Most forecasting texts devote at least one chapter to this approach, which may be used when several expert opinions are to be gathered. Often, when experts meet to discuss issues, one or a few individuals' dominant personalities tend to overwhelm (if not prevent) others' expression of their opinions. Thus, although several experts may be in a room, planners may not obtain the full benefit of their knowledge. A better method is to poll them anonymously; consolidate and synthesize the results; redistribute those results; and continue the process until reaching a consensus (if indeed one ever is achieved). That, essentially, is the Delphi method. The process requires an objective coordinator, who must keep his or her opinion out of the process and function largely in an administrative/facilitating capacity—posing questions to the panel, collecting and consolidating the results, and providing feedback to the panel. As this process unfolds, the facilitator asks successively more precise questions in order to refine the panel's opinions on issues that are either unclear or where the panel has not reached a consensus.

Some useful applications of the Delphi method have been recorded: often results pertain to issues with broad social or economic significance. For instance, a recent Delphi study of Canadian logistics employed a 20-member panel that produced a 30-year forecast (Lynch, Imada, and Bookbinder, 1994). Delphi methods even have been used to resolve accounting questions (Dunn and Hillison, 1980). Moreover, if facilitators interview panelists individually rather than remotely, they may circumvent the principle of anonymity without loss of objectivity or comprehensiveness. With that approach, a clearer understanding of panelists' meanings may be achieved. However, care must be taken to minimize the risk that an interviewer will inject his or her bias into the answers. By limiting the scope of questions to chronological issues (for example time required to commercialize a new technology) and using a highly regimented survey procedure, Preble's (1982) "likelihood of events assessment process" (LEAP) method accomplishes that objective.

Today, with the benefit of recent advances in electronic computing, communications, and data retrieval, it is possible to employ Delphi techniques on a worldwide basis and obtain authoritative answers to a practically unlimited scope of questions. Accordingly, this method is likely to be used with increasing frequency. Whether or not accuracy of results also can be expected remains an open question since rigorous statistical investigations of Delphi forecasts' accuracy have not yet been conducted.

Extrapolation Methods

Because they lend themselves to massive data collection and a broad scope of statistical approaches, extrapolation methods of time series forecasting have gained a great deal of favor among forecasting methodologists. Moving averages and exponential moving averages can be used successfully within a short term. However, short-term forecasts rarely are used for strategic planning purposes. Instead, such methods most often are used for operations control purposes. This is not to say that planners don't employ short-term forecasting methods. Short-term forecasts are a vital tool for planning and controlling implementation programs. But, for purposes of anticipating the future competitive environment, forecasting horizons typically must extend beyond three years. So, short-term extrapolative methods usually are not applicable to strategic planning.

Decomposition Methods

The most important time series methods for strategic planners are those that decompose cyclical data into their trend, seasonal, and cyclical components and use those components in extended forecasting models. Decomposition methods also are used frequently to develop forecasting parameters for the mid- and short-term. The leading economic indicators for short-term forecasting were developed by using such techniques. At the other extreme, Kondratiev (1926) used this technique to discover cycles of 45–55 years in duration. The archetype of such cycles bears his name (the Kondratiev cycle).

Decomposition techniques are among the few that actually can anticipate turning points and recessions (Moore, G.H., 1979: 213; McLaughlin, 1982). Among the most sophisticated of extrapolative methods are auto regressive integrated moving average (ARIMA) techniques employed for short- and mid-term horizons with relative success (Box and Jenkins, 1962). However, recall that simpler techniques may be just as successful (Makridakis and Hibon, 1979). But, ARIMA techniques may be as effective as more elaborate econometric techniques for the mid-term. But, decomposition methods may be as effective as ARIMA techniques for the short-term (Fildes, 1979).

Econometric Models

Econometric forecasting techniques often are misnamed as "causal" methods. This is because their statistical methodologies initially were developed for use in other sciences, such as agriculture and chemistry where controlled experiments can include truly independent and dependent variables in a precedent/consequent relationship. In those cases, it is possible to infer cause and effect. The same statistical methods have been applied to data drawn from economics and commerce in order to identify and describe drivers of economic behavior. However, cause/effect relationships are much more difficult to establish in such applications, and co-relationships often are all that one can establish with confidence. Nevertheless, forecasters frequently use econometric techniques to develop models for predicting short-, mid-, and long-term commercial behaviors, as if cause-effect relationships between hypothesized drivers and economic behavior exist, albeit with questionable reliability (Armstrong, 1978), not to mention invalidity.

Econometric forecasters most frequently employ linear regression techniques to develop mathematic models which are used to explain or predict economic, industrial, and market behavior. Patterson and Walter (1980) have observed that econometric models typically are evaluated based on their structural elegance. But, such evaluations fail to take into account either the validity of causal relationships that the models assume or the quality of input data they use. In fact, forecasting errors may be more attributable to the quality of input data and users' acumen than to the models' mathematics or fundamental logic.

D. Hendry (1997) and Clements and Hendry (1995) found that thorough econometric analysis before their macroeconomic forecasts are constructed can improve their accuracy substantially. In particular, forecasters must assess potential impacts of interruptions in relationships between predictors and fore-casted variables. Such breaks can engender error accumulation due to invalida-tion of the forecasting model. Most forecasting methods do not allow for sys-temic "breaks" which nevertheless are very common in economic nature.

Forecasters may develop more valid comprehensive forecasts by using sys-tems of econometric models and input-output tables. After forecasting eco-nomic aggregates, the input/output tables may be used to infer consequential shifts in the demand for, and production of, industrial goods and services. Con-versely, the tables can be used to infer impacts of industry forecasts on eco-nomic aggregates. Industrial research also can produce more limited input-output tables for specific application within selected industries. However, due to high levels of cost and difficulty, forecasters rarely employ this technique. In summary, with input-output models of inter-industry interactions it is possible, through simulation, to project the impacts of potential shifts in those relation-ships on the general economy—or of shifts in the general economy on specific industries' output.

Growth Curves

For longer-term forecasting, planners also may be able to employ logistic models of industries', markets' or products' life cycles. The term, "logistic," refers to a class of exponential functions that are used to describe S-shaped cu-mulative growth processes that occur in nature. Such functions may be applied to forecasts of new technologies' diffusion, new industries' or markets' emer-gence, and new products' substitution for predecessors—all of which trace S-shaped patterns over time.

A bell-shaped curve, describing symmetrically distributed variations of events about a central tendency, first was defined by the German mathemati-cian, Friedrich Gauss, in 1792. Bell-shaped, and similar distributions have been applied, over the years, to rates of growth manifested by both animate and in-animate behavior. Cumulatively, the bell-shaped distribution takes on an S-shape which can be made into a straight line after logarithmic conversion. Gauss did not intend to create a model of nature with his bell shaped curve and classic Gaussian functions are not "logistic" as that term was defined earlier.

One category of logistic curves was found by a British actuary, Benjamin Gompertz (1820, 1825), to describe the growth and mortality of human popula-tions. Since its discovery, the Gompertz Curve has been used to describe and forecast diffusion of new technologies, industries, and related products that are especially sensitive to differences in population (Prescott, R. 1922; Chow, 1967; Martino, 1975; Lackman, 1978; Franses, 1994; Olshansky and Carnes, 1997).

A second growth function also was named after its discoverer, Raymond Pearl, an American botanist (1921, 1922, 1925). The Pearl Curve typically is used to describe growth patterns of new products or industries which compete for scarce resources against predecessor occupants of the same environment. It is especially interesting that the Pearl Curve's S-shaped exponential growth function first was used to describe non-human biological growth phenomena. But, not long after its discovery, the Pearl Curve's application to economic phenomena became obvious to observers such as Lotka (1925) who used the function to describe diffusion and market saturation of railroad track miles as well as human populations in metropolitan markets.

Since those pioneering applications of Gompertz, Pearl, and their followers, growth curves, and their mathematical models have been used to describe and forecast a wide variety of industries and markets. Today, the Gompertz Curve is used most often to describe diffusion of entirely new products and technologies. The Pearl Curve is best suited to describe substitutions by new products for old ones. These functions can be used to forecast industries' adoption of new technologies and the emergence of new markets (Gompertz Curve) as well as the adoption of improvements in industrial processes (Pearl Curve). The two curves are portrayed in Exhibits 6.1 and 6.2.

Gompertz Curves have been applied successfully in the Automotive and Textile industries (Prescott, R. 1922); Computer industry (Chow, 1967) and the Plastics industry (Lackman, 1978). Pearl Curves have been applied to a much broader scope of industries, including railroads (Lotka, 1925); coal, steel, beer and railroads (Mansfield, 1961); television and other household appliances (I. Hendry, 1972); computers and commercial aircraft (Modis, 1992, 1994, 1998).

Over the years, theorists have wondered about the essential nature of growth curves. Why are they shaped that way? The Gaussian distribution (bell-shaped curve) and its S-shaped cumulative function are purely mathematical, expressing no specific law of nature, yet they serve well as a proxy for natural phenomena. When the Gaussian function is expressed only a little differently, the logistical Pearl and Gompertz functions indeed are reliable models of natural diffusion and adaptation. What characteristics of nature do these functions actually capture in their expressions?

Verhulst (1845) explained the growth curve's shape in terms of environmental capacity limits, as did Lotka (1925). Much later, Bass (1969) explained logistical growth in a model with two separate factors: one, reflecting an initial event of innovation; another, reflecting its imitation. Sahal (1976) explains the sigmoidal nature of growth curves as a more complex product of interactions between adopters and nonadopters; the naturally bell-shaped distribution of driver variables; changes in price elasticity; imitators' learning (which was known to trace a sigmoidal path); and a process of natural selection. Lakhani (1976) described the technological substitution process as equilibrium-adjustment in three stages. Horsky and Simon (1978), on the other hand, discussed impacts of communications media, including advertising, as informational devices that facilitate demand growth.

On balance, it seems that the natural functions which drive growth curves are far from perfectly understood. Nevertheless, practitioners at least should attempt to choose logistic models based on their essential nature as models of innovation (Gompertz Curve) or substitution (Pearl Curve).

Several summaries of growth curves' application to industry analysis and forecasting of new technologies', products', markets' and industries' growth will be found in articles by Fisher and Pry (1971), Hendry (1972), Martino (1975), Mahajan and Muller (1979), and Modis (1994). The texts by Linstone and Sahal (1976) and Modis (1992, 1998) also are helpful.

Hybrid Approaches

Often, the planning managers' ingenuity in making use of multiple techniques will enable them to achieve results that surpass those of more straightforward approaches. Such forecasting methods have been called hybrids because they synthesize different methods. For example, Lewandowski (1982) proposed to integrate mid-term (extrapolative) and longer-term (econometric) forecasting methods. Longer-term models can be used for approximation, while extrapolative models can provide better accuracy for the near term.

When forecasting demand for a new plastic compound used in automotive applications, Lackman (1978) first forecasted growth of the new compound's market share using a logistic function. Next, he forecasted automotive production, and derived demand for parts to be made from the new compound, using an econometric model. A forecast of demand for the new compound then was produced by a simple interaction of the two results (forecasted share multiplied by forecasted market size).

Pollack-Johnson (1995), without empirical verification, argued that the best forecasting techniques (based on forecasts' horizons) are: (1) exponential smoothing for the short term; (2) exponential smoothing adjusted for trend and seasonality, in the medium term; and (3) curve fitting or causal models for the long term. He argued further that forecasters should combine these techniques to achieve the best accuracy. The objective of such hybrid methods is to generate forecasts in which cycles dominate the short term and trend dominates the long term, with smooth transitions between the two. When conjecture about turning points is reasonable, but cannot be inferred from historic data, objective forecasting methods still can incorporate judgmental estimates into the solution space, along with quantitatively derived estimates, to obtain intuitively plausible forecasts.

For many years, General Electric (GE) has employed a multidisciplinary approach to forecasting for strategic planning purposes. Even in its early planning efforts, GE formulated long-range views of the future business environment (I. Wilson., 1973). The scope of each view covered international, defense, social, political, legal, technological, human, financial, and economic issues, all of which were rated for probability and relevance. The result was a series of scenarios describing future business environments. GE's staff then prepared more specific forecasts as needed to evaluate each scenario. Finally, strategies for responding to the most likely scenarios were prepared.

Exhibit 6.1
THE PEARL CURVE

An American biologist and demographer, Raymond Pearl (1870–1940), studied and reported on survival/mortality cycles of humans and other species (1921, 1922, 1925). He found that the same function described these cycles in all species. The use of Pearl curves to describe human demographic and industrial growth patterns was demonstrated by Prescott (1922) and Lotka (1925). Since those initial discoveries and applications, the Pearl function has been found to describe rates of adaptation, diffusion and saturation of both animate and inanimate innovations.

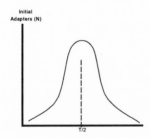
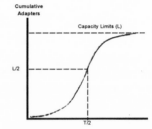

The Pearl Curve is symmetrical. Thus, a new product's ultimate acceptance is half-complete (L/2) midway in the growth term (T/2). At point (L/2, T/2) the growth rate shifts from acceleration to deceleration.

This curve may be used when a new product's sales or (better) market shares have been measured early in its life cycle to anticipate future growth rates and the probable time when specified levels of adoption (e.g., market share) should be achieved.

Exhibit 6.2
THE GOMPERTZ CURVE

Benjamin Gompertz (1779–1865), a British actuary and mathe-
matician, found that he could describe human population distributions and mortality using a unique mathematical function. He
published his findings in 1820 and 1825 (also posthumously in
1872). Subsequently, the function that he discovered has been
called the Gompertz Curve.

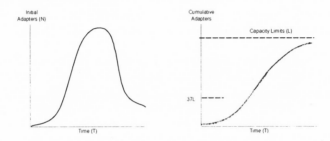

The Gompertz Curve is nonsymetrical. A shift from acceleration
to deceleration of the growth rate occurs when the level of diffusion attains about 37% of its limit (rather than 50% on the Pearl
Curve). Thus, after a relatively fast period of initial adoption,
market saturation takes a much longer time to reach completion.

Behavior patterns that conform to the Gompertz Curve are typical of new technologies' adoption, and the emergence of new industries. In those cases, predecessor technologies or industries
never may be completely extinguished. So, the Gompertz Curve
takes a prolonged time to reach its limit.

LONG-RANGE FORECASTING
WITH GROWTH CURVES

Growth and decline of economies, industries, and markets are fundamental issues with which strategic planning professionals must deal, because these issues profoundly influence the demands for and limits of strategy. Steady-state commercial environments do not exist. The environment is either growing or contracting. It may be difficult, at best, to predict rates of change in commercial activity. Yet, a selection of strategy requires management to commit resources to the anticipated environment, thereby compelling a point of view about the future, however conjectural, to be taken. Resource deployments that are most suitable in an expanding market may be quite unsuited in a stable or contracting one. So, the responsible planning manager must forecast changes in long-term activity of the economy, industries or markets where a firm participates. This challenge is so fundamental to the planning art that we must explore it further in the following sections of this chapter. Fortunately, the forecasting devices discussed earlier provide powerful tools that can be used to meet this challenge. In the present section, the general use of growth curves in long range forecasting is discussed. Then, in the following three sections, other techniques for forecasting variables in specific economic, industrial, and marketing environments will be addressed.

The history of growth curves' application to forecasting methodology is a fascinating exercise in interdisciplinary studies. For instance, Lotka (1918, 1925) demonstrated that the same logistic functions can be used to describe growth patterns in inanimate as well as animate behavior. The same type of curves reflect competition for resources which initially are abundant, but eventually become scarce—such as food, fuel, space, or capital. Of special interest are Lotka's (1925) analyses of demographic (100, 307) and industrial (235, 368) growth phenomena. His mathematical model of growth in U.S. railroad mileage (368) is especially convincing.

Many contributions to the description of growth functions in economic behavior have been made since Lotka's. Readers are referred especially to the application of growth functions by prominent economists, including Kondratiev (1926), Kuznets (1929), Schumpeter (1939), Mansfield (1961), and Ayres (1990a, 1990b). Recall that Kondratiev (1926) employed statistical time series decomposition methods to discover a long wave which transcends shorter-term business cycles. The long wave's duration, in contrast to the typical seven-year business cycle, is about 55 years. Subsequent researchers (e.g., Ayres, 1990 and Modis, 1992) have tended to confirm the long wave especially when data describing fundamental physical phenomena (e.g., energy consumption) rather than monetary variables such as GDP, are measured cumulatively so that they assume sigmoidal functions.

Schumpeter (1939) realized that economic growth cycles overlap in a sequential fashion: one cycle emerges where another matures. At such junctures, environmental turbulence—which he called "creative destruction"—can be cataclysmic in the short-term, albeit progressive in the long run. This is exactly as Kondratiev (1926) had envisioned the process wherein technological crea-tivity is heightened during the later stages of economic declines. Modis (1992) explains this phenomenon using a biological analogy of mutations' role in the process of evolution. During periods of an economy's or industry's growth, technological innovations may appear; but they are unfit to survive in a system which already is working well. However, the same mutations pool will provide vehicles for adaptation to new environmental requirements when the current cycle has run its course. Thus, successful economies and industries probably have large mutation pools of emergent technological innovations.

On a more pragmatic note, Mansfield (1961) studied four industries—coal, steel, beer, and railroads. He found that an innovations' rate of accep-tance, reflected in classic S-shaped logistic functions, differed significantly de-pending on levels of required investment and profitability. The significance here certainly isn't that success of new products and processes depends on their rates of return, but that logistic functions can be used to explain the impacts of investment and return on innovations' rates of adoption. Illustrations of other growth-curve approaches to explaining a variety of industrial development phenomena include those by Lenz (1962), Chow (1967), and Blackman, Selig-man and Sogliero (1973) the latter of which is particularly noteworthy for its treatment of interindustry differences in innovation rates.

Applications of growth curves to market (versus industry) forecasting have been especially productive. Fourt and Woodlock (1960) demonstrated that a simple exponential function can be used to explain consumers' acceptance of grocery products. Mansfield's (1961) work, previously discussed, considered 12 innovations in the coal, steel, beer, and railroad industries. But, Fisher and Pry (1971) are recognized for the first definitive demonstration of logistic functions (Pearl Curves) to explain how new products substitute for and replace others. Their work addressed 17 such substitutions in a variety of industries and mar-kets.

Hendry (1972) described a "three parameter" approach to calculating Pearl functions with which to forecast substitution of consumer appliances such as color for black and white televisions. The three parameters are a starting value, market capacity or growth limit, and the forecast's growth period. The curve's interim values can be calculated where those three variables are given. Black-man's (1974) work characterized differences in rates of new products' substitu-tion between industries using an "innovation index" calculated from factor analysis of eight variables. Stern, Ayres, and Shapanka (1976) also demon-strated a practical procedure for predicting the market values of products in a substitution trade off (e.g., plastic for glass in bottles) by applying growth func-tions to market shares; predicting markets' aggregate values econometrically; and, finally, calculating market segment's values by interacting those two re-sults. Lackman (1978) employed a similar approach, using the Gompertz Curve to forecast demand for a new automotive plastic compound. More recently, Modis (1992) applied a logistic function to predict acceptance of a new com-puter model and sales of commercial aircraft.

The level of skill required to apply growth curves with confidence probably explains their limited use. To reduce the difficulty in applying growth
curves to forecasting tasks, several authors have suggested a few methodological short cuts. Hendry's (1972) "three parameter" approach (initial value, market capacity, and the forecast's growth period) was one of the first. Fisher and
Pry (1971) demonstrated that logarithmic graphic techniques also are quite
useful. Stapleton's (1976) approach to transforming time series data using the
normal distribution table, is especially inviting to mathematically unsophisti-
cated practitioners. After conversion, data will have linear (equal interval)
properties upon which simple regression calculations can be performed. Projections from the resulting regression model will be very close to those obtained
from calculations using the Pearl function. Forecasting software, offering
growth curve-fitting routines, also has begun to emerge.

Ultimately, the value of growth curve forecasting should be reflected in
better strategy. Markets that seem to be growing steadily at some point in time
eventually must slow down. A strategy that is appropriate for rapidly growing
markets is not appropriate for decelerating or declining markets. The planning
manager's challenge is to know when a change in strategy is likely to become
necessary. Foster's (1986) text argues convincingly that managers who understand growth curves can gain valuable insight for purposes of strategy selection.
Blanchard and Waghorn (1997) suggest that firms should divide strategy implementation teams into two categories: one for dealing with the current business cycle and a second to prepare for the next cycle.

There is no question that strategic planning can benefit from the effective
use of growth curve forecasting. Practicing planners who are not acquainted
with these methods should consult texts such as Martino (1975), Linstone and
Sahal (1976), and Modis (1992, 1998), the latter of which are suitable for non-
technicians. Some articles which provide broad overviews of growth curve forecasting include those by Hendry (1972), Mahajan and Muller (1979), Meade
(1985), and Modis (1994).

ECONOMIC FORECASTING TECHNIQUES

It is a rare strategic business plan that does not include a reference to some
kind of economic forecast. Each forecasting method described previously has
been applied to economic forecasting. In the following paragraphs, some applications of these methods are discussed in more detail. We begin with a review
of short- and mid-term economic forecasting techniques and conclude with an
examination of methods employed in preparing longer-term forecasts.

Leading Indicators

Short-term economic forecasting methods, especially, make use of the
leading business cycle indicators (published monthly by the Conference Board,
1997a). During 1996 and the first half of 1997, the Conference Board's
monthly publication, *Business Cycle Indicators*, provided several very helpful
articles to explain how one can employ time series of U.S. economic aggregates

for diagnostic and predictive purposes. Readers who are interested in learning more about the use of business cycle indicators in forecasting should consult that publication's issues from February 1996 to April 1997.

In the mid-1930s, the National Bureau of Economic Research (NBER) originated the practice of constructing composite statistical indicators of leading, coincident, and lagging stages in the business cycle (G. Moore, 1979: 213). Studies of wage and price cycles identified close correlations of such "indicators" to economic recessions and expansions. Although numerous individual variables have been considered as potential leading indicators since then, few of them have met the rigorous tests of validity and reliability to qualify as true indicators. Such tests include (1) conformity to the general economic cycle; (2) consistency in leading, coinciding or lagging the cycle; (3) significance to the economy; (4) statistical reliability; and (5) availability on a timely basis. Because most variables fail to pass all five tests individually, composites of several variables have been constructed for better results. In September 1997, the Conference Board published a review of the current indicators' validity and reported generally favorable results (Conference Board, 1997b).

Business economists use leading economic indicators to predict cycles' peaks and troughs. However, the reliability of leading economic indicators for that purpose has not been very good. The amount of time before or after indicators reach their maximums or minimums, and when the actual economic cycle maximums and minimums occurred, have varied widely. There also have been several false warnings of recessions. Nevertheless, these indicators do tend to move in tandem with the economic cycle, and coincident indicators parallel the cycle closely. Indeed, analysts often use monthly reports of the coincident indicators as a proxy for trends in the GDP. Since coincident indicators are reported monthly, but GDP estimates are reported only quarterly, coincident indicators are of significant value to business analysts, if only for that purpose.

Statistical studies by the Conference Board and NBER have disclosed that the most reliable leading economic indicators include unemployment claims, building permits, stock market prices, the money supply, and interest rate spread (differences between long- and short-term rates). Among all of those indicators, interest rate spread seems to be the most reliable and prescient (Mishkin, 1990; Clark, 1996; Estrella and Mishkin, 1998). Each time the difference between ten-year and three-month treasury bond rates turned negative (reflecting an inverted yield curve) during 1967–1997, a recession followed in about a year.

There is a general misunderstanding that the leading indicators index can predict economic changes 6 to 9 months forward. Statistical evidence has demonstrated that the indicators' reliability at that distance is quite low. One can use the Leading Economic Index (LEI) with limited confidence to predict the national economy's rate of change during a forthcoming quarter, but not much further than that (Conference Board, 1997). There also is good statistical evidence that declines of more than 2% in the LEI and sustained declines in at least half of the LEI's components over six months provide reliable confirmation that a recession either has begun or is about to do so.

The leading indicators' lack of predictive reliability is a source of some disappointment to econometricians. Beckman (1997) demonstrated that the LEI failed to succeed in anticipating five recessions which occurred during 1968–1995. Moreover, the Conference Board's statistical studies (1997) produced regression coefficients, which indicate that—depending on the span of historic LEI data employed—the LEI at best can account for only about 20% of the variance in economic activity 2 to 4 months forward.

Mandel and Coy (1997) observed that in four of the last five recessions, even after the rest of the economy had begun to decline, either employment or consumer spending continued to increase. Thus, shifts in the industrial, rather than the consumer, sector seem to drive downturns in the economy. For this reason, the LEI no longer includes either personal consumption or employment components, but focuses instead on building permits, capital goods orders, and the money supply.

Anticipating or predicting the onset of a recession is the acid test of any short- or mid-term economic forecasting method. Based on the leading indicators' minimal reliability, forecasters obviously need better methods. McLaughlin (1982) suggested that the use of an "indicator pyramid" might be one practical improvement. Figure 6.2 illustrates this technique.

Using the LEI pyramid method, leading indicators are arranged sequentially in a table according to their theoretical average lead times. Months when they actually reach their high points and begin to recede then are plotted against the dates when they are expected to reach their highs.

If several indicators' peaks occur sooner than anticipated, then a recession may arrive early. On the other hand, if indicators are reaching their highs later than expected, the next recession will be delayed. Incidentally, the same pyramid technique should work in reverse. Thus, after a recession has begun, the indicators' successive recoveries can be monitored and used to predict renewed economic expansions.

No empirical test of the pyramid technique has been done to confirm whether or not it can be used reliably. But, because this technique accumulates evidence over time, the analyst ultimately is able to benefit from both the basic leading indicators model and accumulated variances in the current cycle. As successive indicators reach their peaks, the theoretical curve can be adjusted to the left or right, so that the best fitting curve points with increasing credibility to the next recession's most likely onset. Since it lends itself to close monitoring and regular adjustment, this concept is intuitively a very appealing basis for early warning systems that use cumulative control charting methods.

Majani and Makridakis (1977) suggested another LEI technique that is less elegant, but perhaps more pragmatic. They proposed monitoring time series of "cyclical" industries' order lead times to anticipate downturns in customer industries' shipments several months forward. Firms in processing industries—such as basic metals, chemicals, and paper producers—typically publish the data required to implement this simple technique. Similarly, order rates and backlogs of cyclical consuming industries can be used as leading indicators of output from basic materials industries.

Figure 6.2
LEI Indicator Pyramid

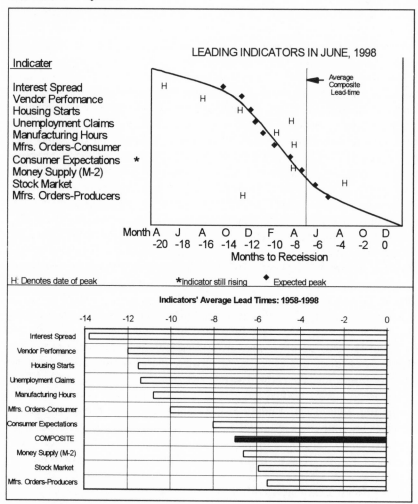

Source: Adapted from McLaughlin, 1982

Short/Mid-Term Econometric Models

Monthly economic data typically are not available sufficiently early in a quarter to be useful for anticipating trends in near term results. However, Ingenito and Trehan (1996) may have developed an efficient short-term econometric model for predicting the ensuing quarter's real GDP growth rate. Using a step-wise regression technique, they analyzed 34 available variables and their combinations during 1967–1995. Although several variables were significant individually, just three variables' growth rates produced the best combined result: non-farm employment, real personal consumption expenditures, and the trend in prior quarters' rates of growth. Separate predictions of employment and consumption are required to use this model effectively. Retail sales are reported about ten days after each month-end. It was found that employment and retail sales together could be used to predict personal consumption quite well. A model developed from employment, retail sales, and a weighted trend of prior periods' GDP predicted three future months' GDP growth rates very closely.

Business planners also can use econometric models for short- and mid-term forecasting purposes. Recall Armstrong's (1978) research, which demonstrated that there seems to be a negative correlation between models' complexity and accuracy. Considering those findings, the complexity of many models in use today is remarkable. Nevertheless, other studies along the same lines have arrived at similar conclusions. Christ (1975) compared the accuracy of models in predicting nominal and real GNP and the GNP deflator, at monthly intervals up to eight quarters forward. As the forecasting horizon lengthened, models' accuracy deteriorated rapidly. However, basic econometric models did outperform more complex ARIMA procedures, which performed poorest of all.

Apparently, the growing sophistication of econometric models has not improved their accuracy during the past two decades, as the popular business press often reports. For instance, Ellis (1997) recently published an analysis of financial institutions' forecasts. The consensus forecast expected below-trend economic growth through 1997, slower consumer spending, higher inflation, and a drop in interest rates. Business fixed investment was forecasted to slow down, but automobile sales were forecasted to be high. Midway through that year, about the only accurate element of those forecasts may have been their anticipation of lower interest rates. Otherwise, the consensus of forecasts already was grossly mistaken at mid-year.

Townsend (1996) studied the accuracy of four leading "consensus" forecasts during 1984–1994, finding that common accuracy rating techniques themselves are prone to substantial error. Using more rigorous statistical techniques than those employed by popular business press writers, he concluded that none of the published econometric forecasts is more accurate than the others.

Long-Range Econometric Models

The abilities of econometric models to anticipate potential changes in the economy deteriorate beyond the mid-term. However, some recent approaches which employ projections of population groups as drivers are promising. Using long range demographic forecasts, econometric models may be used to simulate economic conditions for extended horizons. Cutler et. al (1990) took that approach to forecast long-term shifts of the U.S. economy (and the economies of other industrialized nations) through 2050. Their report begins with a discussion of declining fertility rates since 1960 and resulting shifts in age groups—most prominently manifested by higher proportions of senior citizens and lower proportions of youth. The proportion of employment-age persons versus the total number of dependent persons—including both youth and elderly—should increase as a consequence of declining proportions of children. So, economic dependency ratios in the United States are projected to fall through 2010.

Because the U.S. dependency ratio currently is falling, reflecting lower proportions of children versus wage earners, U.S. living standards probably will continue to rise through 2020. But, due to predictable demographic shifts demand for new homes will decline, and real home prices probably will decline as well.

During 2005–2030, U.S. labor force growth rates will decline and actually turn negative during 2015–2030. Economic implications of such demographic shifts are far-reaching. They include upward wage rate pressures and incentives for industrial automation. Some of those implications already are being realized in Germany, Japan, and other non-U.S. industrialized countries, where labor force growth has dropped to very low or negative rates. However, Japan's dependency ratio (youth and senior citizens who do not work versus the labor force) is rising, with a commensurately adverse impact on Japan's economy.

The U.S. Bureau of Labor Statistics (BLS) publishes long-range population and employment forecasts bi-annually in odd-numbered years (Saunders, 1993). A large macroeconometric model manipulates nearly 300 exogenous variables. Demographic forecasts are important drivers of this model. The BLS forecasts' assumptions in 1997 contemplated declining rates of growth in the labor force, increased foreign trade (the fastest-growing component of real GNP), declining federal defense spending, relatively low unemployment rates, decelerating growth in the over-65 age cohort, a leveling-off of growth in the driving age population (with consequential impacts on new car sales, household formations and demand for housing), and slower growth in personal spending. An extract of the BLS forecast issued in 1997 is provided in Appendix V.

Without any doubt, the BLS economic and population forecasts are among the best buys of any long-range economic and population forecasting information available to U.S. planning managers. The sophistication of these models and the quality of their output is very impressive. Planning professionals who do not avail themselves of this public resource are making a serious mistake. Certainly, those who spend thousands of dollars to purchase comparable information from commercial forecasting sources without first considering what the BLS has available may be wasting their money.

Of course, the work products of commercial forecasting sources can be quite useful, as well. Whereas the BLS issues long-range econometric forecasts only bi-annually, commercial and academic forecasting firms usually issue their forecasts quarterly. Appendix IV provides a listing of several econometric forecasting firms.

Long-Range Cycles

In a paper given at the Economics Institute of the Russian Association of Social Science Research Institutes, the economist, N. D. Kondratiev (1926), initiated an even more extended scope of long-range economic forecasting. Kondratiev performed a conventional statistical decomposition analysis, first removing trend, seasonality, and typical cyclicality from data describing long-term behavior of the French, British, and American economies. What remained were longer waves, with durations of 48–55 years. Kondratiev believed that he was able to explain much of the long waves' behavior in sociological terms. During negative phases, depressions were more likely; but so were technological innovations. In positive phases, such innovations weren't as frequent, perhaps because they weren't needed as much. Also in positive phases, business cycle recessions were relatively mild. But, during negative phases, recessions could turn into depressions.

Since Kondratiev's paper, the concept of long waves in economic history has attracted recurrent attention. The concept is far from generally accepted, and it has been seriously questioned (Mansfield, 1983; Rosenburg and Frischtak, 1983). For a comprehensive discussion of the research and a relatively supportive conclusion regarding the economic validity of long waves, see Snyder (1984). Snyder provides a history of research into long cycles, concluding that the preponderance of evidence is supportive of long waves' existence. The introduction is particularly useful. It describes Snyder's own historic research, which extended back to the year 1260 when the Mayans in Central America chronicled a 54-year cycle. The Romans may have described long cycles, even earlier, according to Snyder.

Mansfield (1983) examined the proposition that, as suggested by Kondratiev, the direction of long waves anticipated the rate of technical innovation. He questioned whether Kondratiev was correct that technological innovations tend to be postponed in good times (when not needed), and are more likely during leaner times when they are needed more. Therefore, he studied 175 innovations in three heavy industries during 1919–1958, and explored relationships of their incidence to capacity utilization rates. Up to a utilization rate of about 70%, there was a direct relationship between the number of innovations and capacity utilization. However, above 70% capacity utilization, the relationship became inverse. This is what Kondratiev's theory contemplates (See Figure 6.3).

More recently, Modis (1992, 1998) has re-examined the nature of such long waves. He concluded that waves' reliability can be confirmed when physical measures, such as energy consumption, are employed in time series analysis rather than monetary measures such as GDP.

Expert Opinion

Expert panels also can be useful in long-term forecasting projects. At extended ranges, the assumptions of quantitative models may be so speculative that simply asking experts to provide their outlooks for the variables to be forecasted is a more practical, and equally reliable, approach. Whether the approach taken employs a Delphi, or some other panel procedure, well informed experts can provide considerable insight into long-term possibilities.

Figure 6.3
Hypothetical Relationship of
Technical Innovation and Capacity Utilization

Level of
Innovation

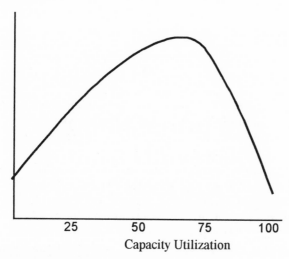

Capacity Utilization

Source: Adapted from Mansfield, 1983

Laczniak (1994) polled 171 of Australia's top corporate executives in 1990. Thirty-one percent of these executives were chief executives or managing directors, 38% held high-level (director or vice president) responsibility for financial or marketing functions, and 40% were other high-placed managers. The survey asked panelists about their expectations for business conditions five years hence, in the year 2000. Topics of inquiry included the world economy, ecology, and technology, as well as the Australian economy.

Some of the propositions to which large majorities of these panelists agreed (and the proportions of their agreement) included the following:

- *Concerning the world economy in 2000*: (1) large corporations will focus more intently on controlling or reducing labor costs through the use of automation (73.7%), (2) worldwide sourcing of materials will gravitate to lower-cost nations from more traditional suppliers (69.0%), and (3) the gap between standards of living in developed and less developed nations will widen (62.5%);

- *Concerning world ecology*: (1) there will be increased levels of global pollution (75.7%), and (2) famine in third-world countries will grow worse, due to their exploding populations (66.2%);

- *Concerning technology*: (1) increasing power of communication and computing technology will result in worldwide inter-connection of data banks (83.7%), (2) high-technology industries will continue their economic ascendance (83.4%), (3) computer-aided manufacturing and design systems will be significantly more important in manufacturing (74.1%),(4) at least 80% of people in developed countries who are less than 30 years old will be computer competent (73.9%), (5) the number of mid-level managers will decline by 15% (72.0%), and (6) productivity levels will increase at least 10% as a consequence of automation (69.3%).

Ten years later, each of these predictions seems likely to come true. More importantly, it is unlikely that econometric or other quantitative forecasting models (except in the case of demographic projections) would have aided these panelists' efforts very much. Instead, the executives in this panel were very well informed and had substantial corporate resources upon which they could draw to gather relevant information. The agreement of so many executives on these (and other) outlooks also suggests that such forecasts may come true if only because they are self fulfilling prophecies.

A steady stream of commercial and academic futurists' products also can be valuable sources of long-range scenarios. For instance, Kiplinger's *The New American Boom* (1986) provided a forward look into impending shifts in population, workforce, energy, communications, biotechnology, construction, consumer marketing, international markets, and national defense through the year 2010. Another valuable study of world markets' potentials appeared in a published study entitled *Crystal Globe* (Cetron and Davies, 1991). Herbert Kahn (1967, 1979, 1983), John Naisbitt (1984, 1996), and the Tofflers (1970, 1994) have been equally productive in formulating thought-provoking scenarios of the extended future.

The Tofflers (1970, 1994) have received considerable recognition for their long term view of economic evolution. They believe that the world's economy has progressed through three rolling waves of change. Agrarian economies characterized the first wave. The second wave brought industrialization and consequential political turbulence. In the United States, the agricultural South and the industrial North fought a Civil War that confirmed accession of the second wave. Throughout modern history, first wave and second wave countries have fought similar wars. The industrialized economies won those wars. But, now, the second wave has reached a peak in the United States, although it continues to spread among less-developed countries.

A third wave began after World War II. In this wave of information and knowledge, technology and service economies, instead of industrial economies, will be the winners. The Tofflers believe that the third wave again has thrust the world into political upheaval and that, once again, forces of evolution will determine which firms are the fittest to survive. However, even today the world's nations still include a few agrarian and many industrial economies. The ability of firms in each nation to grow and prosper is, to a significant extent, constrained by that nation's stage of evolution and its ability to reach the next stage.

In the Third Wave, intellectual assets are especially valuable. Knowledge and skills improve production efficiency and/or reduce the need for raw materials, labor, space, time and capital. Therefore, they can make a critical difference between profit and loss. In a knowledge-based society, critical success factors, which lead to competitive success in global competition, are likely to be different from those that existed in previous waves. They include intangible assets such as patents, specialized workforce skills, and electronic infrastructures. Long-range planners need to appreciate such evolutionary dynamics if they are to select their forecasting assumptions insightfully.

Economic Forecasting Services

Many commercial and academic forecasting services produce annual, semi-annual, and quarterly forecasts of short-term and extended economic behavior. Each of these services employs some kind of an econometric model; and none necessarily is better than the others (Townsend, 1996). Probably, this is because, after the models have been run in all their statistical profusion, their owners invariably tinker with the results to reflect their own best judgment. Since no econometric model yet employs variables that reflect the full range of contingencies in a large nation's economy, and there are significant delays in producing economic data with which to update forecasting parameters, such tinkering is quite understandable if not mandatory. By the time many relevant variables are measured, the fundamentals well may have changed. So, the judgment of the well-informed analysts simply is a necessity in "econometric" forecasting.

To the extent that analysts' judgment typically is superimposed on economic models' results, their forecasts may be as judgmental as they are mechanical. Accordingly, because none of the available models probably can guarantee accuracy that is much better than the others, business analysts are free to select from the commercial products that suit their work styles and budgets. The *Value Line Investment Survey* provides a relatively inexpensive forecasting service. In addition to monitoring some 1,700 companies' stock market behavior, it publishes monthly and quarterly evaluations of the U.S. economy, including a complete forecast of the U.S. economy. The horizon of Value Line's economic forecasts is five years.

Several other commercial forecasting services have more sophisticated capabilities. But, their services also can be quite expensive. The two most prominent firms are the WEFA , Inc. (Philadelphia) subsidiary of Primark, Inc. and the Data Resources, Inc. (Boston) subsidiary of Standard and Poor's. WEFA, previously was known as Wharton Economic Forecasting Associates, a division of the University of Pennsylvania's famous business school, before Primark acquired it. WEFA is the only firm we know of that regularly updates input-output tables. The Conference Board (New York) also is well regarded for its economic analysis and forecasting services. Several other commercial services are listed in Appendix IV.

A few large banks' economics departments also provide forecasting services. First Union, Mellon Bank, and Bank of America are the most prominent. The forecasts from Mellon and Bank of America can be obtained for free. Their internet sites are listed in Appendix IV. But, the analyst must request a password from Mellon's staff. (Don't be surprised if you subsequently receive solicitations of for-profit services.) Investment banking firms have economics forecasting services too; but only their clients may receive them.

Large universities also conduct econometric forecasting programs, some of which sell their forecasting products commercially. Since the Wharton School's service was divested, the Economic Forecasting Center at Georgia State University is probably the most prominent. The University of Michigan's service also is well-regarded. Both of these academic resources are less costly than commercial services (see Appendix IV).

Additional sources of good domestic economic forecasts include trade associations that represent economically sensitive industries, such as the National Association of Home Builders (NAHB) and the American Furniture Manufacturers Association (AFMA). AFMA's quarterly economic forecast is particularly useful to firms engaged in the housing, furniture, and building components industries; but its forecasting term is only two years.

Several international forecasting services also are available. The International Monetary Fund may be the best known. The IMF's forecasts provide predictions of annual economic growth (GDP) and inflation for most countries. The IMF publishes a forecast of the world economic outlook every six months, and it is quite affordable. The IMF's forecast covers approximately 50 of the largest world economies. Discussion topics of semi-annual issues include global economic prospects, nations' economic situations, analyses of growth potentials and inflation, financial policies, foreign trade issues, and short-term forecasts.

DeMasi (1996) recently reviewed the track record of IMF forecasts' accuracy, relying heavily on Artis' (1988, 1996) two studies of forecasts issued during 1971–1994. The results have been disappointing. Even short-term forecasts for the industrialized nations, among others, have had high proportionate errors; and they were not successful in predicting turning points (an acid test of econometric forecasting methods).

Another widely known and highly regarded commercial source of international economic information is the Economist Intelligence Unit (EIU), a division of the British publication, *The Economist*. EIU monitors and reports complete economic information (including forecasts) for 180 countries quarterly. EIU also monitors several world industries such as automotive, health care, and telecommunications. EIU's industry reports often include extended forecasts. Information for contacting EIU is provided in Appendix IV.

INDUSTRY FORECASTING TECHNIQUES

Several forecasting methods may be used to anticipate changes in specific industries' output or conditions of competition. (Some of those methods were discussed in the previous paragraphs.) Forecasted variables typically include industry output volumes or sales, selling prices, costs, profit margins, employment, materials prices or usage, levels of investment, and new technology developments. Results of such forecasts sometimes can determine a firm's strategic success or failure, so specific approaches to forecasting industry variables may become guarded secrets. Because they can be sources of competitive advantage, methodologies for industry forecasting (especially the successful ones) are not very widely publicized.

Input-Output Models

As explained in a previous section of this chapter, input-output (I-O) tables are powerful tools that can be used effectively to describe changes in demand for industries' output. The U.S. Commerce Department's I-O tables are assembled every five years after a U.S. census. Unfortunately, there is an extended delay between census data collection and the publication of input-output tables. In November of 1997, the Commerce Department published tables based on the 1992 census. Therefore, as this text went to press, the current tables were about seven years old when first published. It is risky to assume that the relationships between industries' inputs and outputs will remain valid for such a long time. However, to the extent that validity of such relationships in mature industries is sustained, then it is possible to forecast impacts of changes in federal policy, macroeconomic drivers, and even individual industries' sales and/or production on other industries' sales, costs, outputs, and profitability. In such cases, input-output tables can be fairly faithful structural models of the U.S. economy because of their industry specificity. The U.S. Commerce Department's book of input-output (I-O) tables provides detailed instructions for their correct use.

Blin et al, (1979), have provided a good discussion of difficulties that one may encounter in using I-O tables, including the delay between their data collection and tabulation. In this regard, it is interesting to note that WEFA, the economic forecasting firm, updates input-output tables monthly, quarterly and annually as industry data become available (see Appendix IV for information about WEFA). To our knowledge, no other firm has such up-to-date I-O tables, although other firms make less rigorous attempts.

Life-Cycle Approaches

If the industrial forecast to be prepared covers a long term, life-cycle concepts (Polli and Cook, 1969) may be informative. While the life-cycle model is valid for forecasting growth, maturity, and decline in demand for and output of products and industries, it is also important to recognize that appropriate forecasting methods will change during the life of a product or industry (Mullick et al, 1982) This is because the decisions required at each stage are addressed to different strategic objectives as Table 6.3 demonstrates. (For a further discussion of life-cycle analysis, see Chapter 4.)

The following paragraphs provide some additional comments on several of the forecasting methods mentioned in Table 6.3.

Table 6.3
Evolution of Industrial Forecasting Applications

Life Cycle Stage	Scope of Typical Planning Decisions	Appropriate Forecasting Methods
Pre-product	R&D allocation Product feasibility	Historic analogy, Delphi expert opinion, technology monitoring
Product Development	Product design, amount of development required, market potential	Delphi, historic analogy, learning curves, market research
Market testing and early introduction	Optimum facility size, market timing and indicated strategy	Market tracking, learning curves, market surveys
Rapid Growth	Investment in facilities, marketing strategy, production planning	Statistical prediction of turning points, "S" curve models, I-O models
Steady state	Pricing, production planning, promotion	Time series methods, econometric and I-O models, life-cycle models, trend analysis
Phase-out	Production planning, facilities transfer	Historic analogy, short interval trend analysis

Source: Concept adapted from Mullick et al. 1982

Expert Panels

Notwithstanding the abundance of sophisticated mathematical forecasting methodologies that are available, industrial forecasters probably use executive/expert panels even more frequently than quantitative methods. The most common of such approaches entails assembling a panel of experts. The Delphi method (described previously) is employed to secure equal consideration of all panelists' contributions and to promote a consensus around the most meritorious opinions. Virtually all types of industries have employed this method, which has grown easier to execute with the advent of electronic communications and computing technology. Clouser (1986) reported that a Delphi forecasting project, addressed to ten insurance industry issues, was conducted by a subsidiary of the CIGNA Insurance Companies in 1981. The panel consisted of more than 300 members, all of whom were qualified as experts in risk management. Ono and Wedemeyer (1994) reported the use of Delphi forecasting techniques to evaluate communications trends in Hawaii. In a follow-up examination, the authors found that forecasts prepared nearly two decades earlier were fairly accurate. Expert panel approaches also are used often to contemplate future competitive conditions in technologically dynamic industries, such as aerospace (Chun, 1994; O'Lone, 1990; Sparaco, 1994; Proctor, 1995). Such an approach also can be taken when expert panels are asked to forecast and/or evaluate alternative future business conditions, or scenarios, rather than most likely outcomes.

Analogies

If an industry forecast addresses growth potentials of new products or technologies, then analogies that provide either qualitative or quantitative descriptions of how their markets previously absorbed such products or adopted similar technologies to a point of saturation may be useful (Martino, 1972). Consider the introduction of color television. Prior experience with the introduction of black and white television provided a valuable analogy, which could have been described both qualitatively and quantitatively. In this case, a quantitative approach was used successfully (I. Hendry, 1972).

Demographic Projections

Demographic projections can play an important role in forecasting the availability and cost of industrial labor and other human resources. Availability of labor and skilled talent can be a pivotal determinant of planning decisions, especially in industrialized nations where rates of new entrants into the workforce are declining. This problem exists, and is growing, both in Europe and the United States (Cutler et al. 1990). The Bureau of Labor Statistics publishes employment trends and projections for most U.S. industries. Ten-year forecasts are issued in November of alternate years. These forecasts also include changes in the demand for selected occupations.

Growth Curves

S-shaped growth curves and their mathematical functions are used primarily for industrial forecasting purposes. The history and theoretical foundations of these approaches were examined earlier in this chapter. The logistic functions developed by Pearl (1922) and Gompertz (1825) are used most frequently. Exhibits 6.1 and 6.2 portray these two curve-types. Depending on their assumptions, each function may be used to forecast growth of a new product's sales or market share, or diffusion of a new technology from the early stages of initial introduction to a point of saturation. The planner's challenge is to find a model with theoretical growth assumptions that are appropriate for the variables under study. However, one contingency approach is to employ simulations of alternative models and appreciate how industries might evolve if they assume different growth parameters (Rothermel, 1982; Meade, 1984).

Long-Range Applications

The most extended forecasting methodologies seem to have been developed in very asset-intensive industries. Because payback periods are typically extended, the perceived benefits of comprehensive planning in asset-intensive industries are relatively high. The effort and resources that have been invested in developing long-range forecasting methodologies for those industries also are commensurately high. To illustrate, consider some of the forecasting methods used in the electric power industry. A "smoothed regression" forecasting technique was developed for electric utilities by Bonini (1979). Combinations of demographic and econometric methods also have been employed to forecast energy demand (DeCarmoy, 1982). The National Energy Regulatory Commission projects demand and capacity of U.S. electric utilities ten years in the future (Bopp, 1994). If projected demand and capacity growth rates are not in balance, federal policy makers as well as industry managers are warned of potential surpluses or shortages of capacity in time to respond appropriately.

An Integrating Concept: Porter's Five Forces

Porter's (1980) "five forces" of industry competition were discussed in an earlier chapter. The five forces model provides a conceptual architecture by which industry forecasts of any duration can be built. Thus, a complete forecast should examine (1) the ability and intent of present rivals to meet foreseeable demands for the industry's goods or services; (2) the timing and nature of new competitors' likely entry; (3) the nature and timing of product or service substitutes; (4) foreseeable shifts in resources' quality, availability, or cost; and (5) foreseeable shifts in buyers' abilities to meet resource requirements. Any of the forecasting methods presented in Table 6.2 and 6.3 may be employed to assemble a forecast of competitive conditions in a given industry. The forecast is compete when all five forces are addressed.

MARKET FORECASTING TECHNIQUES

We conclude this chapter by considering how forecasting methodologies may be employed to estimate future consumption of goods or services in specified markets. Approaches to forecasting consumer, industrial, and international markets will be considered in turn. The majority of this discussion is focused on techniques that establish relationships between drivers of demand and ultimate consumption. For a more comprehensive discussion of specific variables that drive purchasing decisions in consumer and industrial markets, the reader is referred to Chapter 5 which covers principles of market analysis.

Consumer Demographics

For reasons explained previously, approaches to forecasting consumer markets often rely on demographic principles. As also explained previously, the U.S. Census Bureau publishes ten-year demographic forecasts bi-annually. Exhibit 6.3 depicts a few extracts from those forecasts. BLS forecasts may be obtained for several age groups. Members of age groups, or "cohorts," are likely to have unique preferences for many goods and services. After cohorts' preferences have been diagnosed, they can be used effectively as drivers to forecast purchasing behaviors (Schonfeld, 1995; Smith and Clurman, 1997). During the decade of 1996–2006, significant increases in the numbers of teenagers and senior working adults have been occurring. But populations of children aged 0 to 9, middle-aged adults aged 35 to 44 and senior citizens over the age of 65 will reach their peaks and/or begin to decline around the year 2000. Declines in the population of young adults aged 20–34 also are occurring.

Exhibit 6.3
United States Population Trends and Forecasts: 1990–2005 (Thousands)

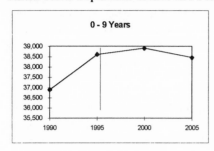

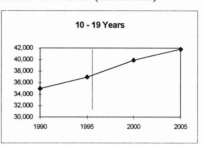

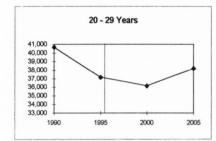

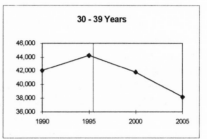

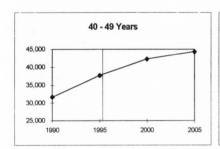

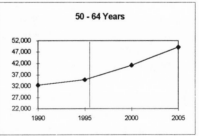

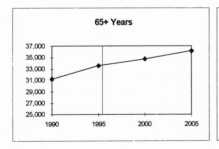

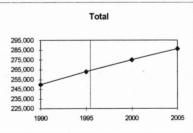

Source: U.S. Bureau of the Census

These trends will have significant impacts on sources of demand for consumer products and services. During 2000–2006, the number of teenagers entering high schools and colleges will rise, while the number of adults entering the workforce is expected to fall short of demand, creating incentives for industry to accelerate the use of automation while igniting inflation in entry-level wages. There are many economic consequences of these, and similar, forecasts to which suppliers of consumer products and services must address their marketing strategies.

The principal sources of error in demographic forecasts are usually exogenous to the forecasting system. For instance, government immigration policies may relax or tighten, thereby changing the working-age population; medical science break-throughs may extend life expectancies; and so on. A change in the birth rate (or, "fertility") is another reason for demographic forecasts to be incorrect. Such changes occur when family formation patterns shift. In fact, demographers have erred substantially in their estimates of fertility. However, insofar as the population of persons already born is concerned, demographers can forecast the sizes and proportionate importance of age groups, as they grow from infancy to maturity, quite accurately.

With somewhat less accuracy, demographers also are able to forecast population shifts between geographic regions. Some of the fastest-growing population centers in the United States include Phoenix, Atlanta, Houston, Washington, D.C. (including surrounding localities in Maryland and Virginia), and Dallas. On the other hand, as this text was written, significant population declines were occurring in metropolitan and rural communities that previously depended on military bases and government expenditures (Terleckyj, 1995). In these cases, demand for new homes, furnishings and all of the consumer markets engendered by regional economic development will be affected extraordinarily.

Beyond the United States, demographic shifts also are occurring on a global scale. Population is migrating between countries as well as within them. About 125 million people recently lived outside their country of birth or citizenship. That number was roughly equal to the population of Japan (Martin and Widgren, 1996).

Consumer Durables

Market analysts commonly use mathematical models to forecast demand for consumer durable goods such as autos or appliances. A typical approach is to build a model representing changes in inventories (or fleets) of durable goods that consumers own. These models reflect driver variables' impacts on consumers' decisions to replace their existing cars, appliances, furniture and so forth—or, in the case of young adults—to make initial purchases. Thus, forecast drivers fall into two classes: those that influence initial purchase decisions (for instance, when new families are formed) and those that elicit replacement purchases (reflecting wear and tear, obsolescence and changing styles).

Recall from a previous chapter, that Katona (1951, 1960, 1975) and Pickering (1978, 1984) explained consumer durables purchasing decisions in terms of ability and willingness to make large purchases. The problem, of course, is to forecast willingness and ability. Forecasts of consumers' incomes, saving rates and indebtedness should be sufficient to detect impending shifts in their abilities to make large purchases and installment debt commitments. Other useful indicators may be developed by projecting relative prices of nondiscretionary goods and services—such as food, fuel, shelter and health care—as well as discretionary items. This is because relatively low inflation rates in nondiscretionary items' prices leave more of consumers' budgets available for discretionary purchases. Forecasts of dependency ratios (Cutler et al., 1990) also should provide a longer term perspective on trends in consumers' discretionary spending power.

Changes in consumer sentiment are more difficult to predict; but forecasts of unemployment rates may provide some indication of consumers' likely economic confidence levels and their willingness to make financing commitments in order to purchase durable goods. Results of consumer sentiment surveys, published monthly by the Conference Board and the University of Michigan, also are useful as short-term leading indicators.

Estimates of consumer sentiment as indicators of willingness to make large purchase commitments are most useful for refining the accuracy of short and mid-term forecasts—but not long range forecasts. Longer range forecasts of consumer durables demand are not likely to benefit from extended estimates of consumer sentiment, because long term shifts in consumers' willingness to make durables purchases follow shifts in spending ability too closely to improve long range forecasts' accuracy.

Consumer Nondurables and Services

Consumer nondurable goods and services must be divided into two very different segments: discretionary and nondiscretionary. *Discretionary* goods and services are not essential for meeting the necessities of nutrition, shelter, health care or transportation. However, a forecast of discretionary items' consumption must be preceded by a forecast of demand for, and consumption of *nondiscretionary* items because purchases of discretionary goods and services can be afforded only after requirements for essentials have been met.

Forecasts of nondiscretionary goods' and services' consumption depend heavily on demographic characteristics of the population under study. Goods and services that are indispensable to young adults with dependents are certainly not the same as those that are essential for single wage earners; and the nondiscretionary budgets of middle-agers are different from those of seniors with "empty nests." So, demographic forecasts, segmented by age groups, are basic prerequisites to forecasts of demand for nondiscretionary items (as well as many discretionary items).

Knowing only the magnitude of physical demand for essential goods and services is not sufficient to complete a forecast of nondiscretionary consumer spending. Also required, is a forecast of prices in each category. Prices of commodities such as food and fuel fluctuate widely; and their rise or fall (usually in response to perceived supply-demand imbalances), combined with physical consumption, determines the level of spending—and, therefore, the portions of consumers' budgets that are absorbed by nondiscretionary purchases. Forecasts of essential commodities' prices may be based on expert opinions, seasonal and cyclical models of commodities' supply versus demand, or econometric models of supply-demand imbalances based on several drivers acting simultaneously.

Forecasting the discretionary consumption of non-essentials is much more difficult than forecasting nondiscretionary items' consumption because a much broader range of choice variables—such as fashion, personal preferences and life styles—is involved. With some modification, models used in forecasting nondiscretionary purchases also may be used to forecast consumption of discretionary items because consumers typically trade up to higher qualities (and prices) of food, shelter, transportation and even health care as their earnings increase. Thus, the quality, rather than scope, of purchased items is at issue in this case.

The sequence in which altogether new items enter consumers' budgets—such as extended vacation travel—is determined by a constellation of economic, social, and psychological drivers. Those drivers often can be discovered by market research. Once identified, drivers may be codified into measurable indicators and employed in statistical models of demand for specific goods or services. If statistically reliable models can be developed, forecasting may be proceduralized by regularly monitoring driver variables, re-running the models, and adjusting them as drivers' importances shift over time.

One approach to forecasting consumer nondurables purchases is to construct a model of the consumer's typical budget. For example, a linear model of the consumer's budget, dynamically adjusted for habit formation, was constructed by Chambers (1990) to predict demand for consumer nondurables in England. To assemble this model, Chambers conducted 108 observations of consumer purchases, deriving seasonally adjusted quarterly data from 1956 to 1982. He then made 14 further observations from 1983 to 1986 to assess the model's post-sample predictive performance, with satisfactory results. The dependent variables in this study were expressed as shares of consumers' budgets for each of four groups of commodities: food, tobacco, and beverages; energy products; clothing and footwear; and other nondurable consumer goods. This is a promising approach since it makes use of reliable methods for forecasting disposable incomes and then produces estimates of markets' composition.

Growth Curves

S-shaped growth curves were discussed earlier in this chapter. The soundness of these long range forecasting models, in both consumer and industrial markets, often has been demonstrated. (Fisher and Pry, 1971; I. Hendry, 1972; Meade, 1984; Mahajan and Muller, 1979; Modis, 1992, 1994, 1998.) Growth curves are used much more extensively (but no more validly) to construct forecasts in the industrial sector than in the consumer sector. Some of the consumer markets that have been forecasted successfully using growth curve models include cars and textiles (R. Prescott, 1922); grocery products (Fourt and Woodlock, 1960); beer (Mansfield, 1961); and household appliances (I. Hendry, 1972). Industrial markets that have been forecasted with growth curves include railroads (Lotka, 1925); coal and steel (Mansfield, 1961); computers (Chow, 1967; Modis, 1992); machinery (Blackman, Seligman, and Sogliero, 1973); tractors (Sahal, 1976); petroleum (Lakhani, 1976); automotive plastics (Lackman, 1978) and transportation (Modis, 1992).

Industrial Markets

Forecasts of demand for industrial goods and services (those that are purchased by producers rather than consumers) typically use primary estimates of producers' output as drivers for secondary projections of producer products' consumption. For example forecasts of demand for automotive components used in assembly plants must begin with forecasts of vehicles' production. There is a second source of demand for auto parts; and that is the "aftermarket" for maintenance and repairs. Similarly, purchases of aircraft create the base for subsequent purchases of replacement parts. Likewise, industrial machinery is purchased for new plants, plant retrofits and replacements; and service parts can be important contributors to machinery producers' earnings. While the two categories of industrial products' consumption—original equipment and aftermarket—must be forecasted independently, they are related. After market demand for parts and services of course depends on the number of original vehicles or equipment in existence, as well as durability and ages of machines or vehicles in the fleet.

Consumption of MRO (maintenance, repair, and operating) supplies and services can be tied closely to producers' output—which sometimes is estimated by extended production schedules substantially ahead of time. Such forecasts may be highly industry-specific—as in the case of MRO supplies for refineries, chemical plants and other processing operations which have unique requirements for materials and supplies. Other MRO markets are much more generalized, however, as in the case of fasteners, lubricants, basic metals, plastic resins and many industrial chemicals. In the former case, econometric models using industry-specific drivers may be employed. In the latter case, time series and decomposition approaches may be more practical.

As the size and cost of industrial expenditures increase, forecasting models are likely to incorporate purchase decisions' timing. Thus, purchases of industrial machinery and commitments to construct new facilities may be forecasted using econometric models with driver variables that include capacity utilization, capital costs, earnings or cash flows. Here, especially, the "willingness-ability paradigm" of demand, explained in Chapter 5, can be very helpful. Industrial producers may have the ability to purchase capital goods or new facilities. But, if their present capacity is not fully utilized, and extended production forecasts do not approach capacity, producers probably will not be willing to make capital commitments unless they are forced to do so by government regulations or a change in technology.

We have found that producers typically defer capital commitments well beyond the time that their markets recover from recessions because rates of capacity utilization remain too low to warrant expansion. To some extent, such deferrals are quite rational. However, they also may be biased by risk aversion. So, rather than basing forecasts of capital spending solely on trends in sales or earnings when an individual industry's aggregate capacity utilization rate is not available, we have found that reasonably accurate forecasts of demand for capital equipment can be obtained from time series that relate cyclicality of industries' cash flows to the trend in capital expenditures. When coverage ratios (which reflect financial risk) exceed certain safety margins that are unique to each industry for some period of time, capital expenditures are likely to accelerate. Thus, willingness to make capital commitments follows ability, in most industries. "Willingness" in this case is reflected in the coverage ratio that compares an industry's cash flows to capital expenditures. The coverage ratio, in turn serves as a proxy for producers' confidence.

Econometric models also have been employed successfully to forecast long term demand for commercial services. Armstrong and Grohman (1972) compared an econometric method used in long-range market forecasting to alternative approaches, including expert judgment and a very simple trend-extending extrapolative method. The econometric method was more accurate in predicting air travel during 1963–1968 than the simple trending method which, however, was more accurate than FAA experts' judgment. As the forecasting horizon lengthened, the predictive advantage of the econometric method increased.

International Markets

International markets warrant a special mention in this discussion. Recall our previous remarks that demographics can have determining influences on consumer markets and that very predictable patterns in America's population age groups are discernible. It would be wrong, however, to generalize such patterns outside the United States. Graphs of age-group trends in several countries are provided in Appendix I. A brief glance at those exhibits will disclose immediately that American demographics are quite different from those of most other nations. So, when formulating product and promotional strategies, planning managers in multi-national corporations that offer consumer products or services must take country-markets' individual demographic characteristics into account. Thus, a market that is mature for demographic reasons, in the United States, may be growing rapidly or declining in other nations and consequently require marketing strategies outside the United States that are completely different from those which are appropriate domestically.

It is beyond the scope of this book to delve deeply into how worldwide differences in consumer or industrial marketing parameters can be forecasted; and we must leave that task to more specialized texts on international marketing. However, it should be mentioned that considerable information is available to describe and forecast country-markets' relative demand for a wide variety of goods and services. Sources of such information include the International Monetary Fund, the United Nations, the U.S. Census Bureau (for population trends), the U.S. Central Intelligence Agency and American embassies throughout the world all collect a wide variety of economic information regarding their host countries. As previously mentioned, several market research firms also assemble such forecasts (see Appendices III and IV).

CHAPTER 7

Assessing Alternative Futures

If we could be certain of future business conditions, planning would be much easier. But, in fact, we can not be certain about future business conditions. Nevertheless, the clearest possible understanding of *potential* economic, industrial, and market environments can be very beneficial to formulating effective strategy. How can we attain such an understanding if the commercial environment often defies prediction? This chapter addresses one answer to that question.

Through careful analysis, forecasters try to arrive at a sufficient understanding of the firm's three environmental dimensions to predict them—for instance, by extending past patterns or by forming causal models. Unfortunately, as observed earlier, the results of extended forecasting efforts rarely have been satisfactory. Forecasters have been especially unsuccessful in predicting turning points when economies', industries' and markets' directions shift from expansive to recessive, and vice versa.

This problem of environmental unpredictability is among the most vexing for planning managers. Strategy texts often prescribe approaches for gaining competitive advantage in growing and declining markets, concentrated and fragmented industries, economic expansions and recessions, and so forth. Typically, such methods for selecting strategy assume that management already knows enough about the essential nature of its future business environment to make appropriate choices. But, management's knowledge of potential shifts in the relevant environment rarely is as well-developed as strategic planning methodologies assume. Reasonableness of this simple fact is suggested by the failures of many previously successful businesses, as Table 7.1 suggests.

These "leaders" at one time or another all enjoyed strong market positions and financial conditions. They even were listed on the Fortune 500. Like dozens of other leading companies, they did not fail due to lack of resources or

Table 7.1
Industry Leaders that Failed

Vehicular	Transportation
Allis Chalmers	Braniff Airlines
American Motors	Eastern Airlines
Fruehauf	Pan Am Airlines
International Harvester	People Express
Studebaker-Packard	Penn Central
Uniroyal	Continental Trailways
Steel	Electronics
Jones & Laughlin Steel	Philco
Kaiser Steel	RCA
National Steel	Retailing
Republic Steel	Wickes
Youngston Sheet & Tube	W.T. Grant

operating skill, but rather, the inability to anticipate correctly how their industries and markets could change fundamentally in the future. Thus, when strategic catastrophes occur, they often reflect failures of management to anticipate fundamental changes—many of them foreseeable as contingencies—in their economic, industrial, and market environments. Rather than failing to implement strategy effectively, these corporations' managers failed to consider alternative futures of their commercial environments until it was too late.

This chapter discusses issues and options that arise when management confronts the uncomfortable fact that it has far less than a perfect understanding of the firm's potential environment and that it has little, if any, ability to predict the timing and magnitude of significant changes in the nature of competition based on a single set of assumptions.

THE IMPORTANCE OF ENVIRONMENTAL
RISK AND UNCERTAINTY

Duncan (1972) proposed three groups of factors that can cause adverse consequences of uncertainty. They reflect critical voids in management's understanding of:

- Environmental factors that drive the firm's basic performance,
- Environmental impacts on competitive success or failure, and/or
- Potential outcomes from making wrong decisions.

In each case, the lack of vital information regarding factors that can influence commercial outcomes, and the inability to anticipate them with some amount of confidence, injects risk into strategic business decisions. The failure to understand these sources of business risk can have significantly adverse consequences. Bourgeois (1985) demonstrated that accuracy of a management team's perception of environmental uncertainty can improve a firm's perform-ance potential, while inaccuracy can impair performance potential significantly.

Considerable research has been done regarding the nature of environ-mental uncertainty and its causes. Returning to Duncan's (1972) research, the three previously mentioned components of uncertainty were measured in five domains: customers, suppliers, competitors, socio-politics, and technology. Each of those five domains was characterized in terms of complexity and dy-namism, and interactions of simple-complex and static-dynamic conditions were contrasted. Dynamic environments were perceived to be more uncertain than static. But differences between the uncertainty in complex versus simple environments weren't always significant. Therefore, Duncan concluded that the static-dynamic dimension was a more powerful contributor to risk than the simple-complex dimension. In other words, the degree to which environments are changing, or subject to change, can contribute more than complexity to their indigenous risk.

Keats and Hitt (1988) examined this question further. They studied 110 manufacturing firms' reactions to environmental instability, complexity, and hostility (versus stability, simplicity, and munificence, respectively). An inverse relationship between environmental instability and firms' operating results was more significant than any other relationship that they found. Importantly, firms reacted to environmental instability by developing simpler structures, that is, by reducing organizational complexity.

Miller and Friesen (1983) also studied the reactions of 50 Canadian and 36 U.S. firms to increases in environmental hostility, complexity, and dynamism. They found that firms' most successful responses to environmental hostility involved analytic approaches to understanding the situation better. The most effective response to complexity, however, tended to be innovative, that is, go-ing beyond the present situation. The most successful responses to environ-mental instability were combinations of both analytic and innovative responses.

Thus, it is fairly well established that environmental instability or turbu-lence can increase levels of business uncertainty and risk to a point where the firm's performance potential is impaired. Depending on its source, appropriate responses to environmentally engendered risk probably differ. But one very likely response to increased risk apparently is to seek a simpler, less difficult situation. (Witness the recent waves of downsizing and restructuring around core businesses.)

Since the formative studies summarized above, strategy theorists have at-tempted to understand the impacts of increasing environmental turbulence. To appreciate the extremes, see Ansoff (1988) and Mintzberg (1994) among many others. Recently, Mangaliso and Mir (1996) offered a two-dimensional frame-work for summarizing environmental turbulence in terms of its socio-cultural and techno-economic sources. They propose that companies can meet differing types of turbulence emanating from each combination of those dimensions most effectively by employing a different strategic response. In their view, conven-tional long-range planning is appropriate only when both socio-cultural and techno-economic environments are stable. However, when both dimensions are unstable, the business environment does not accommodate conventional planning methods. In stable environments, management can be more confident in making long-term resource commitments, whereas that is not true in the case of great turbulence.

Thurow (1995) proposed that five fundamental economic forces recently have increased the socio-economic turbulence of industrialized countries' business environments:

- The end of communism,

- Demographic-mix shifts,

- The shift from economies based on natural resources to those that are based on technology,

- Emergence of a global economy, and

- Disappearance of any single dominant economic, political or military world power.

Among those forces, the accelerating pace of technological change probably has drawn the most attention. This may be because technological change can have a direct and substantial impact on the nature and level of employment opportunities (Papaconstantinou, 1995). As discussed in the two previous chapters, economists recognize that technological change is essential for growth of employment and output. Yet, the resulting structural upheavals, of course, can impose temporarily adverse consequences.

There is general acknowledgment that fundamental change is occurring throughout the global marketplace and that its rate is increasing. This realization is having a profound effect on the way in which management plans to do business. Recognizing that an accurate diagnosis of long-term business conditions may be difficult, if not impossible, to accomplish, companies are beginning to conduct strategic planning in entirely new ways—for instance, by forming ad hoc teams to conceive and accomplish evolving objectives (Theobald, 1994) and planning the creative destruction of their own, successful lines of business before competitors seize the initiative (D'Aveni, 1994).

Thus, as planning managers enter the twenty-first century, they will encounter business environments that are less stable, more complex, less accommodating, and much more turbulent. D'Aveni (1994) has called this type of environment "hypercompetition." In such environments, forecasters, and strategists find it increasingly difficult to provide their clients with definitive assessments of the future economies, industries, or markets in which they will compete. In response, a new approach to environmental assessment has emerged. This approach entails the construction of scenarios, or alternative futures, which provide management with opportunities to consider the realistic range of environmental possibilities. Strategic preparations to conduct a business then may be made in more or less detail, depending on each scenario's apparent likelihood.

USING SCENARIOS TO
PREPARE FOR THE FUTURE

Scenarios can be powerful planning tools because they go beyond the scope of conventional market research, analysis, and forecasting—although such disciplines can contribute materially to the formulation of scenarios. Moreover, scenarios may enable planners to envision sequences of events and discontinuities that conventional extrapolative and econometric models cannot possibly contemplate. However, this is not to say that scenario-based contingency planning is an undisciplined effort. In fact, such planning requires substantial discipline as well as imagination. The following paragraphs explain in greater detail how planning managers can implement scenario-based contingency planning procedures.

The Shell Oil Case

In the late 1960s, a group of strategic planners at the Shell Oil Company began to contemplate possible future environments within which that corporation might have to function. Although these planners did not believe they could forecast future business conditions with certainty, they still believed that it was necessary to prepare for a few alternative futures, any one of which reasonably might occur—even though they could not know the probability of any single future's occurrence. The outcome of this imaginative effort has been widely publicized because it succeeded in anticipating formation of an Arab oil cartel and the shortages of petroleum products that occurred in late 1973.

After evaluating mid-eastern countries' socio-political and economic motives, these planners found it reasonable to conjecture that oil producing nations might begin to manage supplies of petroleum, and their prices, much more aggressively than in the past. Although it was not possible to predict how or when the Arab states' actions would reflect these motives, it was completely reasonable to conjecture that some kind of aggressive economic action soon would be taken to give effect to those motives. That was important because several of Shell's largest contracts were to be renegotiated in 1973 and 1974. Remarkably, the OPEC cartel was formed only a short time afterward, and world oil prices skyrocketed. Because Shell's senior management had been forewarned of the possibility that such an event might occur, it prepared contingency plans to deal with the formation of a cartel and averted disaster.

When OPEC curtailed oil production in 1973–1974, Shell was the only major non Arabian oil producing company to be adequately prepared. Since then, strategic planners have been increasingly interested in the use of scenarios to describe alternative futures and prepare contingency plans for the realistic range of potential environmental business conditions. As such, scenarios are tools for ordering a firm's perceptions about alternative future environments. Hence, they enable management to improve an organization's preparedness for possible shifts in environmental circumstances that can influence performance potential significantly.

Historic Perspective

Zentner (1982) has summarized the methodological history of scenario-based planning. His article provides managers with a history of scenario planning methodology since the initial conceptualizations of Kahn and Wiener (1967). Importantly, he makes a distinction between hard methods that employ quantitative devices and computer models versus soft methods, which are primarily qualitative in nature. The article also summarizes two of Shell Oil Company's long-term energy scenarios.

Military strategists and planners originally developed the methodology of scenario-based contingency planning. After World War II, commercial planners adopted contingency planning techniques (Schwartz, 1991: 7; Edmunds, 1982: 42). But, primarily due to methodological shortcomings, not all attempts have been successful. Simply going through the motions of contingency planning (with or without the mechanism of scenarios) does not guarantee that a firm will enhance its preparedness. Instead, the scenario-drafting procedure must go beyond the scope of conventional wisdom and extrapolative thinking. After the petroleum shortage of 1974, for instance, automobile manufacturers responded by preparing to make smaller cars that consumed less gasoline. However, they generally failed to perceive consumers' shifting tastes back toward larger cars shortly afterward—and then toward more efficient models again, when a recession occurred in 1981. Indeed, as a general matter, in spite of their occasional attempts at contingency planning, American automobile producers seem to have done a poor job of anticipating alternative futures.

By preparing conjectural descriptions of alternative paths along which future business conditions might unfold, strategic planners should be better able to remove the restrictions of their previous assumptions. Therefore, scenarios may provide management with a new learning tool for discovering the realistic range of possibilities that conventional forecasting techniques cannot detect (DeGeus, 1988). Along these same lines, scenarios can provide planners with opportunities to contemplate alternative futures that, although not high in probability, could have large impacts on a firm's performance potential. Rockfellow (1994) refers to such low probability/high impact events as "wild cards." Illustrations include Communist China's alternative policies for control over Hong Kong after 1997 and potential reactions of the world community to impacts of some nations' forestry practices on environmental warming as a result of greenhouse gases' concentration in the atmosphere. Of course, as the planners at Shell discovered in the early 1970s, scenarios' focus need not be too far removed in the future from present-day concerns. By contemplating interactions of predetermined economic events and uncertainties in political circumstances driving oil production and consumption, Shell's planners enabled the company to describe one scenario that, as mentioned earlier, correctly envisioned the world oil shock imposed by OPEC only a short time afterward (Wack, 1985; Schwartz, 1991: 7–9).

Wack's (1985) explanation of Shell's approach to contingency planning contains several other important procedural guidelines. This is a firsthand explanation of the Shell method's development by one of its principal architects, with valuable guidelines taken from actual experience. Most important among those guidelines, perhaps, is the admonition that if scenarios are to be accepted as a basis for strategy formulation, line managers must be involved in formulating them. Managers are far less likely to accept the conceptualizations of staff planners (even if they are sound) that do not reflect line manager's input. A second admonition is to maintain close surveillance over the environment in order to detect clues for refining old scenarios, developing new scenarios/or recognizing the actual emergence of previously defined futures.

Schwartz's Six-Step Model

In his widely distributed text on this subject, Peter Schwartz (1991) has documented the most generally accepted approach to preparing scenarios. The procedure begins with a definition of issues that Management wishes to address. Because the scope of conjecture otherwise could become unpragmatic very quickly, this is an especially important step. Second, planners should define and describe driving forces in terms of their relationships to strategic issues. As such, drivers are independent variables that can influence strategic issues' outcomes. In Schwartz's view, driving forces usually stem from five sources: society, technology, economics, ecology, or politics.

The third step of this procedure entails describing predetermined events likely to occur in any scenario. Demographic patterns of change are among the most likely (if not the most important) predetermined events one should include in any approach to long-term scenario planning. Fourth, a few narrative plots should be written to describe how driving forces and predetermined events could interact within the scope of strategic issues under consideration. Schwartz describes three typical themes for such plots:

- *Winners and losers*—zero sum games, in which players achieve gains only to the extent that competitors sustain corresponding losses;

- *Challenge and response*—for instance, Shell Oil Corporation's predetermined reaction to the possibility of an Arab oil embargo;

- *Evolution*—for instance, the evolution of computing technology, communications, and growing urban density—and their impacts on the emergence of new industries.

The fifth step is where management formulates strategies in response to each plot. Taken collectively, results of the first four steps and management's strategic response constitute a scenario. Depending on plots' likelihood, management should develop strategies more or less completely. Then, in the sixth and final step, management continuously scans the environment in an attempt to detect plots' emergence or to reevaluate plots' probabilities (see Figure 7.1).

Figure 7.1
Scenario Planning Process

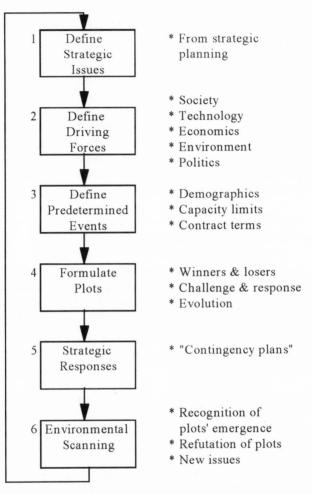

Scenario Planning: Six Steps

1	Define Strategic Issues	* From strategic planning
2	Define Driving Forces	* Society * Technology * Economics * Environment * Politics
3	Define Predetermined Events	* Demographics * Capacity limits * Contract terms
4	Formulate Plots	* Winners & losers * Challenge & response * Evolution
5	Strategic Responses	* "Contingency plans"
6	Environmental Scanning	* Recognition of plots' emergence * Refutation of plots * New issues

Source: Adapted from Schwartz, 1991

During the past two decades, several other procedural guidelines for scenario forecasting have emerged in the literature. MacNulty (1977) suggests an eight-step procedure similar to the original Shell procedure. However, this one is more detailed in its development of an historical data base, selection of organizational objectives, separation of internal versus external driver variables, development of a scenario matrix and analysis of scenarios' implications. Mueller and Smith (1984) offer additional implementation guidelines and cautions. Notwithstanding such improvements, Shell's original procedure is still the generally accepted benchmark; and it is used most often.

State of the Art

Linneman and Klein (1979, 1983, 1985), Klein and Linneman (1981, 1984) and Klein (1983) have performed the most extensive research on scenario planning practices in the United States and Canada. Their surveys of the Fortune 1000 industrial corporations chronicled a growing interest in, and adoption of, multiple scenario analysis by large corporations after the Arab oil curtailment in 1973. Their first report in 1979 defined the general approaches typically employed. They found statistically significant correlations between multiple scenario assessment (MSA) techniques' sustained practice and: (1) corporate management's role in formulating scenarios; (2) experience with formal long-range planning; and (3) size of the planning department. From the summer of 1981 through the fall of 1982, they pursued further MSA studies, ultimately covering the 300 largest Canadian industrial firms as well as the Fortune 500. Their 1983 report disclosed rapid growth in the use of multiple scenarios between 1977 and 1981. The usage rate for such techniques more than doubled from 22% in 1977 to slightly more than 50% in 1981. The latter study also disclosed that companies typically did not use MSA methods to replace conventional forecasting or other analytic techniques but, rather, as a complement to them.

The degree to which companies reported satisfaction with conventional planning approaches in the 1981 and 1983 studies was positively related to the use of scenario methods. Both studies also found that companies with longer planning horizons used scenario techniques most often. Capital intensiveness also correlated directly with the length of planning horizons. Over 72% of survey respondents with planning horizons of ten years or longer used scenario methods. However, these authors concluded that the uncertainty inherent in longer planning horizons, rather than capital intensiveness, was the most important reason for more frequent use of scenario planning methods in capital-intensive industries.

Linneman and Klein's (1985) report delved further into types of scenarios that planners may use, classifying them into five broad categories: global, industry/business specific, exploratory, issue oriented, and internal. These labels are largely self-explanatory. Global scenarios primarily address broad economic issues. Industry/business specific scenarios are more focused. Issue scenarios explore the most specific external themes. Internal scenarios concentrate even more specifically on managerial functions.

Malaska et al. (1984) summarized the incidence of scenario-planning practices in Europe. As in the United States, large corporations in natural resource or resource-dependent industries, such as petroleum, transportation, and electric power generation, tended to be the most frequent users of scenario planning procedures. After the first worldwide oil crisis occurred in 1973, European firms also began to use MSA techniques more often. In Europe, as in North America, scenario planners tend to have had extensive prior experience with formal planning and longer planning horizons. However, these researchers found that only a third of European scenario planners actually used multiple scenarios for contingency planning purposes and developing alternative strategies.

Mason (1994) has offered a somewhat updated view of the scenario planning process and suggested that companies should replace methods developed initially by Shell Oil Company with new ones that are more appropriate for current circumstances. He characterized the scenario forecasting process as being aimed at two objectives: creating a critical mass of managerial intent concerning shifts in environmental business conditions; and stimulating debate among managers to provide a context for planning. He claims that his method, "future mapping," promotes accomplishment of the second objective better than conventional approaches.

The classical approach to scenario planning proceeds by exploring alternative paths from the present into an uncertain future and contemplating where they might lead. A variation of this method (future mapping) begins by defining certain end states that describe the hypothesized condition of an industry at particular points in the future. Then, events likely to lead from the present situation to those end states are defined in detail. To define paths leading toward a single, hypothesized end state, it may be necessary to draft as many as 150 to 200 different events. A *scenario* is defined as one series of events leading to an hypothesized end state. Scenarios then may be evaluated in terms of two criteria: attainability (based on feasibility of the events), and desirability (based on consequences).

Future mapping can be used to test hypotheses: planners estimate the feasibility and strategic impacts of paths leading to hypothesized future states. Then, they select those which are the most probable and/or desirable as a basis for further planning. In either case, a future map or a scenario will provide benchmarks for early recognition that particular end states are increasing or decreasing in likelihood.

One of the most difficult problems with scenario-based planning methods, such as those described so far, is the considerable complexity of environmental alternatives that may require evaluation. Indeed, the scope of alternative futures and responses can be so broad that the process becomes infeasible for all but the largest corporations. Mercer (1995) has proposed an approach to the simplification of this process that makes it more pragmatic for smaller companies as well as large ones. He proposes a simplified arrangement of planning activities divided into three broad stages: (1) environmental analysis; (2) scenario forecasting; and (3) corporate strategy. The first and third steps are self-explanatory. Scenario forecasting divides into six conventional steps, including: (1) selection of drivers and contemplation of their futures for a reasonable term of, perhaps, ten years; (2) developing combinations of drivers that are logical and meaningful; (3) formulating an unlimited number of alternative scenarios broad concepts; (4) reducing those alternatives to two or three final scenarios on their importance or likelihood; (5) documentation of final scenarios; and (6) analysis of strategic issues raised by the final scenarios. Mercer claims that his technique is based on three years of field work with more than 1,000 managers and professionals who have written more than 4,000 complete scenarios.

Scenario Applications

The scope of applications in which planners have employed scenario based forecasting and planning is remarkably broad. Exhibit 7.1 summarizes 18 applications in 12 different industries and the general economy. In that exhibit, the two economic (versus industry) scenarios are especially interesting because they demonstrate differences between the hard and soft methods that Zentner (1982) discussed.

Exhibit 7.1
Scenario Forecasts: Illustrations

Author (Year)	Scope
1. Edmunds (1979)	U.S. Economy
2. Jacobe (1979)	U.S. Economy
3. Klein & Linneman (1981)	8 Cases, Six Industries*
4. Bezold (1982)	U.S. Health Care
5. Matthews (1985)	Hospitals
6. Stokke, et al. (1990)	Norwegian Oil & Gas Industry
7. Schwartz (1991)	Economic Scenarios (3)
8. Kahane (1992)	World Energy
9. Schipper & Meyers (1993)	World Energy
10. Jordon (1994)	Electric Utilities
11. Quinn & Mason (1994)	Computer Industry
12. Bureau of Labor Statistics (1995)	Economic Scenarios
13. Kassler (1995)	World Energy
14. Kaufmann (1995)	World Oil Market
15. Knott (1995)	U.K. Oil Industry
16. Schoemaker (1995)	U.K. Oil Industry
17. Dertouzos (1997)	Information Technology
18. Ross (1997)	U.S. Retailing

* Chemical, food process, petroleum, transportation equipment, steel manufacturing, and recreational equipment.

Schwartz (1991) described three long-range economic scenarios characterized as *new empires*, *market world*, and *change without progress*. These scenarios contrast impacts of alternative political and socioeconomic evolutionary processes. Each is constructed with "soft" theoretical inputs from experts' opinions. In contrast, the U.S. Bureau of Labor Statistics used to prepare three alternative macroeconomic scenario forecasts in great statistical detail, using its econometric model. Each alternative was based on "hard" demographic assumptions regarding fertility and immigration, federal fiscal and monetary policies, and world monetary conditions, among others. The BLS prepared three ten-year forecasts every other year based on three alternative scenarios describing possible combinations of those variables. The 1995 forecast scenarios are provided in Exhibit 7.2. Remarkably, the BLS' scenario forecasting practice was discontinued after 1995 because consumers primarily used the "best guess" version, disregarding optimistic and pessimistic alternatives.

ENVIRONMENTAL SCANNING AND
EARLY WARNING SYSTEMS

In Chapter One, techniques for continuously monitoring the environment were discussed. At that time, the reader's attention was directed to methods and procedures for gathering and evaluating data to describe relevant dimensions of the economy, industry, and markets within which a firm functions. So, here, we simply will acknowledge that environmental scanning and early warning systems are essential complements to scenario-based planning and the evaluation of alternative futures.

Forming environmental scenarios to contemplate the realistic range of potential business conditions is an extremely valuable function for any serious business planning program. However, when a regular program of environmental scanning also is in place, scenarios are much more useful as foundation elements for strategic planning. Through scanning procedures, management can detect the emergence of external business conditions contemplated in one or more scenarios and take action to prepare more carefully as scenarios emerge from potentials to actuals. Experience will not confirm some scenarios; and others, suggested by scanning results, should replace them. Moreover, with new input, planners should modify scenarios to reflect their most current information and thinking.

Narchal et al. (1987) proposed that the objective of a scanning system should be to produce stimuli for developing new scenarios. Analogizing the process to a radar system, planners should monitor important events that may signal emerging opportunities or threats. Events' importance can be disclosed by a screen of qualifying descriptors, which enable management to isolate emerging factors capable of influencing the firm's relevant environment. Reinhardt (1984) reported that this kind of process was developed at the Battelle Memorial Institute. The objective of such procedures is to detect meaningful, albeit faint signals as early as possible, without being distracted by false or random signals.

Jain's (1984) survey of 186 U.S. corporations disclosed that companies usually conduct environmental scanning procedures in four dimensions: economic, technological, political, and sociological. However, he also discovered that a large majority of the 186 companies studied had little more than primitive scanning capabilities. Thus, although it is unquestionable that continuous scanning of the environment sharpens management's ability to keep scenarios current, and to implement contingent strategies on a timely basis, there is still much to learn before environmental scanning can be implemented pragmatically and cost effectively in most firms.

In a survey of large industrial corporations, Roy and Cheung (1985) found that only a third of 52 respondents to a survey of the 250 largest Fortune 500 companies reported having a formal early-warning system. These findings confirmed those reported by Jain in 1984. However, Thomas (1980) claims that his study of nine very large corporations did disclose fairly well-developed pro-cedures, also confirming Jain's (1984) finding that well-developed environ-mental scanning typically is present mainly in the largest corporations.

This seems to be the point where strategic planning's state-of-the-art meets its frontier. If scenario forecasting and contingency planning are to realize their fullest potentials as means of minimizing risk and maximizing performance potential, then management of firms other than the largest corporations must acquire capabilities to: (1) monitor emerging environments; (2) perpetually adjust the scenarios and contingencies for which they prepare; and (3) imple-ment contingent strategy in a timely fashion.

Exhibit 7.2a
BLS Scenario Forecasts: 1996–2005

This exhibit summaries results of three long range forecasts of the US economy
published by the Bureau of Labor Statistics in November, 1995. Each forecast
represented different assumptions about future environments or scenarios. The purpose
of this summary is to provide an example of econometric scenario forecasting.

SCENARIO ASSUMPTIONS

* Population growth will be slow in the Low and Moderate growth scenarios. The high
  growth scenario assumes that faster growth is driven primarily by immigration rates.

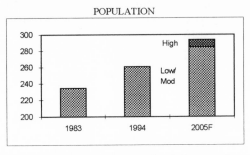

* Increases in Government spending will be modest. Defense spending actually
  would decline in the low and moderate growth scenarios and increase only
  nominally in the high growth scenario.

* Trade balances and producers' investment in plant and equipment increase
  in each scenario. These are among the primary beneficiaries, and secondary drivers
  of economic growth.

RESULTS

* Results of the three scenarios are depicted graphically on the following
  two pages.

* Although there are significant differences in the assumptions of the three
  scenarios, differences in the composition of GDP would be relatively modest.

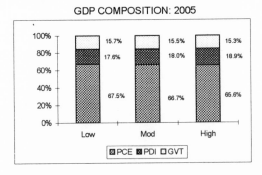

Exhibit 7.2b
BLS Scenario Forecasts: 2005 ($Billions)

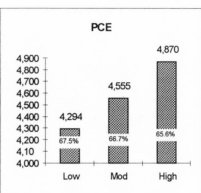

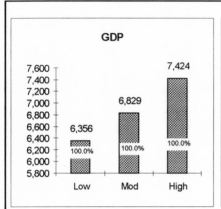

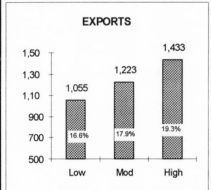

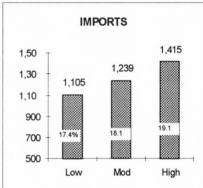

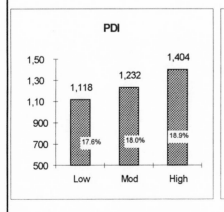

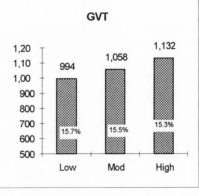

Exhibit 7.2c
BLS Scenario Forecasts: Changes in Expenditures: 1996–2005

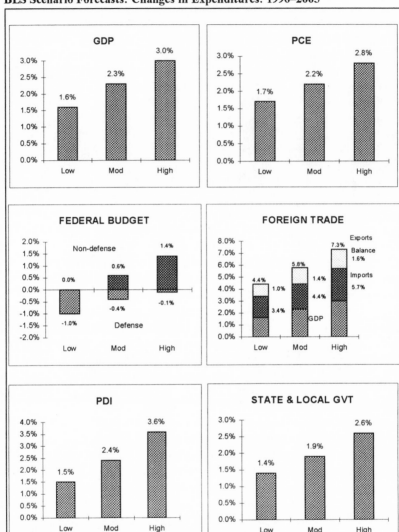

SCENARIOS DIFFER PRIMARILY BECAUSE ...

* Immigration is higher in the "high" growth scenario.
* Defense spending cuts are severe in the "low" growth scenario.
* Business investment leads GDP in the "high" growth scenario.
* Trade balances increase directly with growth.

Source: Bureau of Labor Statistics, November 1995

Part IV

Summary and Conclusions:
What Can We Know?

CHAPTER 8

What We Can Know

These guidelines for strategic planners' use of environmental assessment (EA) methods conclude with an attempt to summarize the state of a very important art. As planning consultants, we often have observed chief executives' hesitation to invest resources in EA functions. The surveys and studies summarized in Chapter 2 confirm our observations (Jain, 1984; Klein and Linneman, 1984; Javidan, 1984). Since environmental assessment provides half of the evidence on which companies should base strategic decisions (the other half being assessment of internal capabilities), it is quite remarkable that Top Management does not commit more resources, or invest more of its own time in assessing the external environment.

We only can conjecture on Top Management's reasons for not developing EA functions more adequately. What we know from published surveys and our own consulting practice seems to indicate that some managers simply don't believe it is possible to understand the business environment very well—let alone to forecast it reliably (Klein and Linneman, 1984). Perhaps that is because the environment appears forbiddingly uncertain and indecipherable. No matter how much information a firm gathers, there is always the possibility that some important element of the economy, industry, or market has been overlooked. Moreover, executives quickly learn that forecasting is an imprecise art, and that forecasts can be wrong as often as they are right. With so little hope of a valid diagnosis or a reliable prognosis, they reason, making an effort is not worth the trouble. Such misguided reasoning is unfortunate because it stems from what management does not know, rather than what it can know.

Top executives, and even planning managers, often have little assurance of just how much they can or cannot know about the present or potential commercial environment. Because they do not understand EA methods, they tend to avoid using them. Therefore, this concluding chapter provides a comprehensive statement of what really can (and cannot) be known about the business environment through formal assessment methods.

SCOPE AND IMPORTANCE
OF THE EA FUNCTION

A complete definition of the firm's business environment must include three dimensions: the economy, industry, and markets within which a firm functions. Also required, are three chronological perspectives: an analysis of the present situation and trends, a forecast of most likely future business conditions to be used for comprehensive business planning, and an assessment of alternative futures that describe the realistic range of contingencies for which management needs to be prepared.

Analysis of present and past environmental conditions often is a matter of statistical description. However, even at this fundamental level, most firms do not perform environmental assessment very comprehensively or skillfully. EA functions are most likely to be well-developed in very large corporations (Thomas, 1980; Diffenbach, 1983; Jain, 1984). But, even in large corporations, a deliberate, systematic approach usually does not exist. Since most firms have only a minimum capability to perform comprehensive environmental assessment, those that have well-developed EA functions should enjoy a competitive advantage (Capon and Hulbert, 1985).

There is an abundance of information with which to describe the economy, industry, and markets where a firm functions. Frankly, the quality and quantity of business-environmental data are more impressive than the theory that exists to interpret them. There are many voids in the framework of theoretical explanations for economic, industry, and market behavior. Often, this is because theorists are unable to conduct controlled experiments with which to test hypotheses about the external business environment. Consider, for instance, a long-held belief that the firm's motive is to maximize earnings. Simply by observing managers' satisficing behavior—for instance, in budgeting—it is possible to disprove that theory (Schoeffler, 1955; Simon, 1957, 1979).

ANALYSIS OF THE
PRESENT ENVIRONMENT

It is difficult, but extremely important, to understand how specific elements of the external environment can affect a firm's performance potential. Environmental elements that significantly influence performance potential are called *drivers*. Planning managers must seek an understanding both of drivers and antecedent factors that can influence drivers' behavior.

Demographics

One class of environmental drivers has a pervasive influence on nearly all others. These variables are demographic—describing age groups' sizes and compositions, geographic migration, cultural characteristics that affect tastes, values, and so forth. Demographic analysis is one of the most powerful tools available for understanding and anticipating economic and market behavior. Therefore, it is surprising that most companies' EA capabilities infrequently include demographic analysis. Demographic characteristics of the United States are dramatically different from those of other economically important nations. The planning functions of multinational corporations must be cognizant of such differences.

Economic Analysis

Economic analysis is probably the most pervasive of EA functions in American corporations. This is because federal and state governments, and an entire industry of commercial economic advisory services, produce an unending stream of statistical reports and interpretations of the U.S. economy. So much information of excellent quality is available that business analysts usually can construct satisfactory diagnoses of macroeconomic aggregates' impacts on the firm, its industry, and its markets. Firms can collect such data from government agencies without relying on more costly commercial services, which usually obtain their data from the same public sources. Moreover, assembling only those data relevant to the firm enhances their usefulness to the analyst and meaningfulness to executive recipients. Thus, if the firm's markets are primarily industrial in nature, it may require less economic information describing the consumer sector. Conversely, firms in the consumer sector probably will prefer to gather data that are focused much less on the industrial sector.

Agencies of the United States' and other nations' governments tend to report economic data according to consistent formats of national income and product accounts. Thus, it normally is possible to describe economic cycles, trends, and seasonal components of industrialized economies, and most regions of the world, with consistency and good reliability. However, even when countries' economic data are recorded the same way, it is important to make adjustments for their relative purchasing power before attempting inter-country comparisons of wealth (Summers and Heston, 1991). Even after exchange-rate translation, the same amount of United States (or another nation's) currency will purchase different amounts of specific goods and services in different countries. Thus, currency translations must reflect purchasing power parity before valid international comparisons can be made.

Whereas, many data resources with which to describe economic trends and patterns are highly developed, theories with which to explain and interpret economic trends and cycles are not nearly as dependable. Most of the techniques developed to analyze economic data have been borrowed from other scientific disciplines, some of which enjoy the ability to conduct controlled experiments and use closed logical systems to explain phenomena of interest. Economists enjoy neither of those luxuries. Thus, their theoretical systems necessarily are open to exogenous influences and cannot support forecasts with nearly the levels of precision obtained in physical sciences. That is a methodological limitation that economists and management theorists simply must accept.

This is not to say that considerable power is unavailable from good descriptive methodology. Consider, for instance, the capability economists have derived by correlating fluctuations in money supply and prices. Findings from that line of inquiry recently have enabled policy makers to impose an unprecedented level of control over inflation in the United States. Whether or not this and other new policy mechanisms developed in recent years will enable central bankers to flatten business cycles and invalidate Kondratiev's long wave remains to be determined.

Linking the Economy
and Industries: I-O Tables

One structural device appears to offer a substantial promise for understanding relationships between macroeconomic aggregates and the dynamics of individual industries. This mechanism consists of input-output tables. Input-output (I-O) tables come closer to providing a closed model of the U.S. economy than any other structural approach to analysis or forecasting economy/industry relationships. I-O models essentially describe the Nation's economy as a collection of interrelated industries. At present, the problem that limits I-O tables' usefulness is a five-year delay between industrial/economic censuses and the time when new tables become available. At some point in the not-too-distant future, updated I-O tables probably will become available in a much more timely manner. When that happens, economics' state-of-the-art will take a significant step forward; then, too business planners' ability to draw tighter relationships between economic aggregates and individual industries' behavior will be greatly enhanced. One economic forecasting firm (WEFA) already has initiated an ongoing function to update the I-O tables monthly, quarterly, and annually, as U.S. industrial data become available. (See Appendix IV.)

Industry Analysis

In describing causes and effects of competition within industries and alternative approaches to achieving strategic advantage, Porter's five forces (1980) and value chain (1985) models have been—and will continue to be—especially useful theoretical aids. Even though these models lack substantial empirical verification, planning managers, and business analysts who study Porter's two definitive works (1980, 1985) on these subjects will be far better equipped to understand competitive dynamics in their industries than otherwise.

More empirical approaches, like that of the PIMS research program (Buzzell and Gale, 1987), are equally encouraging. They can provide planning managers with reliable guidelines by which to evaluate potential impacts of alternative industry positions on the firm's potential performance. Evidentially, rather then theoretically derived, the PIMS principles describe what actually happens, versus what should happen, in specified circumstances. It is just this kind of guidance that planning managers and chief executives desire most.

There is one flaw in both of the previously mentioned approaches to structural industry analysis. To a large extent, they are generic in nature—that is, they describe structural principles that allegedly apply to many or all industries. However, when they propose such general principles of environmental impacts on strategic outcomes, theorists may attempt to accomplish too much. Substantial research has demonstrated that inter-industry differences in strategic behavior (and, of course differences between firms) can have predominant effects on performance potential (Schmalensee, 1985; Dess, 1987; Rumelt, 1991; Roquebert, Andrisani and Phillips, 1996; McGahan and Porter, 1997). Thus, it is vital to know the specific sources of competitive advantage that are unique to each environmental setting. Knowing the general principles of least-cost, differentiated, and focused competition is not enough. At a minimum, the strategist also must discover how and where specific sources of advantage will be found in each industry and market. Such sources have been called critical success factors (Hofer and Schendel, 1978; Leidecker and Bruno, 1984).

Market Analysis

Definitions of customers' motives and choice mechanisms for making purchasing decisions are vital end-products of market analysis. Although that statement may seem self-evident, most firms' managements probably do not really understand how their customers make purchasing decisions or the driving forces that compel those decisions to be made, rather than alternatives. Consequently, planning managers with such knowledge probably can provide their firms with competitive advantages. Moreover, without such knowledge, valid forecasting is nearly impossible.

Analysis of markets for specific products or services often must begin with the most precise segmentation   possible. Market segmentation requires the analyst to pinpoint concentrations of customers who have the same motives and/or means to purchase a firm's (and its competitors') products or services. Industry segmentation addresses the scope of products and services, while market segmentation is customer-focused.

In the consumer sector, one can know a great deal about demographic and psychological variables that significantly influence purchasing motives and decisions. A relatively recent discovery is that situational variables (for example, consumers' time pressures and shopping environments) may influence purchasing decisions as much by as characteristics of the product or service itself. This is especially the case in the purchase of nondurables. In the consumer durables sector, purchasing decision mechanics also are fairly well understood. The use of econometric models that separate initial purchases of durables from purchases of replacements is widespread. However, these models still rely more heavily on economic aggregates than on characteristics of consumers who make decisions to purchase durables. For instance, not much is known about interactions of individuals' willingness and ability to take the risks of long-term purchasing commitments, even though those two dimensions together seem to define the propensity to purchase durable goods.

In the industrial sector, because spending decisions' impacts on the firm's financial performance are subject to formal scrutiny, purchasing behavior probably is more rational than in the consumer sector. Of course, larger expenditures attract the most scrutiny and deliberation. Therefore, producers' profit margins on large transactions tend to be lower than on small transactions (Buzzell and Gale, 1987). Because financial and other strategic motives drive industrial buying decisions, those decisions often are the results of formal analyses, the parameters of which (if known) may be used by a supplier in its marketing strategy. There also are numerous important psychological influences on industrial purchasing decisions. Illustrations include top management's tolerance for risk, habitual payback periods, and hurdle rates for capital expenditures' payback periods, which may not necessarily be consistent with economic logic but nevertheless exert considerable influence on investment decisions.

Willingness/Ability Interactions

The early research of Katona (1951, 1960, 1975) and Pickering (1975, 1981) seems to support a theoretical construct in which buyers' willingness and ability to buy goods or services jointly explain the propensity to make purchasing decisions. Certainly, a buyer must be both willing and able to make a purchase. The timing of consumers' and firms' purchasing abilities (as reflected in income, debt ratios, and other measures of wealth) tends to be cyclical in nature. Similarly, the timing of consumers' and firms' willingness to make purchases (as reflected in measures of confidence, saving, and risk) also is cyclical. But, the two cycles do not proceed in phase; rather, ability precedes willingness. From these simple principles, planning managers can construct and use to practical advantage a fairly comprehensive explanation of purchasing behavior in both consumer and industrial markets. Because of its components' cyclical nature, the willingness/ability mechanism offers encouraging predictive possibilities for strategic planning in asset intensive industries.

CONVENTIONAL FORECASTING

Because economic and management theories must employ open rather than closed theoretical models, it is generally recognized that forecasters' ability to make accurate predictions about the future of economic, industry and market variables is severely limited. Thus, several studies of forecasts' accuracy have tended to be discouraging (Makridakis, 1981; Makridakis and Hibon, 1979). However, there also is substantial evidence to support a more optimistic view of the forecasting art, once its limitations are acknowledged. Most importantly, for forecasting efforts to be successful, they must be valid, that is, forecasting models must contain independent variables that really are mechanical versus circumstantial precursors of the behavior to be predicted. So, thorough analyses of relevant economic, industry and market variables must precede forecasting efforts. Unfortunately, planners often violate this simple, but vital rule.

There are a few techniques for forecasting economies, industries and markets on which the business planner can rely more than others. Most important of these is demographic projection. Because of their life-cyclic nature, one can forecast demographic variables' changes reliably well into the future. Moreover, by making just a few reasonable assumptions regarding fertility, immigration, and infrastructure development, it also is possible to formulate scenarios that describe a realistic range of long term marketing conditions.

Because it often lacks the capability to anticipate turning points (when economic/market cycles' directions change from expansive to recessive or vice versa), forecasting as a methodological discipline has incurred much criticism (Hogarth and Makridakis, 1981). However, to some extent, statistical decomposition methods can provide that ability (Fildes, 1982). Decomposition methods separate trend, seasonal, and cyclical components of time series and are applicable both to mid-term and short-term data. Econometric methods then may be applied to develop leading indicators that have predictive power in the near term. McLaughlin's (1982) leading indicator pyramid then can be used to adjust expectations of cycles' turning points in response to cumulative variances between leading indicators' theoretical and actual lead times. This rolling revision technique offers one possible way to extend leading indicators' predictive horizon. The essential point here is that combinations of mid-term cycle/trend models, short-term econometric models employing leading indicators and pyramid methods of short-term variance analysis may provide a much more reliable approach than any single method alone.

Econometric methods' application to longer-term economic/market data has met with less success. When planners employ econometric methods, evidence seems to argue in favor of simpler, more parsimonious models rather than very elaborate models (Armstrong, 1978). The U.S. Bureau of Labor Statistics' inclusion of demographics among drivers for its econometric forecasting model demonstrates one technical device that should improve long-range forecasts' accuracy.

Some long-range forecasting tasks are less subject to cyclicality, as a source of error, than most. These forecasts assume that growth (or decay) of demand for a product, technology, or service will take place independently of the business cycle. Consider the market-share growth of color television, for instance, and its replacement of black-and-white television. To describe such phenomena, one may use growth curves—mathematical functions of an exponential or S-shape. Using black-and-white television's diffusion as an analog, it was possible to predict the growth and timing of color television's market saturation. Whenever the market's total consumption capacity is estimable, and previous experience provides an analogy, one may use either quantitative and qualitative models to forecast a remarkably broad range of market growth phenomena (Meade, 1984; Rothermal, 1982; Mahajahan and Muller, 1979).

Although the forecasting methods described to this point are quantitative in nature, one should not overlook the roles of experts in anticipating future business conditions. To establish conditional probabilities, Bayesian methods employ expert opinions and formal logic. For forecasting in the near-and mid-terms, these methods can be effective (Fildes, 1979, 1982). Delphi techniques of polling expert panels until reaching a consensus also are quite popular (Diffenbach, 1983; Jain, 1984). Preble's (1982) likelihood of events assessment process (LEAP) provides a means of combining experts' subjective probabilities with regard to the timing of conjectured events; in contrast to the Delphi approach, LEAP does not require achieving a consensus. Widely regarded as an effective approach to forecasting when all of the activities instrumental to reaching an objective are definable, PERT (program evaluation and review technique) is a more rigorous approach to estimating the time to complete long projects (for example, the development of a new car model; design, development, and production of a new class of commercial aircraft; or an electric utility's power plant construction program).

The most effective forecasting techniques probably are hybrids, combining both short-term and extended models (Pollack-Johnson, 1995). Thus, to develop a forecast for the intermediate and long terms, one may take a decomposition approach (perhaps combined with an econometric simulation model). Then, using leading economic indicators, shorter-term elements of the forecast may be developed in greater detail. Alternatively, by interacting input-output tables and econometric models, simulations may be constructed to estimate long-term impacts of changes in economic aggregates on industries' output, or vice versa. Such simulations also can make use of exogenous driver variables, such as S-shaped growth curves and likely demographic shifts, each of which have both high validity and predictive reliability.

SCENARIO FORECASTING

Hybrid forecasting methods that make good use of trend/cyclical time series models, demographics, and other structurally valid independent variables (for example, growth curves) probably will provide the most dependable quantitative approximation of potential long-range environmental conditions. However, even the best forecasting models surely have severe limitations. Accordingly, forecasters and planners now recognize that they often are wise to formulate scenarios describing the realistic range of alternative futures (Linneman and Klein, 1983; Klein and Linneman, 1984; Linneman and Klein, 1985; Wack, 1985; Schwartz, 1991). Here, especially, is where the capabilities of qualitative forecasting methods and expert opinion can be helpful. After taking into account what can be known from quantitative forecasting disciplines, professional futurists may provide great insight into social, technological, political, and regulatory drivers that quantitative methods cannot possibly foretell.

The power of effective scenario forecasting derives partly from its ability to take advantage of both quantitative and qualitative methods. Thus, planners may compose alternative futures by using expert opinions regarding technology, government policy, and various growth analogies such as the Tofflers' (1994) waves. At the same time, they may employ long-term demographics and various quantitative tools, such as I-O tables and econometric simulation. The mix of such scenario-making techniques is left to the planner's imagination. Ultimately, scenario-based planning will be valuable to the extent that top management obtains insight into strategic alternatives, which simpler methods cannot achieve, and formulates more successful plans as a result.

Eventually, management must select one scenario among others to provide assumptions for the prevailing plan of business. However, neither planning nor environmental assessment stops there. Instead, planners must monitor the environment continuously, with a particular focus on forecasts employed in the prevailing plan and, perhaps, a small number of contingency scenarios. As events unfold, they either will confirm prevailing forecasting assumptions or compel revisions. There should be an ongoing process in which planners revise forecasts and scenarios of alternative futures when and as needed. Similarly, plans also should be subject to revision when vital assumptions of the prevailing plan no longer are reasonable.

When it requires long range forecasts to come true, management makes a fundamental mistake. All that one can expect from the forecasting effort is a sound description of forecasting assumptions' future implications. When the assumptions change, so must the forecast—and, probably the plan. However, the firm that conducts these functions comprehensively, routinely, and competently should enjoy a significant competitive advantage.

CONCLUSION: WHAT WE CAN KNOW

This book, and this chapter, began with an indictment of management and the planning profession for grossly underdeveloping EA functions. Competent environmental assessment (of economies, industries, and markets) is vital for sound strategic decisions. Why, then, are EA functions so often poorly developed? Perhaps, as we have conjectured, Management simply is not sure about the scope of feasible approaches and, lacking confidence in its ability to choose EA methods wisely, it chooses none. So, this volume concludes with a straightforward inventory of what can be known by employing environmental assessment methods described in the preceding pages.

Analytic Tools

Usually there are abundant data with which to describe the economy, industry and markets within which a firm competes. Therefore, the business environment usually can be well-described. Most problems with environmental analysis stem not from inability to describe the environment, but rather from inability to understand it. Fortunately a growing number of analytical tools and other resources are available to aid in achieving such an understanding. They include:

- Highly developed systems of regular, detailed reporting by agencies of the US government for the national income and product accounts, monetary aggregates, most industries' output, and many markets' consumption of goods and services;
- Comparable reporting systems in many industrialized nations;
- Techniques for inter-country comparisons and consolidations of country-markets' purchasing power;

- A large number of public and private reporting institutions, including trade associations and commercial services, which monitor and report trends in specific industries and markets;

- Demographic data in comprehensive detail for the total United States, its regions, and metropolitan markets, paralleled by similar (but often less precise) data in many other nations. These data are powerful aids for explaining market trends, and they may be equally powerful aids to forecasting;

- Input-output tables that explain relationships between macroeconomic aggregates and industries, industries' transactions with each other, and industries' dependence on consuming markets;

- Porter's (1980, 1985) models of intra-industry competition, which provide a framework for assessing (1) causes and effects of inter-firm rivalry, substitution, entry by new competitors, customers' bargaining leverage, and suppliers' bargaining leverage; and (2) the relative strength of competitors' positions within an industry based on cost, non-price differentiation or a combination of the two;

- The PIMS program, which provides guidance in assessing a firm's strategic alternatives and performance potential based on several industry/market characteristics including growth rate, concentration, the size of transaction, products' significance to customers, unionization, and standardization versus customization of products, among others;

- Segmentation methods for discerning consumers' motivations and choice-making mechanisms,

- Methods for diagnosing discretionary versus nondiscretionary segments of consumer and industrial markets for durable and nondurable goods and services; and

- Methods for identifying drivers of consumer and industrial markets, based on interactions of cyclical variables that reflect customers' willingness and ability to purchase goods and services.

Those who are frustrated by the business environment's apparent unknowability should review the preceding list and the previous discussions of those topics in this book. For the trained analyst, important behavior in most business environments can be well understood. But, as observed previously, theories with which to explain exactly how molecular events occur in the business environment are far less impressive than our ability to describe them as observed phenomena. We are left, then, with a challenge to develop the most powerful descriptive methodology possible. Tools with which to meet that challenge satisfactorily usually are available.

Forecasting Methods

Since the business environment only can be diagnosed phenomenologically, versus mechanically (in terms of causes and effects), the validity of forecasting methods is constrained accordingly. We cannot build models of environmental mechanics that we do not understand. The most reliable forecasting methods are phenomenological versus mechanistic. They make no attempt to understand why environmental events occur, but simply to anticipate their occurrence over time. Even so, the ability of any forecasting method to foresee turning points accurately in the distant future can be only speculative at best.

The most satisfactory forecasting efforts begin with a careful diagnosis of all three environmental dimensions—economy, industry, market. To be sure that the drivers underlying forecasted market behavior are as consistent as possible, such analysis must be done within the context of accurate industry and market segmentation.

Planning managers may employ any of several very satisfactory forecasting methods; including the following:

- *Demographic projections:* accurate over mid- and long-terms, these drivers of market trends and turning points are available for most U.S. geographic markets and regions as well as most nations;

- *Trend/cycle projections:* including models derived from decomposition of short, mid, long, and very long-term time series that are available for many nations' economies, industries, and markets. These methods can provide acceptable mid-term accuracy, and may succeed in anticipating turning points;

- *Leading indicators and variance analysis procedures:* accurate in the very near-term and (with cumulative variance analysis) perhaps somewhat longer;

- *Growth curves:* may be accurate in predicting the diffusion and saturation of new products, technologies, and infrastructure developments wherever approximate limits on consumption capacity are known and reasonable growth/term analogs exist;

- *Input-output tables:* combined with econometric models, they can be used to simulate impacts of shifts in industries' consumption or output on each other and the total economy—or of the total economy on individual industries; and

- *Extended activity programming methods, such as PERT,* that calculate amounts of time and other resources required to complete extended activity sequences—even those lasting several years. They can be remarkably accurate because they are largely deterministic, making few exogenous assumptions about economic imponderables.

Econometric forecasting methods' reliabilities are much lower than others' because, as observed previously, so little is understood about causes and effects of economic behavior, and because breaks in their relationships can destroy forecasting models' validity. Even though econometric models usually can not provide very accurate forecasts, they still may be useful tools for performing the following tasks:

- Translating assumptions about economic, industry, and market variables into their net potential impacts—for example, when combined with industry input-output tables;

- Formulating scenarios of alternative futures that represent different assumptions about combinations of environmental variables; and

- Constructing pro forma statements of the National Income and Product Accounts, and explaining potential changes in macroeconomic aggregates which may occur in response to specific environmental assumptions such as the federal government's fiscal, monetary, immigration and defense policies.

When using econometric models, forecasters can expect the greatest accuracy when their logic is relatively simple and maximum use is made of non-conjectural independent variables such as demographic projections, federal and state budgets, federal monetary policies, and so forth.

The best forecasting procedures combine more than one of the methods described in this summary. Thus, planning managers can add value to forecasting efforts by being skillful diagnosticians and selecting methods that best match the firm, its industry, and markets.

No matter how skillful a forecaster may be, significant uncertainty and risk still will attend most forecasting efforts. Scenario forecasting procedures are extremely useful for minimizing the adverse consequences of uncertainty. Scenarios define alternative futures for which management can be prepared with contingent strategies. Scenario planning draws upon all of the EA methods described earlier in this summary. In addition, inputs of experts can extend the scope of scenario forecasts far beyond what is attainable solely by the quantitative methods described earlier.

A PLANNING MANAGER'S
EA RESOURCES CHECK-LIST

The following pages contain four check-lists which planning managers may use when taking inventories of their firms' EA resources. (See Exhibit 8.1.) The first three lists contain collections of data resources; the fourth list includes ten important forecasts most of which should be available to Top Management and kept current. Where voids are noted, the firm's EA capabilities may need to be supplemented in order to avoid competitive disadvantage. Each item on these lists is relatively easy and inexpensive to obtain, with the possible exception of item B-2, which prescribes research to obtain competitor intelligence when it is not available from public records, trade associations, and so forth. Such research may require substantial time, effort, and expense.

These lists are far from exhaustive because each firm's EA requirements may be unique. The firm's mix of industries, markets, products or services, planning budget and staff capabilities will require a planning manager to draw appropriately, but uniquely, from the methods discussed in this volume, like a mechanic draws tools from a kit, to meet specific needs of the planning task at hand. However, as a general matter, firms that fulfill the requirements on these four lists, and conduct ongoing programs of environmental monitoring should be reasonably able to assemble and assess environmental evidence relevant to strategic decision making.

Exhibit 8.1
Environmental Assessment Resources
of the Proficiently Planned Firm: A Check-List

A.   Economy

    1.   Subscriptions to regular economic reporting services of the US Government (Appendix III) or a commercial service sufficient to monitor national economic/industry aggregates (Appendix IV);

    2.   Subscription to the Conference Board's monthly publication, *Business Cycle Indicators*;

    3.   Subscriptions to the BLS forecasting services, including bi-annual economic and population forecasts.

B.   Industry

    1.   Subscriptions to industry reports issued monthly by the US Department of Commerce or, more timely, by industry associations;

    2.   A regularly updated census of industry competitors and their performance obtained from reporting services, such as Standard and Poor's, Moody's, Value Line, Dun & Bradstreet and from industry/market research. Identification of the industry's least-cost competitor, claimants to differentiation and focused niche players;

    3.   A profile of performance norms and trends for the firm's industry or segment, obtained from a trade association, commercial reporting service or the firm's own study of competitors' publicly reported financial results;

    4.   A five-forces analysis of industry competition and competitors, updated annually, for each industry segment; and

    5.   A PIMS-type analysis of the firm's industry and the firm's industry-position, also updated annually.

C.   Markets

    1.   National, regional and metropolitan demographic time series relevant to the firm's markets and customers' markets;

    2.   A diagnosis of specific purchase-decision drivers in served markets;

    3.   Trends of revenues and output in each served market segment; and

    4.   A cyclical profile describing willingness and ability indicators of customers' purchasing potentials for each served market segment.

D.   **Forecasts and Forecasting Tools**

1.   BLS' long range economic forecasts for the United States' economy, population and industries' output;

2.   A 3-year economic forecast, updated quarterly, most likely prepared by a commercial forecasting service, a bank, a university or a trade association;

3.   A short-term US economic forecast, based on the leading economic indicators, adjusted for variances from normal lead times;

4.   Relevant demographic projections for served geographic markets;

5.   A long-term trend-cyclical forecast of served markets based on time series' decomposition;

6.   A mid-term forecast of served markets, perhaps based on correlations of willingness-ability variables to consumption;

7.   Growth-curve forecasts of emerging industry and market segments, product lines, technologies or processes, etc.;

8.   Completion time/cost forecasts for long-term development programs that influence served markets (for example, completion of long-term construction programs);

9.   Expert opinions regarding likely turning points in the economic cycle, market behavior, and/or demand for the industry's output; and

10. Scenario profiles of alternative industry/market outlooks for the strategic planning term.

Part V

Appendices:
An Informational Tool-Kit

Introduction

The following pages are divided into six sections. Each section contains referential information which will be useful to planning managers in gathering evidence for planning decisions. The next few paragraphs provide an overview of those sections' contents and purposes.

I. POPULATION TRENDS

This first appendix provides graphic descriptions of population trends in the United States and other industrialized nations of the world. These data were obtained from a base of demographic data for many nations which is maintained by the U.S. Bureau of Labor Statistics. This data base can be accessed through the internet. A web site address also is provided.

Readers should notice the dramatic differences in composition and trends of population age groups between countries. To illustrate some of the starkest differences, consider age group trends in the United States and Japan. Just by glancing at these two pages, you quickly will appreciate dissimilarities of those two countries' demographics.

These graphs provide only a small sample of the BLS' entire international data base. Planners can use these data to obtain demographic projections for business plans which depend on trends in multi-national consumer markets.

II. THE WORLD ECONOMY IN GRAPHS

These exhibits demonstrate the dramatic differences between marketing opportunities of the world's geographic regions and nations. In this illustration, we have chosen to portray data which are relevant to marketing automotive components since the Automotive Industry has become world-wide in nature. Notice especially the differences between nations' highway infrastructures, their population densities, and their wealth. All of these factors are relevant marketing considerations for firms which intend to sell cars, fuel, lodging, automobile repair parts and automotive services multinationally. Once again, reference resources for further research are provided.

III. ECONOMIC DATA SOURCES

This section provides the names of several excellent data resources many of which can be obtained at little or no cost from public and commercial services. These sources contain comprehensive data with which analysts can diagnose most markets and industries. You can obtain all of the information on this three-page list for less than $2,000. From these sources, many firms can obtain economic, industry, and market information that is just as comprehensive as that for which some corporations pay much more.

IV. FORECASTING SERVICES

In this section you will find a list of forecasting services many of which also can be obtained at a modest cost. The list contains eight well-known professional firms which provide economic reporting and forecasting services including the two largest firms of their kind, DRI/McGraw Hill and the WEFA (previously, Wharton Economic Forecasting Associates) subsidiary of Primark Corporation. Three banks also are listed in this section; at this writing, each provided *free* access to its econometric forecasting model: these are extraordinarily valuable resources. Finally, we have listed three well known universities' econometric modeling services.

V. LONG RANGE FORECAST OF the U.S. ECONOMY

The U.S. Bureau of Labor Statistics publishes a long range forecast of the U.S. economy, using its own proprietary econometric model, every other year. An extract from that forecast is included here. The BLS issued this forecast in November 1997; it extends ten years, to 2006, and provides a broad perspective on the Nation's economic outlook. Also see Exhibit 7.2 in Chapter 7 for a similar forecast prepared by the BLS in 1995 which explored impacts of alternative assumptions in three economic forecast scenarios.

VI. CROSS-REFERENCE TABLES:
NAICS VS. SIC CODING SYSTEMS

In the year 2000, the Standard Industrial Classification System (SIC) code, which has been used for many years, will begin to be discontinued. A new North American Industrial Classification System (NAICS), designed jointly by NAFTA's three participants (The United States, Canada and Mexico), then will be implemented. NAICS will provide a much better basis for segmenting industrial markets than the SIC coding system presently provides. This new system will recognize industries which did not even exist when the SIC coding system was designed, and many which were not distinguished by the SIC system. However, while SIC codes are phased out and NAICS is phased in, some analysts undoubtedly will be inconvenienced. This section explains NAICS' structure and provides samples of cross-reference tables for six industries. The Office of Management and Budget (OMB) has prepared extensive cross reference tables in both printed and electronic form. This section contains instructions for obtaining the complete cross-reference tables.

Appendix I

Population Trends and Forecasts of the United States and Other Industrialized Nations

Population of the World (Thousands)

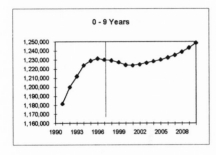

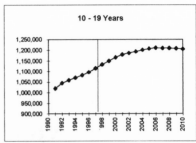

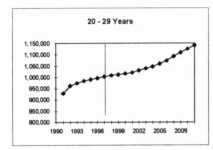

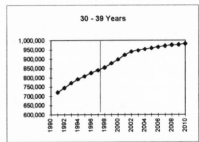

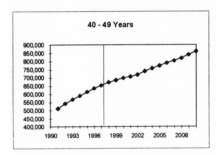

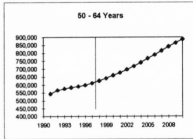

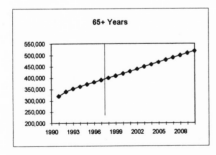

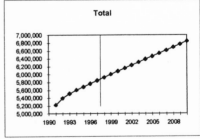

Source: U.S. Bureau of the Census

Population of the United States (Thousands)

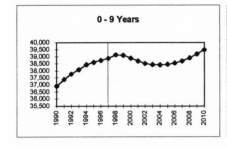

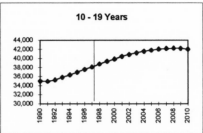

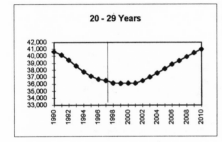

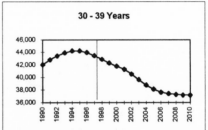

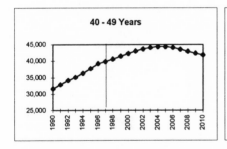

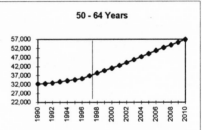

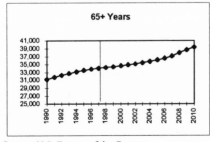

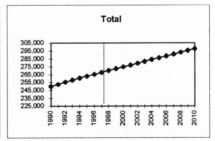

Source: U.S. Bureau of the Census

Population of Canada (Thousands)

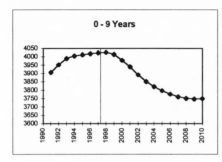

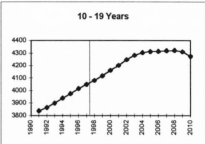

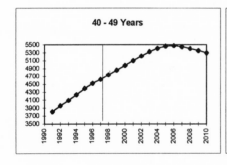

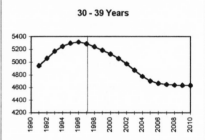

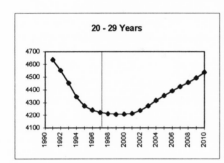

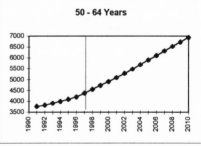

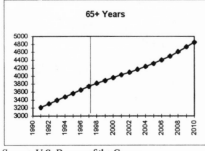

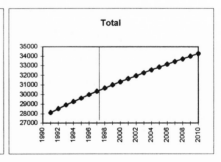

Source: U.S. Bureau of the Census

Population of Mexico (Thousands)

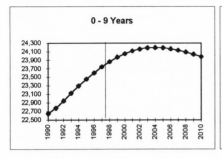

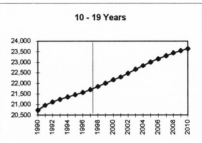

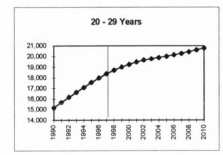

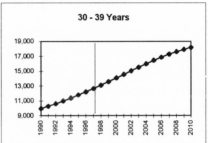

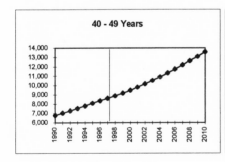

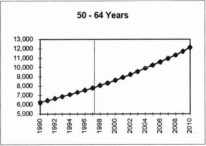

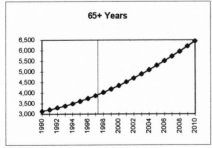

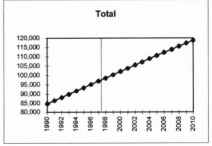

Source: U.S. Bureau of the Census

Population of Brazil (Thousands)

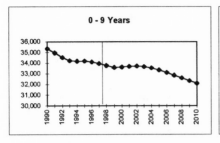

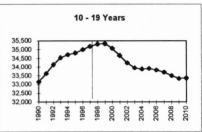

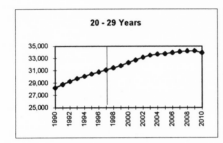

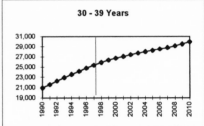

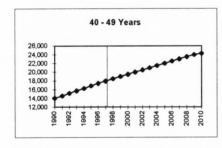

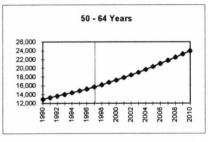

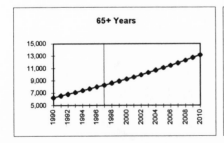

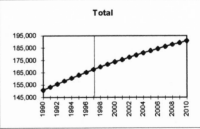

Source: U.S. Bureau of the Census

Population of the United Kingdom (Thousands)

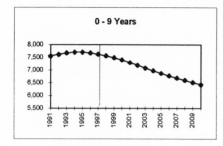

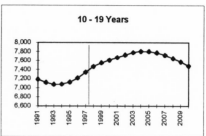

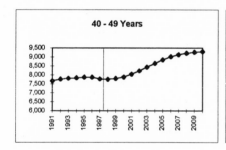

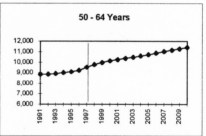

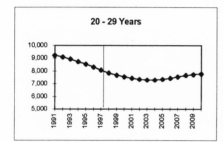

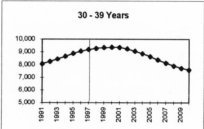

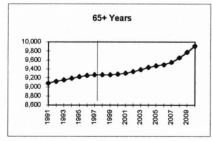

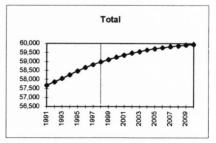

Source: U.S. Bureau of the Census

Population of France (Thousands)

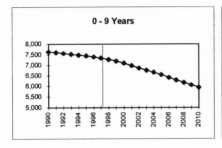

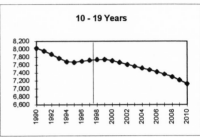

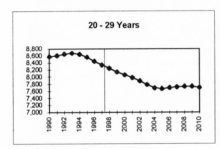

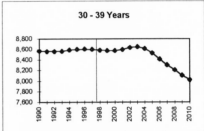

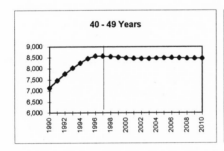

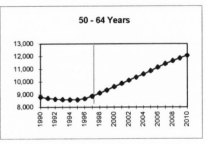

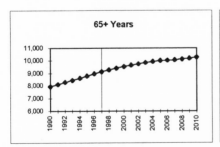

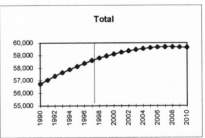

Source: U.S. Bureau of the Census

Population of Germany (Thousands)

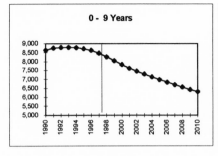

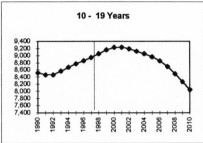

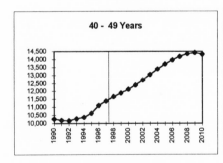

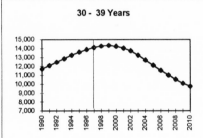

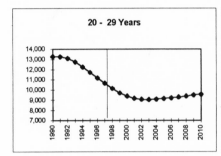

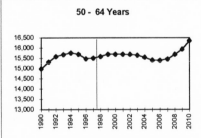

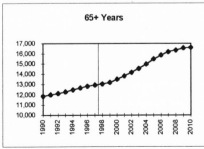

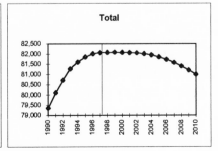

Source: U.S. Bureau of the Census

Population of Japan (Thousands)

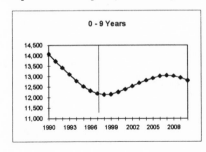

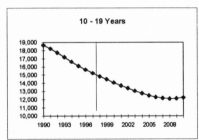

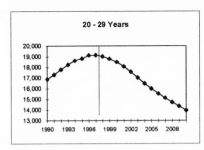

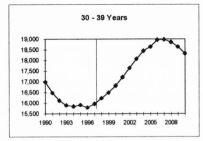

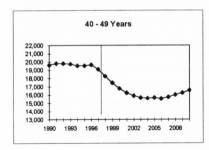

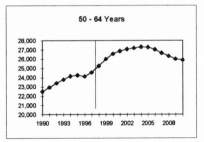

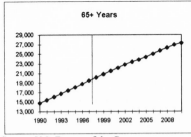

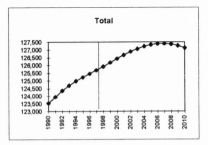

Source: U.S. Bureau of the Census

Population of China (Thousands)

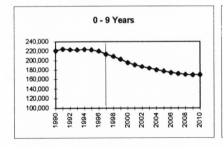

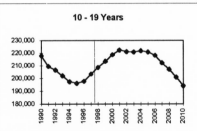

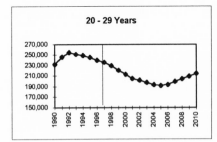

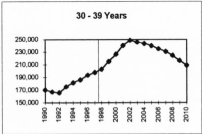

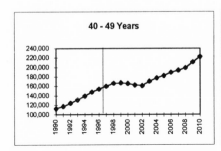

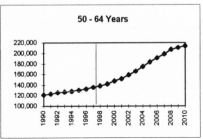

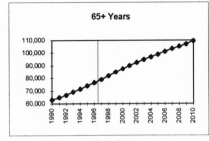

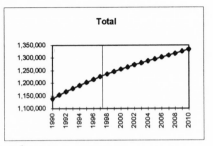

Source: U.S. Bureau of the Census

Appendix II

The World Economy in Graphs

REGIONAL ECONOMIC PROFILES OF POPULATION & WEALTH: 1995

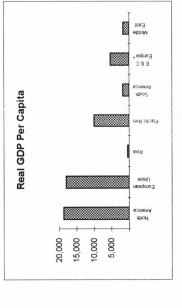

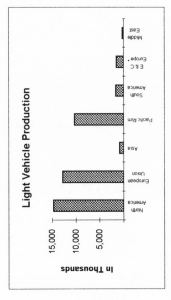

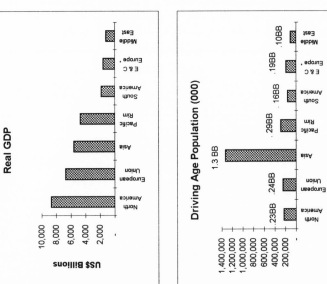

* Eastern & Central

Sources : Real GDP (International Monetary Fund); Real GDP Per Capita (Handbook of International Statistics, 1996);
Driving Age Population (U.S. Census Bureau); and Light Vehicle Production (*The Economist*)

COMPARISON OF NATIONS' WEALTH: 1995
Real GDP Per Capita (Based on Purchasing Power Parity)

Source : Handbook of International Statistics, 1996. CIA

COMPOSITION OF THE WORLD'S TOTAL POPULATION: 1996

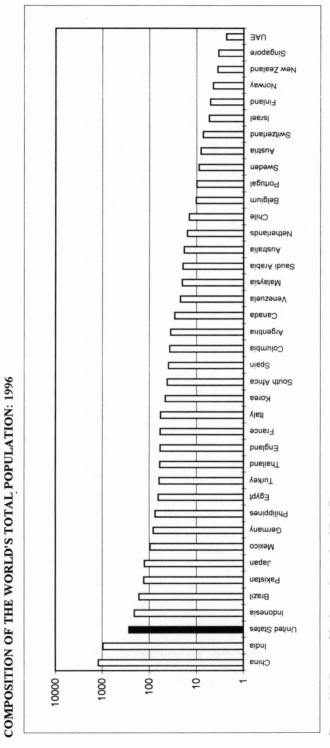

Source : U.S. Bureau of the Census, International Data Base

COMPARISON OF NATIONS' POPULATION DENSITY
Persons Per Kilometer: 1996

Source: Central Intelligence Agency and U.S. Census Bureau

COMPARISON OF NATIONS' ROADWAYS
% Unpaved Roadways: 1996

Spain
Singapore
Belgium
Thailand
Italy
United States
Netherlands
Portugal
Korea
Germany
Malaysia
Egypt
Sweden
Japan
Norway
Finland
New Zealand
France
Pakistan
India
Indonesia
Saudi Arabia
Mexico
Canada
Australia
Venezuela
South Africa
Argentina
Austria
China
Philippines
Chile
Turkey
Columbia
Brazil

100% 90% 80% 70% 60% 50% 40% 30% 20% 10% 0%

Source : Central Intelligence Agency

Appendix III

Economic Data Sources

ECONOMIC DATA SOURCES

TITLE	FREQ.	SOURCE	COST*	CONTENTS
Economic Report of the President www.access.gpo.gov/eop/	Annual	Council of Economic Advisors	$19/yr **	Historic and current statistical tables relating to income, employment and production in the US.
Survey of Current Business www.bea.doc.gov	Monthly	US Dept. of Commerce: Bureau of Econ. Analysis	$39/yr **	Discussion of current economic conditions, including NIPA tables containing both current and historical data.
Business Cycle Indicators www.conference-board.org	Monthly	The Conference Board	$120/yr	Statistical time series including charts and data tables comparing current business cycles with those of the past 30-40 years.
Economic Indicators www.whitehouse.gov/WH/ EOP/CEA/html/CEA.html	Monthly	Joint Economic Committee: Council of Economic Advisors	$37/yr **	Tables and graphs of historic and current economic data, including total output, income & spending, employment, business activity, prices, finance and limited international statistics.
Current Industrial Reports: Manufacturers' Shipments, Inventories and Orders www.doc.gov	Monthly	US Dept. of Commerce: Economics and Statistics Administration	$35/yr	Current value of manufacturers' shipments, inventories and orders by industry group. Some discussion also is included.
Current Business Reports: Advance Monthly Retail Sales www.doc.gov	Monthly	US Dept. of Commerce: Economics and Statistics Administration	Free	Advance estimates of US retail sales by type of business. Contains current and limited historic data, both seasonally adjusted and non-adjusted.

TITLE	FREQ.	SOURCE	COST	CONTENTS
Current Business Reports: Monthly Retail Trade - Sales & Inventories www.doc.gov	Monthly	US Dept. of Commerce: Economics and Statistics Administration	$57/yr **	Total sales and inventories for all retail stores in the US, on a monthly basis. Includes current and limited historical data.
Statistics of Income Bulletin	Quarterly	Internal Revenue Svc.	$30/yr	Provides annual financial statistics from types of tax and information returns filed. Also includes personal income tax data by state and historical data for selected types of taxpayers.
Annual Statement Studies www.rmahq.org	Annual	Robert Morris Associates Philadelphia	$129	Pro forma standardized income statement and balance sheet ratios for 500 4-digit S.I.C. industries, at several size levels, based on survey of 140,000 participating firms (useful benchmarking)
Treasury Bulletin www.ustreas.gov	Quarterly	Department of Treasury	$34/yr	Provides a financial analysis of the US, including federal and public sectors. Also included are international statistics. Some tables provide historic data, but all provide current statistics.
Annual US Economic Data www.stls.frb.org	Annual	Federal Reserve Bank of St. Louis	Free	Historic data tables for major economic indicators including money supply, income and expenditures
National Economic Trends www.stls.frb.org	Monthly	Federal Reserve Bank of St. Louis	Free	Historic data tables and graphs with some discussion of economic variables.
Monetary Trends www.stls.frb.org	Monthly	Federal Reserve Bank of St. Louis	Free	Historic data tables and graphs of monetary indicators. Some discussion is included.
Value Line: Quarterly Economic Review www.valueline.com	Quarterly	The Value Line Investment Survey	$570/yr	Discussion of current and potential economic conditions. Tables of historic, current and forecasted indicators. Data are quarterly and annual. Also, profiles of 1720 companies' financial trends in 95 industry groups.

221

TITLE	FREQ.	SOURCE	COST	CONTENTS
Canadian Economic Observer www.statcan.ca	Monthly	Statistics Canada	$227/yr	Reviews current economic conditions in Canada. Also included are data tables of historic and current data.
Handbook of International Economic Statistics www.cia.gov	Annual	Central Intelligence Agency	$25/yr **	Provides basic worldwide statistics for comparing economic performance of major countries and regions.
World Economic Outlook www.imf.org	Bi-Annually	International Monetary Fund	$36/issue	Provides a discussion of world economic conditions and projections. Data tables are provided for each country, containing historic, current and forecast statistics.
International Financial Statistics www.imf.org	Monthly	International Monetary Fund	$30/issue $246/year	Statistics on all aspects of international finance, including exchange rates, international banking, money, interest rates, and national accounts for every country of the world.
Stat-USA: Internet Site www.stat-usa.gov	NA	US Dept. of Commerce	$150/year	Provides data and market research reports from numerous government departments, including the National Trade Databank.
Penn World Tables www.nber.org	NA	National Bureau of Economic Research	Free	Provides a set of NIPA time series for 152 countries and 29 variables, adjusted for purchasing power parity, based on relative prices within and between countries for 1,500 commodities.

* These costs were representative of quotations we received during a recent survey. No assurance can be given that they will remain in effect at the time of publication.

** Files containing these documents can be down loaded in PDF format, from their web sites, free of charge.

Appendix IV

Economic Forecasting Sources

SELECTED LISTING OF ECONOMIC FORECASTING SERVICES

Part I - Commercial Services

Firm/Organization	Scope	Frequency	Cost*
DRI/McGraw Hill 24 Hartwell Avenue Lexington, MA 02173-3154 (781) 860-6332 (800)933-3374 inside U.S. and Canada www.dri.mcgraw-hill.com	1. US Forecast Summary: complete NIPA tables for alternative forecasts.	Monthly	$3,800/yr
	2. US Economic Summary: complete forecast summary including financial and corporate profiles.	Monthly	$7,500/yr
	3. Review of the US Economy: three year, monthly forecast of 11 macroeconomic sectors. Includes US Forecast Summary and U.S. Economic Summary.	Monthly, except May and November	$21,500/yr
The Conference Board The Consumer Research Center 845 Third Avenue New York, NY 10022-6679 (212) 759-0900 www.conference-board.org.	Consumer market forecast and analysis. Monitors trends in demographics and the consumer marketplace.	Full Membership* Other Membership	$7,500/yr Varies with level of service
	1. North American Outlook Analysis of economic outlook and trends.	Annual	$30/$120/yr
	2. Straight Talk Forecast of U.S economy, interest rates, exchange rates and long term issues. *pricing depends on membership.	Monthly	$195/$395/yr
The Dismal Scientist 600 Willowbrook Lane Suite 600 West Chester, PA 19382 (610) 696-8700 www.dismal.com	Comprehensive data base for the industrialized world.	NA	Free

224

SELECTED LISTING OF ECONOMIC FORECASTING SERVICES

Part I - Commercial Services (Continued)

Firm/Organization	Scope	Frequency	Cost*
Macroeconomic Advisors, LLC 231 S. Bemiston, Suite 775 St. Louis, MO 63105 (314) 721-4747 www.macroadvisors.com	BASIC SERVICES: 1. Macro Service: Washington University PC macro model plus monthly analysis of results.	Monthly	$18,200
	2. Model Service: Washington University PC macro model plus limited analysis.	Quarterly	$9,800
	3. Executive Forecast Service: monthly issues of the US Economic outlook.	Monthly	$11,250
Regional Economic Models Inc. 306 Lincoln Avenue Amherst, MA 01002 (413) 549 - 1169 www.remi.com	Regional and economic forecasting models that reflect impacts of public policy initiatives.		
	Initial Subscription	Annual	Min. $16,000
	Annual Renewal	Annual	Min. $4,200
	Supplemental Forecasts (Annual Subscription Required)	Quarterly	Min. $3,000
	Special Forecasts (for one state)	NA	$1,420
Regional Financial Associates 600 Willobrooklane, Suite 600 West Chester, PA 19382 (610) 696 - 8700 www.fra.com	U.S. macroeconomic quarterly forecast with a 10 year horizon.	Monthly	$5,995
	Same as above with both a regional and U.S. outlook.	Monthly	$9,000
ValueLine Publishing Inc. Church Street Station New York, NY (800) 833-0046 www.valueline.com	Macroeconomic forecast with a four year horizon, including 1720 public company profiles and rankings.	Quarterly	$570/yr

SELECTED LISTING OF ECONOMIC FORECASTING SERVICES

Part I - Commercial Services (Continued)

WEFA, Inc.
800 Baldwin Tower
Eddystone, PA 19022
(610) 490 - 2535
www.wefa.com

Services available include:

1. US Industrial Analysis: forecast of industry output, prices, etc. with quarterly detail. — Monthly — $10,000-$15,000

2. Market Analysis: forecast of industries and U.S.economy using input/output tables. — Monthly — $10,000 $15,000

3. Both services/publications. — $15,000-$20,000

Part 2 - Banks

Firm/Organization	Scope	Frequency	Cost*
BANKS **Bank of America** 555 California St. San Francisco, CA 94104-1502 (415) 622 - 3530 www.bankamerica.com	Economic and Business Outlook: two years of basic macroeconomic data and analysis.	Quarterly	FREE
FirstUnion Bank 1525 West W.T. Blvd. 3C3 Charlotte, NC 28288-1153 (800) 347-1246 www.firstunion.com	Quarterly macroeconomic forecasts.	Quarterly	FREE
Mellon Bank Mellon Bank Center Pittsburgh, PA 15258 (412) 234-5000 www.mellon.com	Econometric forecasts.	Monthly 11 issues Nov/Dec is combined	FREE, but must register for a password

SELECTED LISTING OF ECONOMIC FORECASTING SERVICES

Part 3 - Universities

Firm/Organization	Scope	Frequency	Cost
UNIVERSITIES			
RSQE Forecasting Model **University of Michigan** Ann Arbor, Michigan 48109 (734) 764 - 2355 www.@mqem.econ.lsa.umich.edu	Quarterly U.S. econometric forecasts and analysis.	Quarterly	$550/yr
	A two year forecast and monthly analysis is available at the University's web site. No charge.	NA	FREE
GSU Economic Forecasting Center Georgia State University University Plaza - CBA 220 Atlanta, GA 30303 (404) 651-3287 www-ecfor.gsu.edu	Forecast of economic activity over an eight-quarter period. Forecast table includes over 200 variables.	Quarterly	$150/yr
Yale University Fairmodel Box 208281, Yale Station New Haven, CT 06520-8281 (203) 432 - 3715 http://fairmodel.econ.yale.edu	Two econometric models: 1. US Model: 4 year forecast of the U.S. economy.	Quarterly	FREE
	2. MC Model: three year forecast model which includes multiple countries.	Quarterly	FREE

* These costs were representative of quotations we received during a recent survey. No assurance can be given that they will remain in effect at the time of publication.

227

Appendix V

BLS Long-Range Forecast of the U.S. Economy

November 1997

BLS LONG-RANGE FORECAST
of the U.S. Economy
Part I. Summary

ASSUMPTIONS

Fiscal Policy

1. Real federal defense spending will continue to decline, but at a slower rate.

2. High Medicare costs will force grants to state and local governments to increase.

3. Growth in Medicare expenditures will decelerate due to slower growth of the population older than 65.

4. The trend toward higher gasoline taxes will persist.

5. No major changes in corporate or Social Security taxes are expected.

Monetary Policy

1. Short-term interest rates will be within the range of the last business cycle.

2. Long-term interest rates are projected to drift downward.

Demographics

1. Growth of the total population will decelerate.

2. Hispanic and Asian populations will continue to grow faster than the total.

3. Four major causes for the change in population growth trends over the 1976–2006 period of study are: low birth rates in the years around the Great Depression, the baby boom from the late 1940s to the early 1960s, the small birth rate increase from the late 1970s to the early 1990s and sustained immigration beginning in the 1970s which will continue through the forecast period.

General

No major wars, natural disasters, or oil embargoes will occur during the projection period.

RESULTS

1. Real GDP ($1992) will grow, on average, 2.1% annually, reaching $8.6 trillion by 2006.

2. Exports are projected to increase 3.4 times as fast as GDP.

3. Imports are projected to increase 2.9 times as fast as GDP.

4. By 2006, exports and imports each will approach 20% of GDP.

5. Private investment is projected to increase at 1.5 times the rate of GDP.

6. Federal government expenditures are projected to decrease 15% between 1996 and 2006.

Source: Bureau of Labor Statistics, November 1997

Long-Range Forecasts of the U.S. Economy

ECONOMY	-1986-	-1996-	-2006-	CAGR '86-'96	CAGR '96-'06
Personal consumption expenditures	$3,709	$4,691	$5,773	2.4	2.1
Gross private domestic investment	814	1,060	1,470	2.7	3.3
Exports	362	826	1,686	8.6	7.4
Imports	(526)	(940)	(1,750)	(6.0)	(6.4)
Federal defense expenditures	393	314	257	(2.3)	(2.0)
Federal nondefense expenditures	125	153	142	2.0	(0.8)
State & local government expenditures	617	805	1,006	2.7	2.3
Gross domestic product	$5,494	$6,909	$8,584	2.3	2.2

Billions of chained (1992) dollars

% of GDP	-1986-	-1996-	-2006-	% CHANGE '86-'96	% CHANGE '96-'06
Personal consumption expenditures	67.5	67.9	67.3	0.4	(0.6)
Gross private domestic investment	14.8	15.3	17.1	0.5	1.8
Exports	6.6	12.0	19.6	5.4	7.6
Imports	(9.6)	(13.6)	(20.4)	(4.0)	(6.8)
Federal defense expenditures	7.2	4.5	3.0	(2.7)	(1.5)
Federal nondefense expenditures	2.3	2.2	1.7	(0.1)	(0.5)
State & local government expenditures	11.2	11.7	11.7	0.5	0.0
Gross domestic product	100	100	100	--	--

PERSONAL WEALTH	-1986-	-1996-	-2006-	CAGR '86-'96	CAGR '96-'06
Disposable Personal Income	$3,187	$5,589	$8,997	5.8	4.9
DPI: Chained (1992) $ Billions	4,087	5,088	6,154	2.2	1.9
Per Capita Disposable Personal Income	13,246	21,046	31,165	4.7	4.0
Per Capita DPI: Chained (1992) $ Billions	16,983	19,161	21,318	1.2	1.1
Saving Rate	5.4	4.3	2.7	3.4	0.0

POPULATION	-1986-	-1996-	-2006-	CAGR '86-'96	CAGR '96-'06
Households	109.6	126.7	140.9	1.5	1.1
Population					
Total	240.7	265.6	288.7	1.0	0.8
Age 16+	185.3	204.1	225.5	1.0	1.0

Millions

Source: Bureau of Labor Statistics, 1997

Long-Range Forecasts of the U.S. Economy

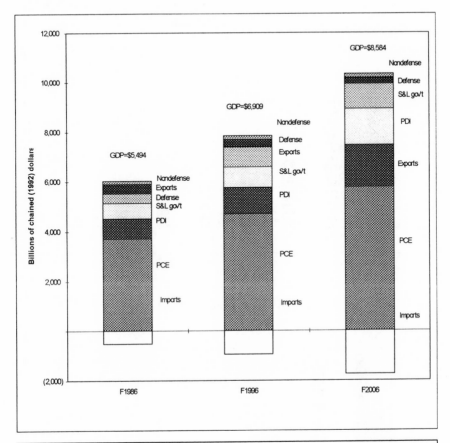

PCE	67.5%	67.9%	67.3%
PDI	14.8%	15.3%	17.1%
Exports	6.6%	12.0%	19.6%
Imports	-9.6%	-13.6%	-20.4%
Gov't	20.7%	18.4%	16.4%
GDP	100.0%	100.0%	100.0%

Long-Range Forecasts of the U.S. Economy

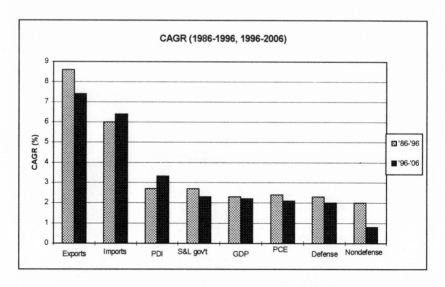

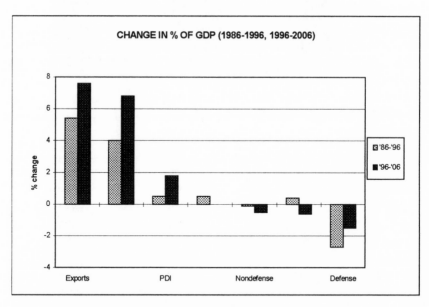

* S&L: State and Local

Appendix VI

NAICS-SIC Code
Cross Reference Tables

Table 1
STANDARD INDUSTRIAL CLASSIFICATION (SIC) CODING SYSTEM

Industry Group	Industry Code *	Description
Agriculture, Forestry and Fishing	01	Agricultural Production-Crops
	02	Agricultural Production-Livestock
	07	Agricultural Services
	08	Forestry
	09	Fishing, Hunting and Trapping
Mining	10	Meal Mining
	12	Coal Mining
	13	Oil and Gas Extraction
	14	Nonmetallic Minerals, except fuels
Construction	15	General Building Contractors
	16	Heavy Construction, except Building
	17	Specialty Trade Contractors
Manufacturing	20	Food and Kindered Products
	21	Tobacco Products
	22	Textile Mill Products
	23	Apparel and Other Textile Products
	24	Lumber and Wood Products
	25	Furniture and Fixtures
	26	Paper and Allied Products
	27	Printing and Publishing
	28	Chemicals and Allied Products
	29	Petroleum and Coal Products
	30	Rubber and Miscellaneous
	31	Leather and Leather Products
	32	Stone, Clay, and Glass Products
	33	Primary Metal Industries
	34	Fabricated Metal Products
	35	Industrial Machinery and Equipment
	36	Electronic and Other Electric Equipment
	37	Transportation Equipment
	38	Instruments and Related Products
	39	Miscellaneous Manufacturing Industries
Transportation, Communications and Utilities	40	Railroad Transportation
	42	Trucks and Warehousing
	43	U.S. Postal Service
	44	Water Transportation
	45	Transportation by Air
	46	Pipeline, Except Natural Gas
	47	Transportation Services
	48	Communications
	49	Electric, Gas and Sanitary Services

*First two, of four digits.

Wholesale Trade	50	Wholesale Trade-Durable Goods
	51	Wholesale Trade-Nondurable Goods
Retail Trade	52	Building Materials and Garden Supplies
	53	General Merchandise Stores
	54	Food Stores
	55	Automotive Dealers and Service Stations
	56	Apparel and Accessory Stores
	57	Furniture and Homefurnishings Stores
	58	Eating and Drinking Places
	59	Miscellaneous Retail
Finance, Insurance and Real Estate	60	Depository Institutions
	61	Nondepository Institutions
	62	Security and Commodity Brokers
	63	Insurance Carriers
	64	Insurance Agents, Brokers and Services
	65	Real Estate
	67	Holding and Other Investment Offices
Services	70	Hotels and Other Lodging Places
	72	Personal Service
	76	Business Service
	75	Auto Repair, Services and Parking
	76	Miscellaneous Repair Services
	78	Motion Pictures
	79	Amusement and Recreation Services
	80	Health Services
	81	Legal Services
	82	Educational Services
	83	Social Services
	84	Museums, Botanicals, Zoological Gardens
	86	Membership Organizations
	87	Engineering and Management Services
	88	Private Households
	89	Services, Not Elsewhere Classified
Public Administration	91	Executive, Legislative and General
	92	Justice, Public Order and Safety
	93	Finance, Taxation and Monetary Policy
	94	Administration of Human Resources
	95	Environmental Quality and Housing
	96	Administration of Economic Programs
	97	National Security and International Affairs

Table 2
NORTH AMERICAN INDUSTRY CLASSIFICATION SYSTEM (NAICS)

Industry Group	Industry Code	Description
Agriculture, Forestry, Fishing And Hunting	11	Raising crops and animals; hunting, fishing and harvesting timber.
Mining	21	Extracting coal, ore, petroleum and gases.
Utilities	22	Generating, transmitting, or distributing electricity, gas, steam, water and/or removing sewage.
Construction	23	Erecting buildings and other structures.
Manufacturing	31-33	Transforming raw material or existing products into new products.
Wholesale Trade	41-43	Selling or arranging the sale of capital or durable non-consumer goods.
Retail Trade	44-46	Selling merchandise to the general public.
Transportation And Warehousing	48-49	Transporting passengers and cargo; warehousing goods.
Information	51	Data processing and communications.
Finance And Insurance	52	Creating, liquidating, selling of financial assets.
Real Estate And Rental And Leasing	53	Selling, leasing, or renting of tangible or intangible assets and related services.
Professional, Scientific, And Technical Services	54	Performing of professional, scientific and technical services for other organizations.
Management Of Companies And Enterprise	55	Holding securities of companies and enterprises to gain controlling interest or in order to influence management decisions.
Administrative And Support And Waste Management And Remediation Services	56	Performing Routine support activities for the day-to-day operations of other organizations.
Educational Services	61	Providing instruction and training.
Health Care And Social Assistance	62	Providing health care and social assistance to individuals.
Arts, Entertainment, And Recreation	71	Providing services to meet the entertainment and recreation interests of their patrons.
Accommodation And Food Services	72	Lodging and/or preparing meals, snacks, beverages for customers.
Other Services (Except Public Administration)	81	Providing services not elsewhere specified -- including religious activities, making repairs, laundry, personal care, etc.
Public Administration	91-93	Administering, managing and overseeing public programs.

SIC-NAICS CROSS-REFERENCE TABLES

The following illustrative SIC-NAICS cross-reference tables demonstrate changes in industrial classification systems that will occur with the transition from SIC to NAICS. Some of the tables show little real change in industrial groupings, while others show some major changes. For the industry researcher or analyst, SIC:NAICS cross-reference tables will be important tools. Some industries' time series will be broken irreparably. However, for other industries, NAICS codes easily can be reclassified. Two-thirds of all 4-digit SICs will be derivable from the NAICS system -- either because the industry will not be changed, or because new and old industries are to be defined with similar structures.

SIC-NAICS CROSS REFERENCE TABLES

TABLE 3	HEAVY CONSTRUCTION CONTRACTORS
TABLE 4	PRIMARY METAL INDUSTRIES (STEEL)
TABLE 5	INSTRUMENTS AND RELATED PRODUCTS
TABLE 6	MOTOR FREIGHT TRANSPORTATION AND WAREHOUSING
TABLE 7	AUTOMOTIVE REPAIR, SERVICES AND PARKING
TABLE 8	FOOD AND KINDRED PRODUCTS (EXCERPT)
TABLE 9	TEXTILE MILL PRODUCTS (EXCERPT)
TABLE 10	RUBBER AND MISCELLANEOUS PLASTICS PRODUCTS (EXCERPT)
TABLE 11	INDUSTRIAL MACHINERY AND EQUIPMENT

Explaination of symbols used in these tables:

pt = "part of" indicates that the NAICS industrial grouping is a combination of former SIC industries.

@ = No cross NAICS code available due to significant reclassification of this industry.

Table 3
HEAVY CONSTRUCTION CONTRACTORS

CODE	SIC DESCRIPTION	CODE	NAICS DESCRIPTION
1611	Highway and Street Construction	23411	Highway and Street Construction (pt)
1622	Bridge, Tunnel, and Elevated Highway	23412	Bridge and Tunnel Construction (pt)
1623	Water, Sewer, Pipeline, and Communications	23491	Water, Sewer, Pipeline Construction, Water, Sewer and Pipelines
	Power and Communication Transmission	23492	Power and Communication Transmission Line Construction (pt)
1629	Heavy Construction, NEC Industrial Nonbuilding Structures Nonbuilding Structures Except Industrial	23493	Industrial Nonbuilding Structure Construction (pt)
		23499	All Other Heavy Construction (pt)

Table 4
PRIMARY METAL INDUSTRIES (STEEL)

CODE	SIC DESCRIPTION	CODE	NAICS DESCRIPTION
3312@	Steel Works, Blast Furnaces (Including Coke Ovens, not Integrated With Steel) Hot Rolled Steel Manufacturing (pt)	324199	All Other Petroleum and Coal Pdcts.
	Except Coke Ovens Not Integrated with	331221	Rolled Steel Shape Manufacturing (pt)
		331111	Iron and Steel Mills (pt)
3313	Electrometallurgical Products, Except Steel Manufacturing	331112	Electrometallurgical Ferroalloy Products
3315@	Steel Wiredrawing and Steel Nails and Spikes	331222	Steel Wire Drawing
	Nails, Spikes, Paper Clips, and Wire	332618	Other Fabricated Wire Product Manufacturing (pt)
3316	Cold-Rolled Steel Sheet, Strip, and Bars	331221	Rolled Steel Shape Manufacturing (pt)
3317	Steel Pipe and Tubes	33121	Iron and Steel Pipe and Tube Manufacturing from Purchased Steel
3321	Gray and Ductile Iron Foundries	331511	Iron Foundries (pt)
3322	Malleable Iron Foundries	331511	Iron Foundries (pt)
3324	Steel Investment Foundries	331512	Steel Investment Foundries
3325	Steel Foundries, NEC	331513	Steel Foundries (except castings)

Table 5
INSTRUMENTS AND RELATED PRODUCTS

CODE	SIC DESCRIPTION	CODE	NAICS DESCRIPTION
3812	Search, Detection, Navigation, Guidance, Aeronautical, and Nautical Systems and System and Instrument Manufacturing	334511	Search, Detection, Navigation, Guidance, Aeronautical, and Nautical
3821	Laboratory Apparatus and Furniture	339111	Laboratory Apparatus and Furniture Manufacturing (pt)
3822	Automatic Controls for Regulating Residential and Commercial Environments and Appliances	334512	Automatic Environmental Control Manufacturing for Residential, Commercial, and Appliance Use
3823	Industrial Instruments for Measurement, Display, and Control of Process Variables;	334513	Instruments and Related Products Manufacturing for Measuring, Displaying, and Controlling Industrial Process Variables
3824	Totalizing Fluid Meters and Counting Device	334514	Totalizing Fluid Meter and Counting Device Manufacturing (pt)
3825	Instruments for Measuring and Testing of Automotive Ampmeters and Voltmeters Except Automotive Ammeters and Voltmeters	334514	Totalizing Fluid Meter and Counting Device Manufacturing (pt)
		334515	Instrument Manufacturing for Measuring and Testing Electricity and Electrical Signals
3826	Laboratory Analytical Instruments	334516	Analytical Laboratory Instrument Manufacturing
3827	Optical Instruments and Lenses	333314	Optical Instrument and Lens Manufacturing
3829	Measuring and Controlling Devices, NEC Motor Vehicle Gauges Medical Thermometers Electronic Chronometers Except Medical Thermometers	334514	Totalizing Fluid Meter and Counting Device Manufacturing (pt)
		339112	Surgical and Medical Instrument Manufacturing (pt)
		334518	Watch, Clock, and Part Manufacturing
		334519	Other Measuring and Controlling Device Manufacturing
3841	Surgical and Medical Instruments and Tranquilizer Guns Operating Tables	332994	Small Arms Manufacturing (pt)
		339111	Laboratory Apparatus and Except Tranquilizer Guns and Operating Furniture Manufacturing (pt)
		339112	Surgical and Medical Instrument Manufacturing (pt)
		322291	Sanitary Paper Product Manufacturing (pt)
	Orthopedic, Prosthetic, and Surgical	339113	Surgical Appliance and Supplies Manufacturing
		334510	Electromedical and Electrotherapeutic Apparatus Manufacturing (pt)
(Continued)			

CODE	SIC DESCRIPTION	CODE	NAICS DESCRIPTION
3843	Dental Equipment and Supplies	339114	Dental Equipment and Supplies Manufacturing
3844	X-Ray Apparatus and Tubes and Related	334517	Irradiation Apparatus Manufacturing (pt)
3845	Electromedical and Electrotherapeutic CT and CAT Scanners Other Electromedical	334517	Irradiation Apparatus Manufacturing (pt)
		334510	Electromedical and Electrotherapeutic Apparatus Manufacturing (pt)
3851	Ophthalmic Goods Intra Ocular Lenses Except Intra Ocular Lenses	339113	Surgical Appliance and Supplies Manufacturing (pt)
		339115	Ophthalmic Goods Manufacturing (pt)
3861	Photographic Equipment and Supplies Photographic Film, Paper, Plates and Manufacturing	333315	Photographic and Photocopying
		325992	Photographic Film, Paper, Plate, and Chemical Manufacturing
3873	Watches, Clocks, Clockwork Operated Devices	334518	Watch, Clock, and Part Manufacturing (pt)

Table 6
MOTOR FREIGHT TRANSPORTATION AND WAREHOUSING

CODE	SIC DESCRIPTION	CODE	NAICS DESCRIPTION
4212@	Local Trucking Without Storage		
	Solid Waste Collection Without Disposal	562111	Solid Waste Collection
	Hazardous Waste Collection Without Disposal	562112	Hazardous Waste Collection
	Other Waste Collection Without Disposal	562119	Other Waste Collection
	Local General Freight Trucking	48411	General Freight Trucking, Local
	Household Goods Moving Without Storage	48421	Used Household andOffice Moving
	Local Specialized Freight Trucking		
		48422	Specialized Freight Trucking, Local (pt)
4213@	Trucking, Except Local		
	Long-distance Truckload General Freight	484121	General Freight Trucking, Long
	Long-distance Less Than Truckload General		Distance Less Than Truckload
	Long-distance Specialized Freight	484122	General Freight Trucking, Local
		48421	Used Household and Ofice Moving
		48423	Specialized Freight Trucking, Long-Distance
4214@	Local Trucking with Storage		
	Local General Freight Trucking	48411	General Freight Trucking, Local
	Local Household Goods Moving		
	Local Specialized Freight Trucking	48421	Used Household and Office Goods Moving
	Local Specialized Freight Trucking		
		48422	Specialized Freight rucking, Local (pt)
4215@	Courier Services Except by Air		
	Hub and Spoke Intercity Delivery	49211	Couriers (pt)
	Local Delivery	49221	Local Messengers and Local Delivery
4221	Farm Product Warehousing and Storage	49313	Farm Product Warehousing and Storage
4222	Refrigerated Warehousing and Storage	49312	Refrigerated Warehousing
4225	General Warehousing and Storage	49311	General Warehousing and Storage
	Miniwarehouses and Self-Storage Units		
		53113	Leasors of Miniwarehouses and Self- Storage Units
4226	Special Warehousing and Storage, NEC		
	Fur Storage	49312	Refrigerated Warehousing
	General Warehousing in Foreign Trade	49311	General Warehousing
	Other	49319	Other Warehousing and Storage
4231@	Terminal and Joint Terminal Maintenance	48849	Other Support Activities for Road Transportation (pt)

Table 7
AUTOMOTIVE REPAIR, SERVICES AND PARKING

CODE	SIC DESCRIPTION	CODE	NAICS DESCRIPTION
7513	Truck Rental and Leasing, Without Drivers	53212	Truck, Utility Trailer, and RV (Recreational Vehicle) Rental and Leasing (pt)
7514	Passenger Car Rental	532111	Passenger Car Rental
7515	Passenger Car Leasing	532112	Passenger Car Leasing
7519	Utility Trailer and Recreational Vehicle	53212	Truck, Utility Trailer, and RV (Recreational Rental Vehicle) Rental and Leasing (pt)
7521	Automobile Parking	81293	Parking Lots and Garages (pt)
7532	Top, Body, and Upholstery Repair Shops	811121	Automotive Body, Paint, and Interior Repair and Maintenance
7533	Auto Exhaust System Repair Shops	811112	Automotive Exhaust System Repair
7534@	Tire Retreading and Repair Shops Retreading Repair	326212 811198	Tire Retreading All Other Automotive Repair and Maintenance (pt)
7536	Automotive Glass Replacement Shops	811122	Automotive Glass Replacement Shops (pt)
7537	Automotive Transmission Repair Shops	811113	Automotive Transmission Repair
7538	General Automotive Repair Shops	811111	General Automotive Repair
7539	Automotive Repair Shops, NEC	811118	Other Automotive Mechanical and Electrical Repair and Maintenance
7542	Car Washes	811192	Car Washes
7549@	Automotive Services, Except Repair and Automotive Window Tinting Lubricating Services, Automotive Towing	811122 811191	Auto Glass Replacement Shops (pt) Automotive Oil Change and Lubrication Shops
	Except Automotive Window Tinting	48841	Motor Vehicle Towing
		811198	All Other Automotive Repair and Maintenance (pt)

Table 8
FOOD AND KINDRED PRODUCTS (EXCERPT)

CODE	SIC DESCRIPTION	CODE	NAICS DESCRIPTION
2099	Food Preparations, NEC		
	Reducing Maple Sap to Maple Syrup	111998	All Other Misc. Crop
	Marshmallow Creme		Farming (pt)
		31134	Nonchocolate Confectionery
	Peanut Butter		Manufacturig (pt)
	Potatoes, Dried and Packaged	311911	Roasted Nuts and Peanut
			Butter Manufacturing (pt)
	Perishable Prepared Food		
	Rice, Uncooked and Packaged with		
	Ingredients	311423	Dried and Dehydrated
	Dry Pasta Packaged with Other		Food Mfg
	Tortillas		
		311991	Perishable Prepared Food Mfg
	Ingredients	311212	Rice Milling (pt)
	Tea	31183	Tortilla Manufacturing
	Vinegar, Prepared Dips Except Dairy	311823	Dry Pasta Manufacturing (pt)
	and Spices and Extracts		
	Other	31192	Coffee and Tea Mfg. (pt)
		311941	Mayonnaise, Dressing, and
			Other Prepared Sauce Mfg (pt)
		311942	Spice and Extract Mfg (pt)
		311999	All Other Miscellaneous Food
			Manufacturing (pt)

Table 9
TEXTILE MILL PRODUCTS (EXCERPT)

CODE	SIC DESCRIPTION	CODE	NAICS DESCRIPTION
2299@	Textile Goods, NEC		
	Broadwoven Fabric of Jute, Linen, Hemp,	31321	Broadwoven Fabric Mills (pt)
	Nonwoven Felt	31323	Nonwoven Fabric Mills (pt)
	Finishing Thread and Yarn of Flax, Hemp,	313312	Textile and Fabric Finishing
			except Narrow Woven Fabric
	Thread of Hemp, Linen, and Ramie	313221	Narrow Fabric Mills (pt)
	Yarn of Flax, Hemp, Jute, and Ramie	313113	Thread Mills (pt)
	Recovery and Processing of Fibers	313111	Yarn Spinning Mills (pt)
		314999	All Other Miscellaneous
			Textile Product Mills (pt)

Table 10
RUBBER AND MISCELLANEOUS PLASTICS PRODUCTS (EXCERPT)

CODE	SIC DESCRIPTION	CODE	NAICS DESCRIPTION
3069	Fabricated Rubber Products, NEC		
	Rubberizing Fabric or Purchased Textile	31332	Fabric Coating Mills (pt)
	Rubber Pants and Raincoats	315299	All Other Cut and Sew Apparel Manufacturing (pt)
	Rubber Bibs, Aprons, and Bathing Caps		
	Rubber Gloves and Life Jackets	315999	Other Apparel Accessories and Other Apparel (pt)
	Rubber Wet Suits		
	Rubber Toys, Except Dolls	339113	Surgical Appliance and Supplies Manufacturing (pt)
	Rubber Resilient Floor Covering		
	Other	33992	Sporting and Athletic Goods Manufacturing (pt)
		339932	Game, Toy, and Children's Vehicle Manufacturing (pt)
		326192	Resilient Floor Covering Mfg (pt)
		326299	All Other Rubber Product Mfg

Table 11
INDUSTRIAL MACHINERY AND EQUIPMENT

CODE	SIC DESCRIPTION	CODE	NAICS DESCRIPTION
3599	Industrial and Commercial Machinery		
	Gasoline, Oil and Intake Filters	336399	All Other Motor Vehicle Parts Manufacturing (pt)
	Flexible Metal Hose		
	Carnival Amusement Park Equipment	332999	Other Misc. Fabricated Metal Product Manufacturing (pt)
	Machine Shops		
	Other Industrial and Commercial	333319	Other Commercial and Service Machinery Manufacturing (pt)
	Industry Machinery	33271	Machine Shops
		333999	Other Misc. General Purpose Machinery Manufacturing (pt)

Bibliography

Akerlof, G.A., W. T. Dickens, and G. L. Perry. The Macroeconomics of Low Inflation. *Brookings Papers on Economic Activity*. Washington D.C.: Brookings Institution. 1996. pp. 1–76

Alexander, D. L. An Empirical Test of the Mutual Forebearance Hypothesis: The Case of Bank Holding Companies. *Southern Economic Journal*. Volume 52, #1. July 1985. pp. 122–140.

Allio, R. J.and M. W. Pennington, eds. *Corporate Planning: Techniques and Applications*. New York: AMACOM. 1979

Ansoff, H. I. *Corporate Strategy*. New York: Wiley. 1965.

———*The New Corporate Strategy*. New York: Wiley. 1988.

Arguea, N. M. Estimating Consumer Preferences Using Market Data—An Application to U.S. Automobile Demand. *Journal of Applied Econometrics*. Volume 9, #1. January—March 1994. pp. 1–18.

Armstrong, J. S. Forecasting with Econometrics Methods: Folklore Versus Fact. *Journal of Business*. Volume 51, #4. 1978. pp. 549–564.

Armstrong, J. S. and M. C. Grohman. A Comparative Study of Methods for Long-Range Market Forecasting. *Management Science*. Volume 19, #2. October 1972. pp. 211–221.

Artis, M. J. How Accurate Is the World Economic Outlook? A Post-Mortem on Short-Term Forecasting at the International Monetary Fund. Washington, D.C.: *International Monetary Fund*. 1988. pp. 1–49.

———How Accurate Are the IMF's Short-Term Forecasts? Another Examination of the World Economic Outlook. Washington, D.C.: *International Monetary Fund*. 1996.

Ayres, R. U. Technological Transformations and Long Waves. Part I. *Technological Forecasting and Social Change*. Volume 36, #1. 1990a. pp. 1–37.

———Technological Transformations and Long Waves. Part II. *Technological Fore-casting and Social Change*. Volume 36, #2. 1990b. pp. 111–137.

Bailey, M. N. and C. L. Schultz. The Productivity of Capital in a Period of Slower Growth: Comments and Discussion. *Brookings Papers on Economic Activity*. Washington D.C.: Brookings Institution. 1990. pp. 369–420.

Ball, R. Assessing Your Competitor's People and Organization. *Long Range Planning*, Volume 20, #2. April 1987. pp. 32–41.

Bass, F. M. A New Product Growth Model for Consumer Durables. *Management Science*. Volume 15. 1969. pp. 215–227.

Baum, J. A. C. and H. J. Korn. Competitive Dynamics of Infirm Rivalry. *Academy of Management Journal*. Volume 39, #2. April 1996. pp. 255–291.

Beckman, B. A. Reflections on BEA's Experience with Leading Economic Indicators. *Business Cycle Indicators*. May 1997. pp. 3–4.

Bersani, K. S. and L. M. Bilenski. Federal Budget Estimates, Fiscal Year 2000. *Survey of Current Business*. Volume 79, #3. March 1999. pp. 12–21.

Bezold, C. Health Care in the U.S.—Four Alternative Futures. *Futurist*. Volume 16, #4. August 1982. pp. 14–18.

Blackman, A. W. The Market Dynamics of Technological Substitutions. *Technological Forecasting and Social Change*. Volume 6, #1. 1974.

Blackman, A. W., E. J. Seligman, and G. C. Sogliero. An Innovation Index Based on Factor Analysis. *Technological Forecasting and Social Change*. Volume 4, #3. 1973.

Blanchard, K. and T. Waghorn. *Mission Possible*. New York: McGraw Hill. 1997.

Blin, J. M., E. A. Stohr, and B. Bagamery. Input-Output Techniques in Forecasting. *TIMS Studies in the Management Sciences*. S. Makridakis and S. C. Wheelwright, eds. Amsterdam: North Holland Publishing. 1979.

Bonini, C .P. and J. R. Freeland. Forecasting by Smoothed Regression. In *TIMS Studies in the Management Science*. S. Makridakis and S.C. Wheelwright, eds. Amsterdam: North Holland Publishing. 1979.

Bonoma, T. V. and B. P. Shapiro. *Industrial Market Segmentation: A Nested Approach*. Marketing Science Institute. 1983.

Bopp, A. E. Comparisons of Recent Growth in Actual Demand, Planned Demand, and Planned Generating Capacity at U.S. Electric Utilities. *Public Utilities Fortnightly*. Volume 132, #22. December 1, 1994. pp. 26–27.

The Boston Consulting Group. *Perspectives on Experience*. Boston: The Boston Consulting Group. 1968.

Bosworth, B. The Decline in Saving: Evidence from Household Surveys; Comments and Discussion. *Brookings Papers on Economic Activity*. Washington D.C.: Brookings Institution. 1991. pp. 183–256.

Boulton, W. R., W. M. Lindsay, S. G. Franklin, and L. W. Rue. Strategic Planning: Determining the Impact of Environmental Characteristics and Uncertainty. *Academy of Management Journal*. Volume 25, #3. 1982. pp. 500–509.

Bourgeois, L. J. Strategy and Environment: A Conceptual Integration. *Academy of Management Review*. Volume 5, #1. 1980. pp. 25–39.

———Strategic Goals: Perceived Uncertainty, and Economic Performance in Volatile Environments. *Academy of Management Journal*. Volume 28, #3. September 1985. pp. 548–573.

Box, G.E.P. and G. M. Jenkins. Some Statistical Aspects of Adaptive Opitization and Control. *Journal of the Royal Statistical Society*. 1962. pp. 297–343.

Bradley, D. G. Managing Against Expropriation. *Harvard Business Review*. Volume 55, #4. July–August 1977. pp. 75–83.

Brock, J. J. Competitor Analysis: Some Practical Approaches. *Industrial Marketing Management*. Volume 13, #4. October 1984. pp. 225–231.

Brock, T. C. Communicator—Recipient Similarity and Decision Change. *Journal of Personality and Social Psychology*. June 1965. pp. 650–654.

Buhler, K. Geodesy and Geometry. *Gauss: A Biographical Study*. Chapter 9. Berlin: Springer–Verlag. 1981.

Bureau of Labor Statistics, U.S. Department of Labor. *Monthly Labor Review*. November 1995.

Business Week. Business Sharpens Its Spying Techniques. *Business Week*. August 4, 1975. pp. 60–63.

Buzzell, R. D. and B. T. Gale. *The PIMS Principles: Linking Strategy to Performance*. New York: The Free Press. 1987.

Capon, N. and J. M. Hulbert. The Integration of Forecasting and Strategic Planning. *The International Journal of Forecasting*. Volume 1, #2. 1985. pp. 123–133.

Capon, N., J. U. Farley, and J. M. Hulbert. *Corporate Strategic Planning*. New York: Columbia University Press. 1987.

Cardozo, R. N. Segmenting the Industrial Market. *Marketing and the New Science of Planning*. R. L. King, ed. Chicago: American Marketing Association. 1968. pp. 433–440.

Carnegie Task Force on Meeting the Needs of Young Children. *Starting Points: Meeting the Needs of Our Youngest Children: The Report of the Carnegie Task Force on Meeting the Needs of Young Children*. New York: Carnegie Corporation. 1994. (Abridged version).

Casper, L. M., M. Hawkins, and M. O'Connel. *Who's Minding the Kids?* U.S. Department of Commerce: Economics and Statistics Administration. Fall 1991.

Cetron, M. and O. Davies. *Crystal Globe: The Haves and Have-Nots of the New World Order*. New York: St. Martin's Press. 1991.

Chambers, J. C., S. Mullick, and D. Smith. How to Choose the Right Forecasting Technique. *Harvard Business Review*. July–August 1971. pp. 45–74.

Chambers, M. J. Forecasting with Demand Systems: A Comparative Study. *Journal of Econometrics*. Volume 44, #3. June 1990. pp. 363–376.

Chen, M. and D. Miller. Competitive Attack. Retaliation and Performance. *Strategic Management Journal*. Volume 15, #2. Feburary 1994. pp. 85–102.

Chow, G. C. Technological Change and the Demand for Computers. *American Economic Review*. 1967. p. 57.

Christ, C.F. Judging The Performance of Econometric Models of the U.S. Economy. *International Economic Review*. 1975. pp. 54–76.

Chun, S. K. Commercial Aircraft Production: Jockeying for Position. *Business Korea*. Volume 11, #7. January 1994. pp. 38–40.

Clark, K. A Near-Perfect Tool for Economic Forecasting. *Fortune*. Volume 134, #2. July 22, 1996. pp. 16–17.

Clements, M. and D. F. Hendry. Macro-Economic Forecasting and Modeling. *The Economic Journal*. July 1995. pp. 1001–1013.

Clouser, E. R. How The Delphi Panel Prognosticates the Future. *Risk Management*. Volume 33, #9. September 1986. pp. 30–41.

Collis, D. J. How Valuable Are Organizational Capabilities? *Strategic Management Journal*. 1994. pp. 143–152.

Conference Board, The. The Cyclical Indicator Approach. *Business Cycle Indicators*. March 1997a. p. 2.

———Predicting Growth with the Leading Indicators: The Composite Versus the Diffusion Index. *Business Cycle Indicators*. March 1997b. pp. 3–4.

—————— *Consumer Confidence Index* (Series #122). www.crc-conquest.org. Monthly
—————— *Business Cycle Indicators.* Volume 4, #7. July 1999.

Cooley, J. R., D. W. Jackson, and L. R. Ostrom. Analyzing the Relative Power of Participants in Industrial Buying Decisions. *Contemporary Marketing Thought: 1977 Educators' Proceedings.* B. A. Greenberg and D. N. Bellenger, eds. Chicago: American Marketing Association. 1977. pp. 243–246.

Council of Economic Advisors. *Economic Report of the President.* U.S. Government Printing Office. Washington, D.C. 1999.

Cripps, J. D. Heuristics and Biases in Timing the Replacement of Durable Products. *Journal of Consumer Research.* Volume 21, #2. September 1994. pp. 304–318.

Crock. S., J. W. Smith, R. A. Melcher, and L. Himelstein. They Snoop to Conquer. *Business Week.* October 28, 1996. pp. 172–176.

Cutler, D. M., J. M. Porterba, L. M. Sheiner, and L. H. Summers. An Aging Society: Opportunity or Challenge, Comments and Discussion. *Brookings Papers on Economic Activity.* Washington D.C.: Brookings Instituion. 1990. pp. 1–73.

Cyert, R. M. and J. G. March. *A Behavioral Theory of the Firm.* Englewood Cliffs, NJ: Prentice-Hall, Inc. 1963.

Daft, R. L., J. Sormunen, and D. Parks. Chief Executive Scanning, Environmental Characteristics, and Company Performance: An Empirical Study. *Strategic Management Journal* (UK). Volume 9, #2. March–April 1988. pp. 123–139.

Dalkey, N. *The Delphi Method: An Experimental Study of Group Reaction.* Rand Memorandum RM-58888-PR. Santa Monica, CA: Rand Corporation. September. 1964.

Daly, M. The "Shrinking" Middle Class. *FRBSF Economic Letter.* March 7, 1997.

Datta, Y. Market Segmentation: An Integrated Framework. *Long Range Planning.* Volume 29, #6. December 1996. pp. 797–811.

D'Aveni, R. *Hypercompetition.* New York: Free Press. 1994.

De Carmoy, G. Energy Forecasting. *The Handbook of Forecasting: A Manager's Guide.* Chapter 21. S. Makridakis and S.C. Wheelwright, eds. New York: Wiley. 1982.

De Geus, A. Planning as Learning. *Harvard Business Review.* Volume 66, #2. 1988. pp. 70–74.

De Masi, P. The Difficult Art of Economic Forecasting. *Finance & Development.* Volume 33, #4. December 1996. pp. 29–31.

Denning, B. W. and M. E. Lehr. The Extent and Nature of Corporate Long Range Planning in the United Kingdom. *Journal of Management Studies.* Volume 8, #2. May 1971. pp. 145–161.

Dertouzos, M. What Will Be: How the New World of Information Will Change Our Lives. Chicago, IL: HarperCollins Publishers. 1997.

Dess, G. G. Consensus on Strategy Formulation and Organizational Performance: Competitors in a Fragmented Industry. *Strategic Management Journal.* Volume 8, #3. May–June 1987. pp. 259–277.

Desta, A. Assessing Political Risk in Less Developed Countries. *The Journal of Business Strategy.* Volume 5, #4. Spring 1985. pp. 40–53.

Dickson, P. R. and A. G. Sawyer. The Price Knowledge and Search of Supermarket Shoppers. *Journal of Marketing.* Volume 54, #3. July 1990. pp. 42–53.

Diffenbach, J. Corporate Environmental Analysis in Large U.S. Corporations. *Long Range Planning.* Volume 16, #3. June 1983. pp. 23–30.

Drucker, P. F. *The Age of Discontinuity.* New York: Harper & Row. 1969.

Duncan, R. B. Characteristics of Organizational Environments and Perceived Environmental Uncertainty. *Administrative Science Quarterly.* Volume 17, #3. September 1972. pp. 313–327.

Dunkelberg, W. C. Small Business Economic Trends—February 1996. *Small Business Economic Trends*. 1996. pp. 1–21.

Dunn, M. and W. Hillison. The Delphi Technique—Adapted for the Management Accountant. *Cost and Management*. Volume 54, #3. May–June 1980. pp. 32–37.

Economic Report of the President. Washington, D.C.: United States Government Printing Office. 1997.

The Economist Intelligence Unit 1997 World Model Productions Forecasts. London. *The Economist*. 1998.

Edmunds, S. W. Which Way America? Six Scenarios for the Future of the United States. *The Futurist*. Volume 13, #1. February 1979. pp. 5–12.

———The Role of Futures Studies in Business Strategic Planning. *The Journal of Business Strategy*. Volume 3, #2. Fall 1982. pp. 40–46.

Ellis, D. F. Consensus Forecasts of Financial Institutions. *Journal of Business Forecasting Methods & Systems*. Volume 15, #3. Fall 1997. pp. 34–37.

Estrella, A. and F. S. Mishkin. Predicting U.S. Recessions: Financial Variables as Leading Indicators. *The Review of Economics and Statistics*. Volume 80, #1. February 1998. pp. 295–306.

Ettorre, B. Managing Competitive Intelligence. *Management Review*. Volume 84, #10. 1995. pp. 15–19.

Evans, F. B. Selling as a Dyadic Relationship—A New Approach. *The American Behavioral Scientist*. May 1963. pp. 76–79.

Fahey, L. Application in Strategic Management: Identifying Potential New Industry Entrants. *Strategic Planning Management*. July–August 1984. pp. 6–7.

———Integrating Macroenvironmental Analysis into Strategy Analysis: Some Problems. *Strategic Planning Management*. June 1985. pp. 1–3.

Fahey, L. and W. R. King. Environmental Scanning for Corporate Planning. *Business Horizons*. Volume 20, #4. August 1977. pp. 61–71.

Fahey, L., W. R. King, and V. Narayanan. Environmental Scanning and Forecasting in Strategic Planning: The State of The Art. *Long Range Planning*. Volume 14, #1. February 1981. pp. 32–39.

Fifer, R. M. Understanding Competitors through Financial Analysis. *Strategic Planning Management*. October 1984a.

———Understanding Your Competitors' Personality. *Strategic Planning Management*. December 1984b.

———Understanding Your Competitors' Functional Strategies. *Strategic Planning Management*. February 1985.

Fildes, R. Quantitative Forecasting—The State of the Art: Extrapolative Models. *Journal of the Operational Research Society*. 1979. pp. 691–710.

———Forecasting: The Issues. *The Handbook of Forecasting: A Manager's Guide*. Chapter 7. S. Makridakis and S. C. Wheelwright, eds. New York: Wiley. 1982.

Fildes, R. and S. Howell. On Selecting a Forecasting Model. *TIMS Studies in the Management Sciences*. S. Makridakis and S. C. Wheelwright, eds. Amsterdam: North-Holland. 1979.

Fisher, J. C. and R. H. Pry. A Simple Substitution Model of Technological Change. *Technological Forecasting and Social Change*. 1971. pp. 75–88.

Foster, R. *Innovations: The Attacker's Advantage*. New York: Macmillan. 1986.

Fourt, L. A. and J. W. Woodlock. Early Prediction of Market Success for New Grocery Products. *Journal of Marketing*. Volume 25. 1960. pp. 31–38.

Franses, P. H. Fitting a Gompertz Curve. *Journal of Operational Research*. Volume 45, #1. 1994. pp. 109–113.

Friedman, J. A. A Conceptual Model for the Analysis of Planning Behavior. *Administrative Science Quarterly.* September 1967. pp. 225–252.

Friedman, Y. and E. Segev. Horizons for Strategic Planning. *Long Range Planning.* October 1976. pp. 84–89.

Fuld, L. A Recipe for Business Intelligence Success. *The Journal of Business Strategy.* Volume 12, #1. January–February 1991. pp. 12–17.

Gadel, M. S. Concentration by Salesmen on Congenial Prospects. *Journal of Marketing.* April 1964. pp. 64–66.

Gause, G. F. Experimental Studies on the Struggle for Existence. *Journal of Experimental Biology.* Volume 9. 1932. p. 389.

Gauss, C. F. Disquisitiones Generales Circa Superficies Curvas. *Carl Friedric Gauss' Werke, Volume IV.* 1828. pp. 344–345.

Gelb, B. D. M. J. Saxton, G. M. Zinkhan, and N. D. Albers. Competitive Intelligence: Insights from Executives. *Business Horizons.* January–February Volume 34, #1. 1991. pp. 43–47.

Gilad, B. and T. Gilad. Strategic Planning: Improving the Input. *Managerial Planning.* Volume 33, #6. May–June 1985. pp. 10–13, 17.

Gilad, B., G. Gordan, and E. Sudit. Identifying the Gaps and Blind Spots in Competitive Intelligence. *Long Range Planning.* Volume 26, #6. December 1993. pp. 107–113.

Gimeno, J. Reciprocal Threats in Multimarket Rivalry: Staking Out Spheres of Influence in the U.S. Airline Industry. Paper presented at the Academy of Management Annual Meeting. Boston. 1997.

Ginter, P. M. and W. J. Duncan. Macroenvironmental Analysis for Strategic Management. *Long Range Planning.* Volume 23, #6. December 1990. pp. 91–100.

Godiwalla, Y. M., W. A. Meinhart, and W. D. Warde. Environmental Scanning—Does It Help the Chief Executive. *Long Range Planning.* Volume 13, #5. October 1980. pp. 87–99.

Gompertz, B. A Sketch on an Analysis and the Notation Applicable to the Estimation of the Value of Life Contingencies. *Philosophical Transactions of the Royal Society of London.* Volume 110. 1820. pp. 214–294.

———On the Nature of the Function Expressive of the Law of Human Mortality and on a New Mode of Determining Life Contingencies. *Philospophical Transactions of the Roal Society of London.* 1825. pp. 513–585.

———On One Uniform Law of Mortality from Birth to Extreme Old Age, and on the Law of Sickness. *Journal of the Institute of Actuaries.* 1872. pp. 329–344.

Gordon, R. J. The Time-Varying NAIRU and its Implications for Economic Policy. *NBER Working Paper.* #5735. August 1996.

Grant, J. H. and W. R. King. Techniques for Environmental Assessment. *The Logic of Strategic Planning.* Chapter 10. Boston: Little Brown and Company. 1982.

Gross, C. W. and R. T. Peterson. *Business Forecasting.* Boston: Houghton Mifflin Company. 1979.

Guide to Economic Forecasts. *Industrial Relations Review and Report.* May 1994. pp. 8–11.

Haley, R. I. Benefit Segmentation: A Decision-Oriented Research Tool. *Journal of Marketing.* July 1968. pp. 303–315.

Hambrick, D. C. An Empirical Typology of Mature Industrial-Product Environments. *Academy of Management Journal.* Volume 26, #4. June 1983. pp. 213–220.

Hambrick, D. C. and D. Lei. Toward Empirical Prioritization of Contingency Variables for Business Strategy. *Academy of Management Journal.* Volume 28, #4. December 1985. pp. 763–788.

Hambrick, D. C., I. C. MacMillan, and D. L. Day. Strategic Attributes and Performance in the BCG Matrix—A PIMS Based Analysis of Industrial Product Businesses. *Academy of Management Journal*. Volume 25, #3. September 1982. pp. 510–531.

Hamel, G. and C. K. Prahalad. *Competing for the Future: Breakthrough Strategies for Seizing Control of Your Industry and Creating Markets for Tomorrow*. Boston: Harvard Business School Press. 1994.

Handy, C. *The Age of Paradox*. Boston: Harvard Business School Press. 1994.

Harrigan, K. R. *Strategies for Declining Businesses*. Lexington, MA: Heath. 1980.

Hedley, B. Fundamental Approach to Strategy Development. *Long Range Planning*. Volume 9, #6. December 1976. pp. 2–11.

———Strategy and the "Business Porfolio." *Long Range Planning*. Volume 10, #1. February 1977. pp. 9–15.

Helmer, O. Problems in Futures Research—Delphi and Causal Cross-Impact Analysis. *Futures*. Volume 9, #1. 1977. p. 71.

———The Utility of Long-Term Forecasting. *Studies in Management Sciences: Forecasting*. S. Makridakis and S. C. Wheelwright, eds. Asterdam: North Holland Publishing. 1979.

Henderson, B. D *Henderson on Corporate Strategy*. New York: New American Library. 1982. pp. 54–60.

Hendry, D. F. The Econometrics of Macroeconomic Forecasting. *The Economic Journal*. September 1997. pp. 1330–1357.

Hendry, I. C. The Three-Parameter Approach to Long Range Forecasting. *Long Range Planning*. Volume 5, #1. March 1972. pp. 40–45.

Herring, J. P. The Role of Intelligence in Formulating Strategy. *Journal of Business Strategy*. Volume 13, #5. September–October 1992. pp. 54–60.

Hershey, R. Commercial Intelligence on a Shoestring. *Harvard Business Review*. Volume 58, #5. September–October 1980. pp. 22–30.

Heston, A. and R. Summers. International Price and Quantity Comparisons: Potentials and Pitfalls. *The American Economic Review*. Volume 86, #2. May 1996. pp. 20–24.

Hill, R. M., R. S. Alexander, and J. S. Cross. *Industrial Marketing*. 4th edition. Homewood, IL: Irwin. 1975.

Hofer, C. W. Conceptual Constructs for Formulating Corporate and Business Strategies. *Intercollegiate bibliography: 1977 New Cases in Administration*. J. Burleson, ed. Boston: Intercollegiate Case Clearing House. 1977.

Hofer, C. W. and D. Schendel. *Strategy Formulation: Analytical Concepts*. St. Paul, MN: West Publishing. 1978.

Hogarth, R. M. and S. Makridakis. Forecasting and Planning: An Evaluation. *Management Science*. Volume 27, #2. Feburary 1981. pp. 115–138 .

Horsky, D. and L. S. Simon. Advertising in a Model of New Product Diffusion. Presented at the TIMS/ORSA National Meeting. New York. 1978.

Hoyer, W. D. An Examination of Consumer Decision Making for a Common Repeat Purchase Product. *Journal of Consumer Research*. Volume 11, #3. December 1984. pp. 822–829.

Hymans, S. H. Consumer Durable Spending: Explanation and Prediction. *Brookings Papers on Economic Activity*. Washington, D.C.: Brookings Institution. 1970. pp. 173–206.

Ingenito, R. and B. Trehan. Using Monthly Data to Predict Quarterly Output. *FRBSF Economic Review*. 1996. pp. 3–11.

Isenman, A. W. Managing Suppliers: The Strategic Implications. *Strategic Planning Management.* December 1986. pp. 90–95.

Jacobe, D. The Earnings Squeeze of 1979 Could Make 1974–1975 Look Good. *Savings & Community Banker.* Volume 100, #3. March 1979. pp. 38–41.

Jain, S. C. Environmental Scanning in U.S. Corporations. *Long Range Planning.* Volume 17, #2. April 1984. pp. 117–128.

Javidan, M. The Impact of Environmental Uncertainty on Long-Range Planning Practices of the U.S. Savings and Loan Industry. *Strategic Management Journal.* Volume 5, #4. October–December 1984. pp. 381–392.

Jones, L. Competitor Cost Analysis at Caterpillar. *Management Accounting.* Volume 70, #4. October 1988. pp. 32–38.

Jordan, D. D. Emerging Trends in the U.S. Electric Utility Industry. *Executive Speeches.* October–November 1994. pp. 17–21.

Jorgenson, D. W. The Productivity of Capital in a Period of Slower Growth: Comments and Discussion. Brookings Papers on Economic Activity. M. N. Bailey and C. L. Schultz, eds. Washington D.C.: Brookings Instituion. 1990. pp. 369–420.

Jun, M. and R. T. Peterson. Medium and Long Range Forecasts Computer vs. Paint Industry. *Journal of Business Forecasting.* Volume 10, #2. Summer 1991. pp. 12–18.

Kahane, A. Scenarios for Energy: Sustainable World vs. Global Mercantilism. *Long Range Planning.* Volume 25, #4. August 1992. pp. 38–46.

Kahaner, L. *Competitive Intelligence: From Black Ops to Boardrooms: How Businesses Gather, Analyze, and Use Information to Succeed in the Global Marketplace.* New York: Simon & Schuster. 1996.

Kahn, H. and A. Wiener. *The Year 2000.* New York: Macmillan. 1967.

Kassler, P. Scenarios for World Energy: Barricades or New Frontiers? *Long Range Planning.* Volume 28, #6. December 1995. pp. 38–47.

Katona, G. *Psychological Analysis of Economic Behavior.* New York: McGraw Hill Book Company. 1951.

———*The Powerful Consumer: Psychological Studies of the American Economy.* New York: McGraw-Hill Book Company. 1960.

———*Psychological economics.* New York: Elsevier Scientific Publishing. Co. 1975.

Kaufmann, R. K. A Model of the World Oil Market for Project LINK: Integrating Economics, Geology and Politics. *Economic Modeling.* Volume 12, #2. April 1995. pp. 165–178.

Keats, B. and M. A. Hitt. A Causal Model of Linkages among Environmental Dimensions, Macro-Organizational Characteristics and Performance. *Academy of Management Journal.* Volume 31, #3. September 1988. pp. 570–598.

Kiechel, W. Corporate Strategists Under Fire. *Fortune.* Volume 106, #13. December 27, 1982. pp. 34–39.

King, W. R. Strategic Issue Management. *Strategic Planning and Management Handbook.* W. R. King and D. I. Cleland, eds. New York: Van Nostrand Reinhold. 1987. pp. 252–264.

King, W. R. and D. I. Cleland. Environmental Information Systems for Strategic Marketing Planning. *Journal of Marketing.* October 1974. pp. 35–40.

Kiplinger's Washington Letter staff. *The New American Boom.* Washington, D.C: Kiplinger. 1986.

Klein, H. E. *Incorporating Environmental Examination into the Corporate Strategic Planning Process.* Doctoral Dissertation. Columbia University. 1973.

————The Role of Environmental Forecasting/Assessment in Formal Corporate Planning Processes. Paper delivered at the Third International Symposium on Forecasting. Philadelphia. 1983.

Klein, H. E. and R. E. Linneman. The Use of Scenarios in Corporate Planning—Eight Case Histories. *Long Range Planning*. Volume 14, #5. October 1981. pp. 69–77.

————Environmental Assessment: An International Study of Corporate Practice. *Journal of Business Strategy*. Volume 5, #1. Summer 1984. pp. 66–75.

Knott, D. Four Scenarios for U.K. Oil in 2010. *Oil & Gas Journal*. Volume 93, #26. June 26, 1995. p. 27.

Kondratiev, N. *The Long Wave Cycle*. New York: Richardson and Snyder. 1926. Translated by Guy Daniels.

————The Long Wave in Economic Life. *Review of Economics Statistics*. Volume 17. 1935. pp. 105–115.

Kudla, R. J. The Components of Strategic Planning. *Long Range Planning*. Volume 11, #6. December 1978. pp. 48–52.

Kukalis, S. Determinants of Strategic Planning Systems in Large Organizations: A Contingency Approach. *Journal of Management Studies*. Volume 28, #2. March 1991. pp. 143–160.

Kuznets, S. Retardation of Industrial Growth. *Journal of Economic & Business History*. August 1929. pp. 534–560.

Lackman, C. L. Gompertz Curve Forecasting: A New Product Application. *Journal of the Market Research Society*. Volume 20, #1. January 1978. pp. 45–47.

Laczniak, G. R. Towards 2000: A Tougher Future for Australian Business? *Asia Pacific Journal of Management*. Volume 11, #1. April 1994. pp. 67–90.

Lakhani, H. Diffusion of Environment-Saving Technological Change: A Petroleum Refining Case Study. *Technological Substitution: Forecasting Techniques and Applications*. H. A. Linstone and D. Sahal, eds. New York: American Elsevier. 1976. pp. 197–220.

Landefeld, J. S. and R. P. Parker. Preview of the Comprehensive Revision of the National Income and Product Accounts: BEA's New Featured Measures of Output and Prices. *Survey of Current Business*. Volume 75, #7. July 1995. pp. 31–38.

————BEA's Chain Indexes. Time Series and Measures of Long-Term Economic Growth. *Survey of Current Business*. May 1997. pp. 58–68.

Lebel, D. and O. J. Krasner. Selecting Environmental Forecasting Techniques from Business Planning Requirements. *Academy of Management Review*. Volume 2, #3. July 1977. pp. 373–383.

Leidecker, J. K. and A. V. Bruno. Identifying and Using Critical Success Factors. *Long Range Planning*. Volume 17, #1. Feburary 1984. pp. 23–32.

————Critical Success Factor Analysis and the Strategy Development Process. *Strategic planning and Management Handbook*. W. R. King and D. I. Cleland, eds. New York: Van Nostrand Reinhold. 1987.

Lenz, R. C. *Technological Forecasting*. 2nd ed. USAF Aeronautical System Division, Technical Report ASD–TDR–62–414. June 1962.

Lev, B. Industry Averages as Targets for Financial Ratios. *Journal of Accounting*. 1969. pp. 290–299.

Lewandowski, R. An Integrated Approach to Medium- and Long-Term Forecasting. *The Handbook of Forecasting: A Manager's Guide*. S. Makridakis and S. C. Wheelwright, eds. New York: Wiley. 1982.

Lindsey, W. M. and L. W. Rue *Environmental Complexity in Long Range Planning*. Oxford, OH: The Planning Executives Institute. 1976.

Linneman, R. E. and H. E. Klein. The Use of Multiple Scenarios by U.S. Industrial Companies. *Long Range Planning.* Volume 12, #1. February 1979. pp. 83–90.

———The Use of Multiple Scenarios by U.S. Industrial Companies: A Comparison Study, 1977–1981. *Long Range Planning.* Volume 16, #6. December 1983. pp. 94–101.

———Using Scenarios in Strategic Decision Making. *Business Horizons.* January– Volume 28, #1. Feburary 1985. pp. 64–74.

Linstone, H. A. and D. Sahal, eds. *Technological Substitution: Forecasting Techniques and Applications.* New York: American Elsevier. 1976.

Lotka, A. J. *Elements of Physical Biology.* Baltimore: Williams & Wilkins Co. 1925.

Lown, C. S. and R. W. Rich. Is There an Inflation Puzzle? *Economic Policy Review.* Volume 3, #4. December 1997. pp.51–69.

Lynch, M. E., S. J. Imada, and J. H. Bookbinder. The Future of Logistics in Canada: A Delphi-Based Forecast. *Logistics and Transportation Review.* Volume 30, #1. March 1994. pp. 95–112.

MacNulty, C.A.R. Scenario Development for Corporate Planning. *Futures.* Volume 9, #2. April 1977. pp. 128–138.

Mahajan, V. and E. Muller. Innovation Diffusion and New Product Growth Models in Marketing. *Journal of Marketing.* Volume 43, #4. Fall 1979. pp. 55–68.

Majani, B. and S. Makridakis. Can Recessions Be Predicted? *Long Range Planning.* Volume 10, #2. April 1977. pp. 31–40.

Makridakis, S. If We Cannot Forecast, How Can We Plan? *Long Range Planning.* Volume 14, #3. June 1981. pp. 10–20.

———*Forecasting, Planning, and Strategy for the 21st Century.* New York: Free Press. 1990.

Makridakis, S. and M. Hibon. Accuracy of Forecasting: An Empirical Investigation. *Journal of the Royal Statistical Society.* 1979. pp. 97–125.

Makridakis, S. and S. C. Wheelwright, eds. *TIMS Studies in Management Sciences: Forecasting.* Asterdam: North Holland Publishing. 1979.

Makridakis, S. and S. C. Wheelwright. Forecasting: Framework and Overview. *TIMS Studies in the Management Sciences.* S. Makridakis and S. C. Wheelwright, eds. Asterdam: North Holland Publishing. 1979a. pp. 1–15.

———Forecasting in the Future and the Future of Forecasting. *TIMS Studies in the Management Sciences.* Asterdam: North Holland Publishing. S. Makridakis and S. C. Wheelwright, eds. 1979b. pp. 329–352.

Makridakis, S. and S. C. Wheelright, eds. *The Handbook of Forecasting: A Manager's Guide.* New York: Wiley. 1982.

Malaska, P., M. Malmivirta, T. Meristo, and S.–O. Hansen. Scenarios in Europe— Who Uses Them and Why. *Long Range Planning.* Volume 17, #5. October 1984. pp. 45–49.

Mandel, M .J. The New Business Cycle. *Business Week.* Volume 32, #4. March 31, 1997. pp. 58–68.

Mandel, M. J. and P. Coy. Economic Trends. *Business Week.* June 23, 1997. p. 28.

Mangaliso, M .P. and R. A. Mir. Environmental Turbulence and Firm Responsiveness: Crisis or Opportunity? Paper presented at the Annual Meeting of the Academy of Management. Cincinnati. August 1996.

Mannering, F. Brand Loyalty and the Decline of American Automobile Firms: Comments and Discussion. *Brookings Papers on Economic Activity.* Washington, D. C.: Brookings Institution. 1991. pp. 67–114.

Mansfield, E. Technical Change and the Rate of Imitation. *Econometrica.* Volume 29. 1961. pp. 741–766.

————Long Waves and Technological Innovation. *American Economic Review*. Volume 73, #2. May 1983. pp. 141–145.

March, J. G. and H. A. Simon. *Organizations*. New York, NY: Wiley. 1958.

Marchetti, C. The Automobile in a System Context: The Past 80 Years and the Next 20 Years. *Technological Forecasting and Social Change*. Volume 23. 1983. pp. 3–23.

Martin, P. and J. Widgren. International Migration: A Global Challenge. *Population Bulletin*. Volume 51, #1. April 1996. pp. 2–48.

Martino, J. P. An Experiment with the Delphi Procedure for Long Range Forecasting. *IEEE Transactions on Engineering Management*. 1968. pp. 138–144.

————Forecasting by Analogy. *Technological Forecasting for Decision Making*. New York: American Elsevier Publishing. 1972. pp. 65–102.

————Growth Curves. *Technological Forecasting for Decision Making*. New York: American Elsevier Publishing. 1975. pp. 103–127.

————*Technological Forecasting for Decision Making*. New York: American Elsevier Publishing. *Co.*, 1983.

Mason, D. H. Scenario-Based Planning: Decision Model for the Learning Organization. *Planning Review*. Volume 22, #2. March–April 1994. pp. 6–11.

Mattey, J. Capacity Utilization and Structural Change. *FRBSF Economic Letter*. November 15, 1996.

Matthews, M. B. The Use of Scenario Generation for Examining Future Hospital Utilization. *Health Care Management Review*. Volume 8, #3. Summer 1983. pp. 57–60.

Mauri, A. J. and M. P. Michaels. Firm and Industry Effects within Strategic Management: An Empirical Eamination. 1998. pp. 211–219.

McGahan, A. M.. and M. E. Porter. How Much Does Industry Matter, Really? Working Paper of the Harvard Business School. Boston. 1997.

McGrane, J. M. Going On-Line for Planning and Competitive Intelligence. *Management Review*. Volume 76, #10. October 1987. pp. 55–56.

McLaughlin, R. L. Leading Indicators: A New Approach for Corporate Planning. *Business Economics*. Volume 6, #3. 1971. pp. 7–12.

————Forecasting Recessions. *The Handbook of Forecasting: A Manager's Guide*. S. Makridakis and S. C. Wheelwright, eds. New York: Wiley, 1982. pp.289-302.

Meade, N. The Use of Growth Curves in Forecasting Market Development—A Review and Appraisal. *Journal of Forecasting*. October–December 1984. pp. 429–451.

————Forecasting Using Growth Curves. *The Journal of the Operational Research Society*. Volume 36, #12. December 1985. pp. 1103–1115.

————Forecasting with Growth Curves: The Effect of Error Structure. *Journal of Forecasting*. Volume 7, #4. October–December 1988. pp. 235–244.

Mercer, D. Simpler Scenarios. *Management Decision*. Volume 33, #4. 1995. pp.32–40.

————Scenarios Made Easy. *Long Range Planning*. Volume 33, #4. August 1995. pp. 81–86.

Merritt, T. Forecasting the Future Business Environment—The State of the Art. *Long Range Planning*. Volume 7, #3. June 1974. pp. 54–62.

Mester, L. J. Multiple Market Contact Between Savings and Loans. *Journal of Money, Credit and Banking*. Volume 19, #4. November 1987. pp. 538–549.

Miller, D. and M. Chen. A Study of Sources and Consequences of Competitive Inertia. *Administrative Science Quarterly*. Volume 29, #1. March 1994. pp. 1–23.

Miller, D. and P. H. Friesen. Strategy Making and Environment: The Third Link. *Strategic Management Journal*. Volume 4, #3. July–September 1983. pp. 221–235.

Mintzberg, H. That's Not "Turbulence." Chicken Little, It's Really Opportunity. *The Planning Review.* Volume 22, #6. November–December 1994. pp. 7–9.

Mishkin, F. S. The Information in the Longer Maturity Term Structure About. *The Quarterly Journal of Economics.* Volume 105, #3. August 1990. pp. 815–828.

MIT Commission on Industrial Productivity. Working papers of the MIT Commission on Industrial Productivity. Cambridge, MA: MIT Press. 1989.

Mockler, R. J. A Catalog of Commercially Available Software for Strategic Planning. *Planning Review.* May–June 1991. pp. 28–35.

Modis, T. *Predictions: Society's Telltale Signature Reveals the Past and Forecasts the Future.* New York: Simon & Schuster. 1992.

———Life Cycles: Forecasting the Rise and Fall of Almost Anything. *The Futurist.* September—October 1994. pp. 20–25.

———*Conquering Uncertainty: Understanding Corporate Cycles and Positioning Your Company to Survive the Changing Environment.* New York: Business Week Books (McGraw Hill). 1998.

Moore, G. H. Inflation's Turn. *TIMS Studies in the Management Sciences.* S. Makridakis and S. C. Wheelwright, eds. Amsterdam: North Holland Publishing. 1979.

Moore, J. F. *The Death of Competition: Leadership and Strategy in the Age of Business Ecosystems.* New York: HarperCollins Publishing. 1996. pp. 213-226.

Moore, W. L. Individual Differences in Search Behavior for a Nondurable. *Journal of Consumer Research.* Volume 7, #3. December 1980. pp. 296–307.

Morrison, I. *Second Curve.* London: Nicholas Brealey Publishing. 1996.

Mueller, G. and J. B. Smith. Six "Commandments" for Successful Futures Studies for Corporate Planning. *The Journal of Business Strategy.* Volume 5, #2. Fall 1984. pp. 88–92.

Mullick, S. K., G. S. Anderson. R. E. Leach and W. C. Smith. Life-Cycle Forecasting. *The Handbook of Forecasting: A Manager's Guide.* Chapter 17. S. Makridakis and S. C. Wheelwright, eds. New York: Wiley. 1982.

Naisbitt, J. *Megatrends: Ten New Directions Transforming Our Lives.* New York: Warner Books. 1984.

———Global Paradox. *Executive Excellence.* Volume 13, #5. May 1996. pp. 3–4.

Narayanan, V. K. How the Broader Environment Can Shape Industry Elements. *Strategic Planning Management.* June 1984. pp. 1, 3, 6.

Narayanan, V. K., and L. Fahey. Environmental Analysis for Strategy Formulation. *Strategic Planning and Management Handbook.* W. R. King and D. I. Cleland, eds. New York: Van Nostrand Reinhold. 1987.

Narchal, R. M., K. Kittappa. and P. Battacharya. An Environmental Scanning System for Business Planning. *Long Range Planning.* Volume 20, #6. December 1987. pp. 96–105.

Newbold, P., and C.W.J. Granger. Experience with Forecasting Univariate Time Series and the Combination of Forecasts. *Journal of the Royal Statistical Society (A).* 1974. pp. 131–164.

O'Lone, R. G. Air Transport: U.S. Manufacturers Expect Strong Long-Range Demand. *Aviation Week & Space Technology.* Volume 132, #12. March 1990. pp. 101–105.

Olshansky, S. J and B. A. Carnes. Ever Since Gompertz. *Demography.* Volume 34, #1. February 1997. pp. 1–15.

Olshavsky, R. W. Consumer Decision Making—Fact or Fiction? *Journal of Consumer Research.* Volume 6, #2. September 1979. pp. 93–100.

Ono, R. and D. J Wedemeyer. Assessing the Validity of the Delphi Technique. *Futures.* Volume 26, #3. April 1994. pp. 289–304.

Papaconstantinou, G. Technology and Jobs. *OECD Observer.* June–July 1995. pp. 6–9.

Patchen, M. The Locus and Basis of Influence on Organizational Decision. *Organizational Behavior and Human Performance*. 1974. pp. 3–10.

Patterson, F. S., and J. D. Walter. Jr. Planning Models and Econometrics. *Managerial Planning*. Volume 28, #5. March–April 1980. pp. 11–15.

Pearl R. Experimental Studies on the Duration of Life. *The American Naturalist*. 1921. pp. 481–509.

———A Comparison of the Laws of Mortality in Drosophila and in Man. *The American Naturalist*. 1922. pp. 398–405.

———*The Biology of Population Growth*. New York: Alfred A. Knopf. 1925.

Peppers, D. and M. Rogers. *Enterprise One to One: Tools for Competing in the Interactive Age*. New York: Bantam Doubleday Dell Publishing Group. 1997.

Phillips, A. W. The Relation between Unemployment and the Rate of Change of Money Wage Rates in the United Kingdom, 1861–1957. *Econometrica*. 1958. pp. 283–300.

Pickering, J. F. Verbal Explanations of Consumer Durable Purchase Decisions. *Journal of the Market Research Society*. Volume 17, #2. 1975. pp. 107–113.

———The Durable Purchasing Behaviour of the Individual Household. *European Journal of Marketing*. Volume 12, #2. 1978. pp. 178–193.

———A Behavioral Model of the Demand for Consumer Durables. *Journal of Economic Psychology*. 1981. pp. 59–77.

———Purchase Expectations and the Demand for Consumer Durables. *Journal of Economic Psychology*. Volume 5, #4. December 1984. pp. 341–352.

Pine, B. J. Peter Schwartz Offers Two Scenarios for the Future. *Planning Review*. Volume 23, #5. September–October 1995. pp. 30–32.

Pol, L. G. and R. K. Thomas. *Demography for Business Decision Making*. Westport, CT: Quorum Books. 1997.

Pollack-Johnson, B. Hybrid Structures and Improving Forecasting and Scheduling in Project Management. *Journal of Operations Management*. Volume 12, #2. Feburary 1995. pp. 101–117.

Polli, R. and V. Cook. Validity of the Product Life Cycle. *The Journal of Business*. Volume 42, #4. October 1969. pp. 385–400.

Porter, M. E. How Competitive Forces Shape Strategy. *Harvard Business Review*. Volume 57, #2. March–April 1979. pp. 137–145.

———*Competitive Strategy Techniques for Analyzing Industries and Competitors*. New York: Free Press. 1980.

———*Competitive Advantage: Creating and Sustaining Superior Performance*. New York: Free Press. 1985.

Preble, J. F. Future Forecasting with LEAP. *Long Range Planning*. Volume 15, #4. August 1982. pp. 64–69.

Prescott, J. E. Environments as Moderators of the Relationship between Strategy and Performance. *Academy of Management Journal*. Volume 29, #2. June 1986. pp. 329–346.

———A Process for Applying Analytic Models in Competitive Analysis. *Strategic Planning and Management Handbook*. W. R. King and D. I. Cleland, eds. New York: Van Nostrand Reinhold. 1987. pp. 222–251.

Prescott, R. D. Law of Growth in Forecasting Demand. *Journal of the American Statistical Association*. 1922. pp. 471–479.

Proctor, P. Market Factors Favor Business Jet Makers. *Aviation Week and Space Technology*. Volume 142, #11. March 13, 1995. pp. 76–78.

Pugliese, T. and S. McCulloch. *World model production forecasts: the outlook for production of passenger car by model and plant to 2002*. London: The Economist Intelligence Unit. 1997.

Putsis, W. P., Jr. and N. Srinivasan. Buying or Just Browsing? The Duration of Purchase Deliberation. *Journal of Marketing Research*. Volume 31, #3. August 1994. pp. 393–402.

Quinn, L. L. and D. H. Mason. How Digital Uses Scenarios to Rethink the Present. *Planning Review*. Volume 22, #6. November–December 1994. pp. 14–17.

Reimann, B. C. Decision Support Software for Value-Based Planning. *Planning Review*. Volume 16, #2. March–April 1988. pp. 24–32.

Reinhardt, W. A. An Early Warning System for Strategy Planning. *Long Range Planning*. Volume 47, #2. October 1984. pp. 25–34.

Rigney, M. Shoppers Crave Experiences. *Advertising Age*. Volume 66, #27. July 10, 1995. p. 21.

Rink, D. R. and J. E. Swan. Fitting Business Strategic and Tactical Planning to the Product Life Cycle. *Strategic Planning and Management Handbook*. W. I. King. and D. I. Cleland, eds. New York: Van Nostrand Reinhold. 1987.

Risley, G. *Modern Industrial Marketing: A Decision-Making Approach*. New York: McGraw-Hill. 1972.

Robinson, R. B. and J. A. Pearce. Research Thrusts in Small Firm Strategic Planning. *Academy of Management Review*. Volume 9, #1. January 1984. pp. 128–137.

Robinson, S. J. Q., R. E. Hitchens and D. P. Wade. The Directional Policy Matrix—Tool for Strategic Planning. *Long Range Planning*. June 1978. pp. 8–15.

Rockart, J. Chief Executives Define Their Own Data Needs. *Harvard Business Review*. Volume 57, #2. 1979. pp. 81–93.

Rockfellow, J. D. Wild Cards: Preparing for the Big One. *Futurist*. Volume 28, #1. January–Feburary 1994. pp. 14–19.

Roquebert, J. A., P .J. Andrisani, and R. L. Phillips. The Relative Contribution to SBU Profitability of Industry, Corporate, and SBU Effects. Working Paper of the University of Texas. Austin, TX. 1996.

Rosenberg, N. and C. R. Frischtak. Long Waves and Economic Growth: A Critical Appraisal. *American Economic Review*. Volume 73, #2. May 1983. pp. 146–151.

Ross, J. R. Four Contrasting Scenarios Seen for Retail Industry in 2010. *Stores*. Volume 79, #3. March 1997. pp. 34–35.

Rothermel, T. W. Forecasting Resurrected. *Harvard Business Review*. Volume 60, #2. March–April 1982. pp. 139–147.

Rothschild, W. E. Competitive Analysis: Understanding Winners and Losers. *Strategic Planning Management*. May 1984. pp. 1–3.

———Evaluating a Competitor's Product Strategy. *Strategic Planning Management*. Volume 4, #6. June 1986. pp. 41, 44–46.

Roy, S. P. & J. K. Cheung. Early Warning Systems: A Management Tool for Your Company. *Managerial Planning*. Volume 33, #5. March–April 1985. pp. 16–21.

Rue, L. W. Tools & Techniques of Long Range Planners. *Long Range Planning*. Volume 7, #5. October 1974. pp. 61–65.

Rumelt, R. P. How Much Does Industry Matter? *Strategic Management Journal*. Volume 12, #3. March 1991. pp. 167–185.

Rummel, R.J. and D. A. Heenan. How Multinationals Analyze Political Risk. *Harvard Business Review*. January–Feburary 1978. pp. 67–76.

Sahal, D. The Multidimensional Diffusion of Technology. *Technological Substitution: Forecasting Techniques and Applications*. H. A. Linstone and D. Sahal, eds. New York: American Elsevier. 1976.

Saunders, N.C. The U.S. Economy: Framework for BLS Projections. *Monthly Labor Review.* Volume 116, #11. November 1993. pp. 11–30.

Schipper, L.. and S. Meyers. Using Scenarios to Explore Future Energy Demand in Industrialized Countries. *Energy Policy.* Volume 21, #3. March 1993. pp. 264–275.

Schmalensee, R. Do Markets Differ Much? *American Economic Review.* 1985. pp. 341–351.

Schoeffler, S. *The Failures of Economics: A Diagnostic Study.* Cambridge, MA: Harvard University Press. 1955.

Schoemaker, P. J. H. Scenario Planning: A Tool for Strategic Thinking. *Sloan Management Review.* Volume 36, #2. Winter 1995. pp. 25–40.

Schonfeld, E. Betting on the Boomers. *Fortune.* December 1995. pp. 78–87.

Schumpeter, J. A. *Business Cycles.* New York: McGraw-Hill. 1939.

Schwartz, P. *The Art of the Long View: Planning for the Future in an Uncertain World.* New York: Doubleday. 1991.

Scientific American. *How Industry Buys, 1970.* New York: Scientific American. 1969.

Segev, E. How to Use Environmental Analysis in Strategy Making. *Management Review.* Volume 66, #3. March 1977. pp. 4–13.

Shepherd, W. G. The Elements of Market Structure. *The Review of Economics and Statistics.* Volume 54, #1. Feburary 1972. pp. 25–37.

Shermach, K. Coupons, In-Store Promotions Motivate Consumer Purchasing. *Marketing News.* Volume 29, #21. October 9, 1995. p. 6.

Simon. H. *Models of Men: Social and Rational.* New York: Wiley. 1957.

———— Rational Decision Making in Business Organizations. *The American Economic Review.* Volume 69, #4. September 1979. pp. 493–513.

Simos, E. O. International Economic Outlook. *Journal of Business Forecasting.* Volume 9, #3. Fall 1990. pp. 32–35.

Slywotzky, A. J. *Value Migration: How to Think Several Moves Ahead of the Competition.* Cambridge, MA: Harvard Business School Press. 1996.

Smith, J. W. and A. Clurman. *Rocking the Ages: The Yankelovich Report on Generational Marketing.* New York: Harper Collins. 1997.

Smith, K. G., T. R. Mitchell, and C .E. Summer. Top Level Management Priorities in Different Stages of the Organizational Lifecycle. *Academy of Management Journal.* Volume 28, #4. December 1985. pp. 799–820.

Snyder, J. M. *Introduction to the Long Wave Cycle.* New York: Richardson & Snyder. 1984.

Snyder, N. H. Can Environmental Volatility Be Measured Objectively? *Academy of Management Journal.* Volume 25, #1. March 1982. pp. 185–192.

————Environmental Volatility, Scanning 220. *Journal of Business Forecasting.* Volume 4, #3. Fall 1985. pp. 19–23.

Sparaco, P. Airbus: Partners Settle On A3XX Configuration. *Aviation Week & Space Technology.* June 13, 1994. p. 32.

Spiers, J. Where Americans Are Moving. *Fortune.* Volume 132, #4. August 21, 1995. pp. 38–39.

Stapleton, E. The Normal Distribution as a Model of Technological Substitution. *Technological Substitution: Forecasting Techniques and Applications.* H. A. Linstone and D. Sahal, eds. New York: American Elsevier. 1976. pp. 47–56.

Stern, M., R. U. Ayres, and A. Shapanka. A Model for Forecasting the Substitution of One Technology for Another. *Technological Substitution: Forecasting Techniques and Applications.* H. A. Linstone and D. Sahal, eds. New York: American Elsevier. 1976. pp. 119–141.

Stobaugh, R. B., Jr. How to Analyze Foreign Investment Climates. *Harvard Business Review*. September–October 1969. pp. 100–108.

Stoffels, J. D. *Strategic Issues Management: A Comprehensive Guide to Environmental Scanning*. Oxford, OH: The Planning Forum. 1994.

Stokke, P. R.. W. K. Ralsonn.. T. A. Boyce. and I. H. Wilson. Scenario Planning for Norwegian Oil and Gas. *Long Range Planning*. Volume 23, #2. April 1990. pp. 17–26.

Summers, L. Why Is U.S. National Saving So Low? Comments and Discussion. *Brookings Papers on Economic Activity*. Washington D.C.: *Brookings Institution*. 1987. pp. 602–642.

Summers, R.. and A. Heston. The Penn World Table (Mark 5): An Expanded Set of International Comparisons, 1950–1988 *Quarterly Journal of Economics*. Volume 106, #2. May 1991. pp. 327–368.

Terleckyj, N. E. The Price of Peace. *Forecast*. November–December 1995. pp. 40–46.

Theobald, R. New Success Criteria for a Turbulent World. *The Planning Review*. Volume 22, #6. November–December 1994. pp. 10–13, 43.

Thomas, P. S. Environmental Scanning—The State of the Art. *Long Range Planning*. Volume 13, #1. Feburary 1980. pp. 20–28.

Thorelli, H. B.. and S. C. Burnett. The Nature of Product Life Cycles for Industrial Goods Businesses. *Journal of Marketing*. Volume 45, #4. Fall 1981. pp. 97–108.

Thurow, L. C. Surviving in a Turbulent Environment. *Planning Review*. Volume 23, #5. September–October 1995. pp. 24–29.

Toffler, A. *Future Shock*. New York: Random House. 1970.

Toffler, A. and H. Toffler. *Creating a New Civilization*. Atlanta: Turner Publishing. 1994.

Townsend, H. A. Comparison of Several Consensus Forecasts. *Business Economics*. Volume 31, #1. January 1996. p. 531.

Trends to Watch in Retail: All Eyes on Fun. *Discount Store News*. Volume 34, #11. June 5, 1995. p. 23.

U.S. Bureau of the Census. *Household and Family Characteristics*. March, 1991 Report #458. Series P-20.

———*Statistical Abstract of the United States*. 1967–1998 (inclusive) Web site www.census.gov.

U.S. Department of Commerce: Bureau of Economic Analysis. Benchmark Input-Output Accounts for the U.S. Economy, 1987. *Survey of Current Business*. April 1994. pp. 73–115.

———Benchmark Input-Output Accounts for the U.S. Economy, 1987: Requirements Tables. *Survey of Current Business*. May 1994.

———*Benchmark Input-Output Accounts of the United States, 1987*. Washington. D.C.: U.S. Government Printing Office. November 1994.

———Benchmark Input-Output Accounts for the U.S. Economy, 1987. *Survey of Current Business*. Volume 78, #9. September 1998. p. D-45.

———*Survey of Current Business*. Volume 79, #7. July 1999.

Value Line Investment Survey. New York: Value Line. 1983–1992 (Inclusive).

Verhulst, P. F. Recherches Mathematiques sur la loi d'Accroissement de la Population. *Nouveaux Memoires de l'Academie Royale des Sciences et des Belles-Lettres de Bruxelles*. Volume 18. 1845. pp. 1–40.

Volterra, V. *Lecons Sur 1s Theorie Mathematique de la Lutte pour la Vie*. Paris: Gauthier-Villars. 1931.

Wack, P. Scenarios: Shooting the Rapids. *Harvard Business Review*. Volume 63, #6. November–December 1985. pp. 139–150.

Wall, J. L. What the Competition Is Doing: Your Need to Know. *Harvard Business Review*. Volume 52, #6. November–December 1974. pp. 22–24, 28–38, 165–169.

Walsh, C. E. What Caused the 1990–1991 Recession? *FRBSF Economic Review*. 1993.

———A Primer on Monetary Policy Part 1: Goals and Instruments. *FRBSF Weekly Letter*. August 5, 1994a.

———A Primer On Monetary Policy Part 2: Targets And Indicators. *FRBSF Weekly Letter*. August 19, 1994b.

Wasson, C. R. The Importance of the Product Life Cycle to the Industrial Marketer. *Industrial Marketing Management*. Volume 5, #6. December 1976. pp. 299–308.

Webster, F. E., Jr. Interpersonal Communication and Salesman Effectiveness. *Journal of Marketing*. July 1968. pp. 7–13.

———New Product Adoption in Industrial Markets. *Journal of Marketing*. July 1969.

Webster, J. L., W. E. Reif, and J. S. Bracker. The Manager's Guide to Strategic Planning Tools and Techniques. *Strategic Planning Process*. Chapter 30. P. Lorange, ed. Brookfield, VT: Dartmouth. 1994.

Weigand, R. E. Identifying Industrial Buying Responsibility. *Journal of Marketing Research*. Feburary 1966. pp. 81–84.

Weinstein, A. *Market Segmentation*. Chicago, IL: Probus Publishing. 1987.

Wheelwright, S. C. and D. G. Clarke. Corporate Forecasting: Promise and Reality. *Harvard Business Review*. Volume 54, #6. November–December 1976. p. 40.

Wilson, D. T. Industrial Buyers' Decision-Making Styles. *Journal of Marketing Research*. Volume 8, #4. November 1971. pp. 433–436.

Wilson, D. T., H. L Matthews, and D. J. Sweeney. An Analysis of Industrial Buyers Risk Reducing Behavior: Personality Correlates. Presented at The Annual Conference of the American Marketing Association. 1973.

Wilson, I. H. Futures Forecasting for Strategic Planning at General Electric. *Long Range Planning*. Volume 6, #2. June 1973. pp. 39–42.

———Wilson, I.H. The Current State of Planning in North America: Introduction to the Special Issue. *Long Range Planning*. 1983. pp. 2–3.

Winer, R. S. A Price Vector Model of Demand for Consumer Durables: Preliminary Developments. *Marketing Science*. Volume 4, #1. Winter 1985a. pp. 74–90.

———A Revised Behavioral Model of Consumer Durable Demand. *Journal of Economic Psychology*. Volume 6, #2. June 1985b. pp. 175–184.

Woo, C. Y. and A. C. Cooper. The Surprising Case for Low Market Share. *Harvard Business Review*. Volume 60, #6. November–December 1982. pp. 106–113.

Zaichkowsky, J. L. Consumer Behavior: Yesterday, Today, and Tomorrow. *Business Horizons*. Volume 34, #3. May–June 1991. pp. 51–58.

Zeisset, P. T. and M. E. Wallace. How NAICS Will Affect Data Users. *Economic Planning and Coordination Division: Bureau of the Census*. December 1997.

Zentner, R. Scenarios: Past, Present, and Future. *Long Range Planning*. Volume 15, #3. June 1982. pp. 12–20.

Index

About the Author

C. W. RONEY is managing principal of Commercial Planning Consultants, Dayton, Ohio. Over a career of more than 30 years he has served as both a member of senior corporate management and as a strategic planning consultant. He is the author of several journal articles.

ISBN 1-56720-235-7

90000>

EAN

9 781567 202359

HARDCOVER BAR CODE